MIDNIGHT
in SIBERIA

*A Train Journey into
the Heart of Russia*

DAVID GREENE

W. W. NORTON & COMPANY

New York · London

Midnight in Siberia is a work of nonfiction. Some of the names
and certain identifying details have been changed.

TO MY WIFE, ROSE

CONTENTS

AUTHOR'S NOTE ON THE MAP

The Trans-Siberian Railway is Russia's spine, a thin line of constancy that holds this unwieldy country together. It's more than just a map that underscores this. The railroad connects families, bringing distant relatives together more affordably than air travel. And it connects different chapters in this country's journey—today, high-speed luxury trains carry Russia's uber-elite and standard-class trains carry business travelers, tourists, and families, all following the same path used by Stalin to ship political prisoners to the Siberian gulags.

While the Trans-Siberian, as broadly defined, includes a number of different routes, the primary two connect Moscow to Ulan-Ude, where one route continues east to Vladivostok and the other (the Trans-Mongolian) dips south to Beijing. I decided to stick—mostly—to the all-Russia route, using the train as a vehicle and guide, seeing Russia from west to east. I did take a few detours, as you can see. I jogged over to Yaroslavl, not a stop on the main route. Same goes for Izhevsk. And I took a bus down to Chelyabinsk, hoping to pick up a southern branch of the Trans-Siberian to reconnect with the main route in Omsk. That plan fell apart when I realized I would need a Kazakh visa for a bit of that trip. It proved far more efficient to backtrack to Ekaterinburg than to take a last-minute gamble at the Kazakh consulate. From Ekaterinburg, it was a rather straightforward trip eastbound (save for a heart-thumping hovercraft ride across Lake Baikal and a late-night jump back on the train in the village of Baikalsk). Then we hugged the Chinese border, before swinging a sharp right turn and completing the home stretch into the Pacific port of Vladivostok. There we arrived, after 5,772 miles (if we'd stayed on course), more tea than vodka (not by much), more instant noodles than fresh meals (by a lot), and a whole lot of conversation.

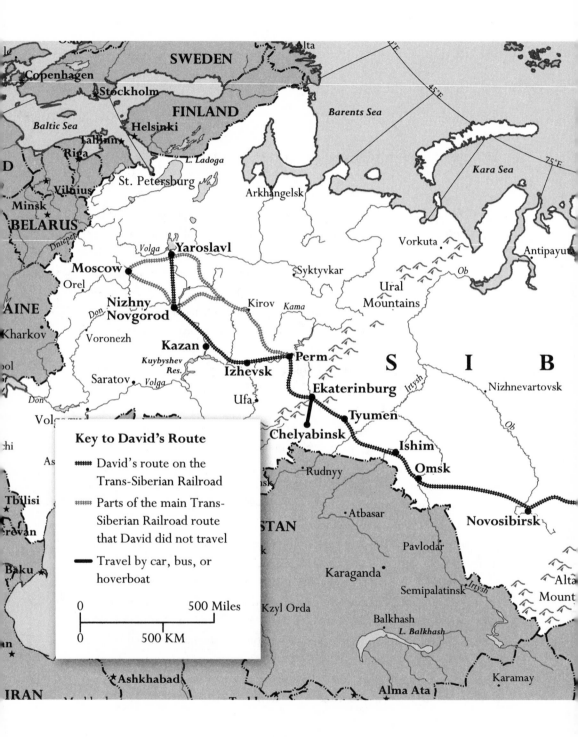

Key to David's Route

▬▬▬ David's route on the
Trans-Siberian Railroad

▬▬▬ Parts of the main Trans-
Siberian Railroad route
that David did not travel

▬▬▬ Travel by car, bus, or
hoverboat

0   500 Miles
|——————————————|
0   500 KM

PROLOGUE

Wasn't history supposed to end in 1991?

Apocalyptic at that sounds, it was essentially the prediction of a political scientist named Francis Fukuyama who two years before that had penned an essay called "The End of History?"

As anti-Communist fervor was building around the world, Fukuyama argued that the East-West battle of ideas which fueled the Cold War was finally coming to an end. He favored nuance over finality, predicting that the world had not seen the last of totalitarian regimes and community ideology. They would ebb and flow and influence events here and there. But the trend was unmistakable: Liberal democracy, parliamentary-style governments, and market-driven economics were taking hold in more and more countries of the world. That would more or less continue. The great debate was over.

Fukuyama sure seemed prescient in December 1991, when the Soviet Union was dissolved.

The question worth asking in 2014 is whether we've arrived at the *end* of the End of History.

Russia, led by its enigmatic, macho leader, Vladimir Putin,

blatantly ignored pleas and warnings from the West and forcibly annexed Crimea, which was (and remains, if you ask the most wishful thinkers) part of the sovereign nation of Ukraine. To foreign policy alarmists, this marked the resumption of the Cold War. To even the coolest minds, it was a seminal event likely to poison the West's relations with Russia.

Henry Kissinger, former U.S. secretary of state and one of the world's most influential foreign policy minds, wrote in the *Washington Post* following the Crimea annexation that it is dangerous to view Ukraine "as a showdown" over whether the sovereign nation "joins the East or the West." Ukraine has to function, Kissinger wrote, "as a bridge between them."

He went on to argue that the West certainly has interests in Ukraine—growing economic and cultural ties—but that so does Russia, perhaps even more. Kiev was the birthplace of the Russian Orthodox religion. Ukraine has been strategically important to Russia for centuries, especially Crimea, where Russia maintains its Black Sea naval fleet. And in Crimea and eastern Ukraine, many people speak Russian and feel a closer cultural connection to the East.

Kissinger wrote that each side has to recognize the interests of the other. He didn't hold out much hope for that: "Putin is a serious strategist—on the premises of Russian history. Understanding U.S. values and psychology are not his strong suits. Nor has understanding Russian history and psychology been a strong point of U.S. policymakers."

His casting of this modern conflict represents just one view. But it's hard to argue with the reality he underscores: At worst, Ukraine could become a colossal misunderstanding that morphs into a new "showdown." At best, Ukraine can be used as a "bridge" between competing interests and philosophies. Either way, the old fault line and the East-West battle over ideas, territory, and influence remain present today.

All of this has been building of course. The United States and its allies were furious when Russia invaded its neighbor Georgia in 2008. Likewise, Russia was furious in 2011 when it agreed under enormous pressure to abstain rather than veto on a UN vote to approve NATO military action in Libya, given assurances that NATO was going to tread delicately. NATO bombs were dropping within days.

There are reasons to think these tensions may die down. Russia and the West have shared interests, and they've worked together effectively at times—on space exploration and pressuring Syria to hand over its chemical weapons stockpile. Russia's global dominance in energy may also be fading, and that could weaken Russia's economy to a point where it must either get along with the West or face economic deprivation and collapse from within. But for now, Putin clearly believes that a stand-off with the West is in Russia's strategic interest and that he's strong enough to pull it off.

Just as notable as Russia's aggressiveness abroad is Putin's management of the home front. In recent years, he has solidified the Kremlin's control over local and regional governments, pressured news organizations, curtailed the right to protest, and targeted minorities—most glaringly, Russians who are gay and lesbian. He has also threatened human rights organizations, especially those that receive funding from the United States and elsewhere abroad.

Most stunning? By all accounts—and admittedly, polling in Russia is often unreliable—Putin is more popular than ever.

On May 1, 2014, more than one hundred thousand Russians descended on Red Square to celebrate their president and cheer his conquering of Crimea. It was arguably the most impressive display of Russian patriotism since the Soviet collapse and quite a counterpoint to the anti-Putin protests of 2011 that received plenty of attention from Western media but appear, for the moment, largely forgotten.

If we think of 2014 as a snapshot, what do we see? A Russian leader moving further away from Western democratic values. An East-West divide marked by growing mistrust. A military stand-off that has seen both NATO and Russian forces mobilizing and carrying out exercises with the aim of intimidating.

This moment may not mark the end of Fukuyama's End of History. Perhaps this is one of those moments he predicted when the Cold War enemy would score a blow, on the ultimate path to defeat.

I'm tempted to look at this moment differently: as a reminder that culture and history matter, values and traditions endure, peoples of the world have different instincts, wishes, priorities, and dreams. It is easy to see Vladimir Putin as an authoritative leader with his own selfish motivations who has been able to squash anyone who wants to protest and dupe everyone else into letting him lead. That portrayal may hold some truth. But Putin, popular as ever, shrewd as always, also embodies a Russian soul that is unfamiliar to many in the West.

During the Cold War, Soviet citizens were nearly impossible for Americans and others in the West to understand. Authors and journalists—Hedrick Smith among them with his book *The Russians*—took us into apartments in Russia, into the lives of people, giving us a rare window into the culture of a place that seemed so cold and threatening.

Part of understanding history and events is understanding people. And I feel lucky to have had that chance, living in Russia and, more recently, taking a wild and eye-opening trip across the vast country on a train.

Inside cramped sleeping quarters on trains, in homes, apartments, and cafés, while soaking in a Russian bathhouse or chasing debris from a meteorite, I got to meet Russians, bringing with me an ear, a deep curiosity, and no agenda.

I learned about a culture and way of life different from my own and began to understand how dangerous it is to assume that one way of thinking or any one system of government can apply everywhere.

So many Russians welcomed me into their lives. I would like to introduce you to some of them in the pages ahead.

MIDNIGHT IN SIBERIA

INTRODUCTION

I STRUGGLE AWAKE, and there she is.

Russia.

A silver-haired grandmother in a flowered nightgown. She's framed by the morning sunlight flooding through the dusty windowpane. And she's holding a glass of water before my crusted eyes and parched lips.

Russia is Aunt Nina.

Here she stands, fresh and awake, despite last night's marathon conversation about politics, childhood, dogs, snow, soccer—whatever her nephew Sergei served up next—that lasted far beyond my vodka-laced endurance. Forty years younger and barely mobile, I could be jealous of her energy or humiliated by it. Above all I just need that water. I blame Russia. No, Russia didn't ram seventeen shots of vodka down my throat. But Aunt Nina's family is *so* warm, and *so* persuasive. That's what Russia does to the uninitiated at night. And now she's greeting me in the morning—not very forgivingly.

"Dobroe utro!" That's Russian for "Good morning," delivered in a tone that mixes sweet and stern. Her pursed lips, tight with impatient disappointment, indicate I have only five minutes to roust myself from this bed.

What fond memories of the night before! The table was crowded with Aunt Nina's creations: Piping hot borscht (the venerable Slavic soup made of beets) usually with dollops of sour cream to make it creamy, potato pancakes stacked in towers, tender stewed chicken drowning in some addictive red sauce, and vegetables pickled to perfection. Serving dishes inhabited every open piece of real estate. And the night was crowded with Russian proverbs—which I am convinced Sergei's family members were authoring on the spot.

"David, it is bad luck to only have one shot."

"David, you know what they say in Russia? A horse can't walk on three legs. He must have a fourth."

"David, in Russia, even numbers like eight are bad luck. We must go to nine."

Nights around the dining room table don't end. In Soviet times this was sacred ground, a hiding place where it was safe to smile and laugh and talk openly. And traditions don't die easily in this country. Why should they, when they're this merry and liberating? More vodka means more stories, which mean more laughter, which mean more vodka, which brings us to the morning.

I am guzzling water, peering sheepishly over the rim of the glass at Aunt Nina and Sergei, my friend and colleague. They are vertical, staring down at the patient with a combination of bewilderment (vodka is rarely *this* damaging around here) and hope (if my hangover progresses to the next stage, it will be messy for all involved).

It's 9:30 a.m., and Sergei and I have a meeting in an hour, so I promise to shower promptly.

"Dvadtsat minoot [20 minutes]?"

I'm begging for mercy.

"Bystro [Go quickly]!" Nina says, clapping her hands twice for emphasis.

I limp into the shower, turn on the faucet, and let the stream of water serve as a masseuse for my aching head. Beyond therapy, hangover showers serve another purpose in life, and that's reflection. And here in Aunt Nina's shower, I can't stop thinking about how my experience of the past twelve hours has been so . . . *Russian*.

My morning nurse is the embodiment of the Russian babushka, or grandmother—the term really applies to any older Russian woman. A word of caution: When you say "babushka" out loud, put the emphasis on the first syllable—"BAH-boosh-kah." (By comparison, a "bah-BOOSH-ka"—an English-language invention that doesn't exist in Russian—is a scarf. And calling a tough old woman a scarf doesn't get you far around here).

If Russia had a mascot, it could well be a babushka. In paintings or photos that capture Russia, you may have seen older women, selling fruit along the road, wearing babushkas (yes, this time, scarves). That's one rendition of the babushka. There is also the urban babushka, like Aunt Nina. She lives in the western Russian city of Nizhny Novgorod, in the apartment she and her late husband were assigned to during Soviet times. Rural, urban, or otherwise, babushkas are known to be strong and self-sufficient. Many lost their men years ago to hard work or alcoholism, in many cases both. They are the engine and spirit of Russia's older generation, and in some ways of the whole country.

Aunt Nina has boundless energy, can talk for hours about literature, loves to cook, and gives tough love. She lectured me and Sergei for drinking too much, then talked soused Sergei to sleep (I needed no help), and then rushed in the morning to deliver me water and sympathy.

Of course, all the warmth and love I felt during this visit was within the confines of a family's home, which brings up an important point: On first impression Russians are generally *not* friendly people.

It's the first thing international visitors notice: The streets are filled with nervous, blank faces. In public many Russians don't seem to acknowledge that other humans are sharing their space. They are indifferent if, say, you want to squeeze past on a crowded sidewalk. They avoid eye contact as if they might get a disease from it. (A not-unrelated point: Russians who visit the United States are equally perplexed by Americans, and their obsession with smiling at people they've never met.)

You come to understand these tendencies. In Soviet times being in public was risky. If you accidentally spoke to a stranger who was under suspicion from the government, or told a joke about Stalin, or appeared too friendly with a foreigner, it could mean interrogation or in extreme cases worse—a journey to a Siberian prison camp. Many Russians developed coldness in public as defense, suppressing thoughts and feelings, not letting their true selves escape. And while the risks of putting yourself out there are far less severe in today's Russia, remnants of that behavior remain. During three years living in Moscow, my wife, Rose, and I slowly adjusted to this. If someone slipped on the ice or was otherwise in need of help, strangers would often just walk by pretending not to notice. Why risk getting involved, especially if the police were being called? Rose and I would be the only people coming to someone's aid, doing all we could with limited Russian-language skills. A British diplomat friend once saw two teenage girls hit by a speeding car as they were running across a street. One of the girls was decapitated. The driver just sped from the scene. Our friend stopped his car, called an ambulance, and ran to the other girl, who was screaming uncontrollably next to her friend's body. All the while, cars passed and pedestrians walked by as if nothing was out of order.

While seemingly cold and vacant to strangers on the outside, many Russians are beautiful and generous on the inside. Their public disengagement can be shocking, but they are some of the warmest people on earth. Once they get to know you and invite you into their homes, many Russians will freely share their stories, traditions, and food. When you enter a home, two things happen: You are offered a pair of slippers—polite encouragement to take off your shoes and make yourself comfortable—then you are offered tea or vodka. I spent many days hoping for tea and getting vodka. Whatever is in the glass or on the plate, however, there is no higher honor in Russia than to be welcomed to a family's table and treated as one of their own, which was the case in Aunt Nina's apartment.

As the shower slowly melts the hangover, I am feeling grateful. To be in Russia. To be on a journey with a Russian colleague who became my dearest friend in the country, Sergei Sotnikov. He has brought me to Nizhny Novgorod to spend time with his family. We are a few days into a five-week trip aboard the Trans-Siberian Railway. It's the journey on which I hope you will join me in this book.

I am on this trip to see Russia, to experience it, to satisfy my curiosity and to answer enduring questions. My wife and I were Midwestern children of the eighties: She hails from northwestern Ohio, and I grew up in Pittsburgh. We were both raised by college professors who explained world events as best they could. Rose vividly remembers watching the Berlin Wall crumble on her family's first color television, rabbit ears protruding in her living room, as her father told her what was unfolding—"This is the beginning of democracy spreading to the Soviet Union." I was given the same expectation. So were millions of Americans.

Democracy *has* come to countries that were prisoners of the Soviets—Hungary, Poland, and the Czech Republic—and to countries that were actually annexed by the Soviet Union, like Latvia, Lithuania, and Estonia. But elsewhere in the former Soviet space—and especially in Russia itself—not so. And if you are like me and Rose, raised to believe in the so-called "end of history," taught to expect democratic change to sweep the former Soviet Union and then move beyond, the course of history has been a surprise.

Rose and I moved to Russia in 2009. I was taking over as the Moscow bureau chief for NPR News, and Rose was giving up a successful career in public policy to relocate temporarily for her husband (making no secret of her expectation that he'd spend the better part of his life repaying her). We were eager to understand where Russia was going. The home of Tolstoy and Dostoevsky, ballet dancers and supermodels, Russia is more than a cultural epicenter. It has a massive economy, holding much of the world's oil and natural gas. It remains a country with influence, and when given a motive can easily threaten the strategic interests of the United States.

Most worrisome is the nation's leader, Vladimir Putin, recently reelected after serving two terms between 2000 and 2008. Forced out by term limits, he handed the reins to a protégé—Dmitri Medvedev—but after a few years was ready to take his job back. Putin is accustomed to Russians showering him with love and affection. But there have been hints that that may be changing. Russians, mostly in Moscow, took to the streets by the thousands in 2011, chanting anti-Putin slogans and calling for a new leader. Some have grown tired of a man who once said that protesters taking to the streets without a permit deserved to be "clubbed in the head." But Putin withstood that outburst of opposition and seems, as of this writing, as securely in power as ever.

Russian scholars and writers have long spoken of their country's confounding nature, how it takes wild turns and goes through periods of upheaval but always seems to return to a cruel, dysfunctional resting place. The novelist Nikolai Gogol once compared the country to an out-of-control troika—a traditional Russian carriage pulled by three harnessed horses—intimating that it could crash and burn at any moment. "Russia, where are you flying?" he asked in his novel, *Dead Souls.* "Answer me . . . there is no answer." The contemporary Russian novelist Mikhail Shishkin said recently that Gogol's metaphor is as applicable as ever. Shishkin just updated the mode of transport. "Now Gogol would compare Russia with a metro train, which travels from one end of a tunnel to the other—from order dictatorship to anarchy-democracy, and back again. This is its route. And you don't go anywhere else on this train."

But come with me on a train ride, and let's see where it goes. Maybe we won't answer the largest questions about Russia definitively. But we'll try as best we can, and along the way, meet people who will make us laugh, reveal their pain, and teach us about a country that plays a big role in the world and is important to understand. In this book—along this ride—I will interject snippets of analysis, insights from historians and fellow journalists, and observations I made during my time in the country. But mostly this book will be a journey and an adventure, a wild ride on one of the world's epic train routes, 6,000 miles from Moscow to far East Asia, taking us into the heart of a country and into the lives of its people. From all the Russians we meet, we'll make connections and learn whatever we can.

SCHOLARS IMMERSED in Russian studies have written innumerable, groundbreaking books about life, history, and politics. Spending a few years living and working in the country keeps me squarely in their shadows. But during that time I watched Russia closely with fresh eyes and innocent curiosity. With its cruel leaders, history of tragedy, harsh weather and boisterous personalities, Russian life can play out almost like a stage drama. And I always like to think of myself as a quiet character, sharing the stage and taking in the surroundings. It's an approach I have used as much as possible in my on-air storytelling at NPR. In 2009 the United States seemed to be at an inflection point: The economy was in shambles, just as a historic political moment arrived. Americans had just voted for their first black president. During the first three months of 2009, I hit the road in an SUV, equipped with a recorder and notebook, fueled by caffeine and gas-station food. I traveled from northern Michigan to Florida, then from New York to San Francisco, mostly just listening as people shared their personal struggles and hopes for their families and communities. None of my reporting would have deserved a "breaking news" headline on cable news, but I learned a great deal about America in a difficult and defining moment.

This was on my mind in December 2011, as Rose and I began what would be our first trip on the Trans-Siberian Railway. (This book brings you along on our second.) I was wrapping up my tenure in Moscow for NPR, and my editors and I believed the train trip might offer me one wild, romantic way to take our listeners to an unfamiliar place and provide clues about Russia's journey as a country. By turns, the train trip was in-your-face, unpredictable, grueling, loud, poetic, humorous, and deflating—all of which could describe Russia itself. The conversations I had along the way opened a window on a culture long shrouded in mystery and misunderstood by the West. My fellow passengers talked to me about the wounded soul of their once-great nation, baring their anger about Russia's present and their fear about what the future would bring. They taught me how years of hardship—under czarist, Communist, and capitalist rule—had taken their toll on Russia's people and made their mark on everything from Russian folklore and traditions to politics and family life.

TWO DECADES AGO, when the Soviet Union collapsed, the Western media focused heavily on the promise of capitalism and democracy. Today the glue holding the country together seems to be eroding. As I traversed Russia in a train, I couldn't help but feel I was traveling on the only concrete thing holding this nation together. For years Russians *had* an identity, shaped in all ways by Soviet culture. But modern Russia seems to be living in a void: a place where the powerful and connected can rake in eye-popping amounts of money, where a $275,000 bottle of champagne is on the menu at a Moscow hotel thirty miles from impoverished villages, where ordinary families go about their daily lives hoping to survive, unable to dream of any higher purpose.

That feeling of emptiness has many Russians turning to the past for answers and guidance. To live in Soviet times often meant not being able to define your own future. You could not travel, determine how much money you made, or decide where you lived. But many people had stable jobs, quality education, and a sense of pride that their country was respected in the world. Today the social safety net from Soviet times is gone, and Russians are not confident that anything has replaced it. The reality is harsh: Russia seems to stand for little besides wealth at the top, corruption, an uneven playing field, and the repression of civil rights. Russians today are free to travel and free to express their views in public, but the Soviet Union has been replaced by a system eerily similar in some ways—featuring the same repression and inequality that existed before, only without the Communist ideology that at least put food on the table.

The Russia I saw was very much as Gogol described it more than 150 years ago: careening down an uncertain path. On the Trans-Siberian Railway I began to see a thin line of constancy, connecting Russia's cities and its steppes, its problems and its potential, its past and its future. Cultural heritage seems to pervade a nation that stretches from Europe to Pyongyang and Alaska, making some customs and ways of thinking feel the same through all of Russia's extremities. And across this vast country the emotion that remained constant was an uneasy frustration: Here are millions of people across different landscapes, climates, and communities, all with families they love and ideas to offer, but almost universally unable to answer some simple questions: Where is your country going? And what do *you* want for its future?

I learned a lot from that trip in 2011, but not nearly enough. I wanted to see more, wanted to meet more people. I knew that even though my career had taken me back home, my time in Russia was far from finished. I would be getting back on that train.

· · ·

I LANDED BACK in Washington in 2012, around the same time as a friend and colleague, Julia Ioffe. She was born in Russia, moved to the United States in grade school, went to Princeton for college but never got rid of the Russia bug. She returned as a journalist, writing for *Foreign Policy* and *The New Yorker* magazines while living with her grandmother in the family's Soviet-era flat in Moscow. Our time as foreign correspondents overlapped, but Julia—having been born in the country and learned Russian before English—knew the place intimately. I took whatever work Julia produced seriously—and one of the first things she did after returning to the United States was to translate an essay by Mikhail Shishkin. His essay, published by Julia's current employer, the *New Republic*, is called "Poets and Czars: From Pushkin to Putin, the Sad Tale of Democracy in Russia."

In czarist times, Shishkin wrote, Russia was a "Holy Fatherland" surrounded "on all sides by an ocean of enemies." And to live in Russia meant being a "child and soldier" of the czar. But the protection you received in return made all that worthwhile. As Shishkin put it, "the unconscious slavery was bitter for the body, but life-sustaining for the spirit." This was a convenient arrangement for Russia's all-powerful czars. People believed that in a dangerous and uncertain world, to be in Russia was the best one could hope for. But, "everything changed with Peter the Great," Shishkin wrote. Czar Peter had worthy intentions. He wanted to throw open the doors to eighteenth-century Europe, with its new ideas and theories about science and technology. But Peter could not pick and choose who came through the door, and poets and thinkers entered as well, with European ideas about individual rights and human dignity.

As Shishkin put it, Peter "wanted to 'cut a window to Europe,' but instead, he cut a hole in the Russian ark." Suddenly Russian thinkers and writers were armed with progressive ideas.

The great poet Pushkin may have owed his literary genius to his Russian blood, but his ideas were shaped by the West. This led him to challenge the power vertical in Russia, writing in the poem *Exegi Monumentum*, "I've set up to myself a monument not wrought by hands. The public path to it will not grow weedy. Its unyielding head soars higher than the Alexandrine Column." This was a direct challenge to the czar. Shishkin points to those words as Pushkin's "declaration of independence."

Then something funny happened.

The czar who ruled during Pushkin's time courted the poet, realizing and fearing his influence. Nicholas I named Pushkin the country's "First Poet," and the poet obliged. Shishkin writes of a tragic calculation that Pushkin faced. He was convinced that democracy would never really flourish in Russia. Undermining the czar would only create a power vacuum, and the new reality would be uglier than what it replaced. "Pushkin saw that in Russia, the choice between dictatorship and democracy was beside the point: the only choice was between bloody chaos and ruthless order." More specifically Pushkin "understood that in a Russian revolution, the first things to burn [would] be the libraries."

Shishkin uses this history as an appetizer for his bitter main course: recognition that history in his country can't stop repeating itself. Shishkin's novels drill into universal human themes and questions—love, pain, decency—and he's been compared to some of the great Russian writers of the past—Pushkin, Chekhov, Tolstoy. And in 2013 Shishkin himself faced an impossible calculation.

His government helped arrange an annual trip to the United States for Russian literary moguls. Having gone the year before, Shishkin declined this time. A critic of Putin and the Kremlin, he refused to be showcased by a government he found unpalatable. I can't help but see his predicament as comparable to Pushkin's, facing the czar three centuries ago. Historical parallels are tenuous, but make no mistake: Russia today exists in a bizarre purgatory, not unlike the country Pushkin knew. Pushkin then, Shishkin now, faced a terrible choice: Stand for change that could be messy and unpredictable, or settle for and endorse a status quo that is unsavory but somehow safe?

In Shishkin's time, after Soviet rule, Russia opened to the West and seemed on a path to democracy. But the dust has now settled, and Russia has an autocratic, power-hungry leader. What happened? In Shishkin's mind the brief flirtation with democracy after Soviet times "ended with everyone returning to their barracks. We had to live, after all. And order returned on its own, the very same order, because no one in Russia knows a different one."

If anything came through on my first train trip, and in my time in Russia, it's that people in this country dream of change—in the abstract—but have little or no faith that they can contribute to it or control it. And that has been ingrained in the psychology for generations. I always turn back to an essay called "The Image of Dual Russia," written more than five decades ago by the late Robert Tucker, a Princeton scholar who studied Russia and the Soviet Union. He writes that over centuries—from the 1400s straight up until the 1917 Bolshevik revolution that ushered in Soviet times—Russia became divided. On the one hand there was "official Russia": the state, in Russian, the *gosudarstvo*. Quite separately there was "popular Russia": the people, many of them peasants in far-flung communities, taught to make sacrifices Shishkin described in order to feel protection and a sense of purpose. Most strikingly, Tucker explained how there was no relationship between the two. They existed and lived in entirely separate worlds. Russian leaders and bureaucrats viewed the people as soldiers in some us-against-them war against the world, but didn't value them as human beings. And the people saw the government as "alien"—a distant, conquering force whose vision, cruel as it seemed, was intractable, inevitable, and inescapable. And so popular apathy prevailed. In 1917 the Bolsheviks arrived and, in the eyes of the outside world, brought their Marxist vision into a fight on behalf of the *people*. But Tucker believed that the Russian people—most of them, at least—were apathetic and not really ever involved. The Bolsheviks were able to topple the czar fairly easily, he said, because in reality, the czar had little support from the uninvolved and apathetic masses. But neither did Lenin and the Bolsheviks. They took power and began a new chapter in Russian history, in large part by making themselves a "self-appointed organ of consciousness," Tucker wrote. The Russian people themselves saw little if any personal stake in the way things played out—they were innocent and detached bystanders to history.

That's alarming. But Tucker's conclusions from decades ago, like Shishkin's insights today, nevertheless paint a broad picture of the Russia I saw. At a moment when there could be a fight for change, history's handcuffs remain on this proud country that's full of warm, creative, strong people. At the very moment when countries in the Middle East—Tunisia, Egypt, Libya—were rising up and overthrowing leaders in the Arab Spring, Russians made a bit of noise and then settled down again. Why did they not see things through? How can Russians accept the harsh reality they live in—a country with low life expectancy, rampant health problems, gaping inequality, and a dwindling population? What is holding people back? Is it fear? Fatigue? Fatalism? Public apathy? An innocent but false belief in country? A paternalistic faith that leaders are there to protect you? Or, most likely, a recipe of all these ingredients—a recipe written by the czars, cooked for generations, and infused so deeply in Russians that they would struggle to exist without it.

ALL THESE QUESTIONS lingered when I finished my assignment in Russia and returned home in 2012, as did one more: How can I *love* such a maddening place? For all its troubles there's an inner energy and warmth and unpredictability that make Russia as addictive as Aunt Nina's stewed chicken. Spend enough time there, and for all the pain you witness, you don't want to leave. I yearned to go back to Russia because of my love for the place and the unfinished business of understanding it. So, I returned in 2013 for another Trans-Siberian journey. This book is that journey.

1 · ROSE

ROSE WAS CONVINCED it would be snowing when we landed.

It was September 2009, and the two of us were about to begin a new life in Russia.

Snowing? Sure, I thought. It's *always* cold in Moscow. It even snows in September. What are the other clichés, honey? All Russians do is drink vodka, wear fur hats, and train for the Olympics?

It was snowing.

We could see it as our Delta 767 from JFK made its final descent into Moscow.

"You know I'm a warm-blooded Mediterranean, right, Greene?" I did. But this question wasn't meant to offer new information, rather to underscore the meteorological sacrifice my Sicilian-Lebanese-American wife was making in beginning this new chapter.

In our *warm* apartment in New York City's East Village, Rose and I had spent endless hours talking about the job that opened at NPR: Moscow bureau chief.

I had covered the White House for eight years, done some economic reporting in New York, and was hankering for a foreign assignment. Rose had gotten a master's degree in public policy, launched into a great job as a policy adviser for the New York City Council, and was always hungry for a new adventure—she loves to explore and travel—but Russia?

Rose grew up in rural Ohio. Her Lebanese-American mom raised four kids, taught school, and opened a family restaurant in a small town along Interstate 75. Her Sicilian-American dad taught college law and pharmacy for four decades. I grew up in Pennsylvania. My late mom, another academic, was a beloved psychology professor. My dad is a physician in the pharmaceutical industry who shares my passion for late-night chats about politics or yesterday's Pittsburgh Steelers game. Our parents all worked to make us worldly. Rose and I talked about current events growing up, we traveled, and we read the Dostoevsky and Tolstoy required in class.

Covering the White House, I certainly took my swims in foreign policy, attending numerous summits between Russia's Vladimir Putin and America's George W. Bush, who once famously remarked that he looked into Putin's soul and liked what he saw (a moment when I could almost hear Putin, a former KGB spy, saying to himself, Got him!).

And yet neither Rose nor I could escape feeling this naive confusion about Russia, as if we were missing something. The summits we saw on television as kids, with Ronald Reagan and Mikhail Gorbachev—weren't they setting Russia on a path to becoming a Western democracy and true American ally? Why hasn't Russia gotten there? Isn't that what Russians *want* their country to be?

We talked about the risk of moving to a new country, especially one known for being cold and unwelcoming. And Rose was quick to remind me of the risks. She's not a woman who holds much back or shies away from debate. (Her Lebanese-Sicilian good looks may have gotten her *into* beauty pageants in high school, but the event she always won was the interview.)

"Okay, so let's get this straight here," she said in one of our many conversations, sitting in our tiny Manhattan apartment. "We moved to New York for my job a year ago. Now you're asking me to leave my new job, move to Russia, be cold for several years, and live in a country that may not even give me a visa to work?"

I felt she captured things pretty well. "Yes?"

"I like the idea of an adventure . . . especially before we have kids. But Greene? You understand you're going to owe me."

The decision wasn't easy, and the two of us talk to this day about what might have been different had we turned Russia down. In the end it may have been our curiosity that won out. Rose put it best: "I don't know a damn thing about Russia, except for its food and culture. But I . . . I have always thought that seeing a new place, experiencing it, learning about it as a couple—together—could be a fun adventure, and who knows if we'll ever get this chance again?"

After walking off the plane, through a bitterly cold jetway that did nothing for marital peace, Rose and I were hit in the face by Russia. Russians, as it turns out, don't like lining up for anything. It may come from a sympathetic place: During Soviet times the difference between being first or sixth in line at a poorly stocked store could be the difference between your family having bread on the table that night, or not. Lines became free-for-alls.

But I would love for someone to explain to me why this practice must endure at the immigration line at Moscow's Sheremetyevo

International Airport. Rose and I were bumped rudely, trampled on, yelled at in Russian, pushed aside, and frowned at until we just decided to let the whole horde of Russian passengers go ahead of us. Then we calmly walked up to the Russian immigration officer, a scowling woman dressed in a pale blue government uniform.

"Iz N'iu Iorka?" she seemed to grumble. We assumed it was Russian for "From New York?"

"Yes," I said.

"Da," Rose said, surprising even herself by what just came out of her mouth. In a single word she gave me a sign that she really was going to try to make the best of this.

We found our luggage and exited into the terminal. "Whatever you've done to us, Greene—it's all happening." Rose gave me a this-is-all-your-fault smile. "Welcome to Russia."

Our first task was to find Boris and Sergei. When NPR told me that my first task upon arrival in Russia was to locate Boris and Sergei, I thought it was either a joke or some kind of funny code. Does everyone in Russia have two best friends named Boris and Sergei? Rose and I wondered in jest. But indeed, Boris Ryzhak and Sergei Sotnikov are NPR's office manager and producer in Moscow. And they were picking us up at the airport.

I had Sergei's mobile number, called it, and finally located the two men. Sergei is five foot seven, slightly shorter than I am, meaning that Boris towers over him. Boris is a former semiprofessional basketball player, a giant with graying hair, floppy lips, rich, dark eyes, and a deep voice that soothes even when I have no idea what he is saying in Russian.

"Zdrast-vui-tyeh!" he said, giving me a hearty handshake. "Hellooo," Sergei said, at once translating Boris and offering his own greeting. They led us to a van, loaded our luggage, and drove us into the city we would now call home.

Everything looked foreign—especially because the Cyrillic alphabet is entirely different from the Latin alphabet used in so many languages—English, Spanish, French, Portuguese, German—a distinction not lost on my wife ("You really had to pick a county with a whole new alphabet to learn?"). The job offer and decision to move all happened so quickly that there was no time for language classes back in New York. As an English-speaking newcomer in Russia, you find yourself scanning buildings and signs, looking for words written in good old Latin letters—or at least appearing to be.

"Pectopah?" I said out loud in the van, noticing a word with familiar lettering on plenty of buildings. "What's pectopah?"

Sergei and Boris burst into laughter. "David," Sergei said. "You have fallen into the trap! Those are actually all Cyrillic letters. The letter that looks like a *p* is *r* in Russian. The *c* is an *s* sound. And the *h* is actually our version of *n*.

I was sheepish. "Oh. So that's actually—'restaurant'?"

"You got it!"

I felt like a contestant on *Wheel of Fortune* who figured out the phrase well after the entire viewing audience.

Language challenges aside, being in the hands of these two men gave me and Rose our first sense of comfort—one that lasted for our nearly three years in the country, and helped us through the most difficult days.

On its face our arrangement gave us little reason to trust Boris and Sergei. They are employed by UPDK, a semiprivate real estate agency that, during Soviet times, offered Western news organizations everything they needed—housing, office space, drivers, translators—and then proceeded to spy on them and control their movements. Agreeing to work this way was the only way Western news outlets could do business in the Soviet Union.

Fast-forward to today, and Western news outlets like NPR *can* operate independently. But partly for convenience, and partly because being fully transparent to the authorities tends to raise less suspicion, many outlets have continued to work this way, including NPR. The bureau chief's apartment and office are in a building owned and managed by UPDK and very likely still bugged. (Our apartment had more "smoke detectors" hanging from the ceiling than a firehouse.) And officially Boris and Sergei are employed by the agency—though, to be clear, they are in their jobs because they love NPR and they are in every way part of the fabric of our news organization. The arrangement is by NPR's choice and—save for the bugging—is purely bureaucratic. Not once did I question Sergei's and Boris's loyalty to me and to Rose. They became our protectors, our family, even de facto parents, available on the phone at any hour if Rose or I had a crisis—or even just needed to ask Sergei the Russian translation for lamb or beef while shopping at the supermarket. (We would finally get sick of making baaa and mooo sounds at the meat counter).

2 · SERGEI

OUR TRAIN TRIP begins on a chilly, not oppressively cold, February night. It is just after 10:00 p.m. in Moscow, a city that sleeps as infrequently as New York does.

Sergei and I packed light, a single roll-aboard suitcase each. We drag them over hard chunks of ice on the sidewalk and stand on the busy street in front of NPR's office to hail a taxi—well, actually, just someone's car.

Real taxis *are* available. But calling one is pointless because it can take hours for a driver to beat the traffic and reach you. So the quickest way to get from point to point is to do what amounts to hitchhiking. If you stand in the road and put your hand up, a Russian driver will usually pull over within minutes, hoping to give you a ride and make a few extra rubles before or during his or her commute.

Moscow traffic jams are notorious and can immobilize drivers for hours. *The New Yorker* had a wonderful piece in 2010 about a pedestrian who got mad at a driver on the road and felt so confident the offending car would not move much that he walked blocks and blocks home, grabbed a baseball bat, and returned to vent his anger by smashing up the offending vehicle which, as he predicted, was still stuck in traffic in roughly the same spot.

Its not that public transportation isn't available. Moscow has one of the biggest and most efficient subway systems in the world. It's just incredibly unpleasant. Whatever the temperature outside happens to be in Moscow, there seems to be some rule that the temperature will always be fifty degrees warmer in the metro. So if it's about freezing outside and you're bundled up in winter wear, it's a veritable sauna on the subway, making the whole place stink of sweat and sweat-soaked fabric. The subway is also crowded with Russians who have no interest in improving a stranger's travel experience. A passenger needing access to the door to get off at the next station will simply walk into you, expecting that the fleshy obstacle in the way will get the message and move.

Rose, who likes to stand her ground, learned about the city's unspoken rules of the road the hard way. As we approached a metro stop during one morning rush-hour ride, a herd of sweaty passengers squeezed through the crowd toward Rose and me. I nudged Rose, motioning that we should retreat as far from the door as possible, but she resisted, not wanting to condone rudeness. She waited in vain for someone to politely ask or at least politely motion that they would like to get by. Her determination was both admirable and hazardous. As the train came to a stop and the door slid open, the exiting wave of humanity slammed into her—this human standing in their path—flinging her airborne, out of the train and onto the platform. I rushed off the train and helped her up. By the time she had collected herself and cursed Russia, our train was on its way to the next station.

. . .

IN THE CITY people who are warm and generous to family and friends in the safe confines of home become rushed, mean, selfish, and unpleasant in the anonymity of public spaces. Selfish drivers refusing fellow drivers room to enter side streets or willfully blocking busy intersections routinely create traffic nightmares. Selfish, uncaring commuters on the metro create the chaos that landed Rose on her backside on the train platform. So whenever you leave a family's warm and inviting apartment or a meal at a comfy café in Moscow, it's worth reminding yourself that you're about to encounter coldhearted bedlam on the streets.

Cars are buzzing by Sergei and me on the twelve-lane avenue outside our office, but within a few seconds of putting our hands in the air, a black Mitsubishi with tinted windows comes to a sharp stop in front of us, skidding the final two feet over ice. The driver rolls down the passenger-side window, releasing a plume of cigarette smoke into our faces. "Yaroslavsky Vokzal," Sergei says. "Chetyresta," the driver demands. That's four hundred rubles—about thirteen bucks. A bit pricier than usual, but it's late, and I feel like the majesty of setting off on a Trans-Siberian journey is a little like heading off on your honeymoon—don't let fussing over money detract from the occasion.

"Price okay?" Sergei asks.

"Sure." I climb into the backseat. Sergei gets in front with the driver, who is curious about why Sergei asked the American in the back if the price was acceptable.

"Moi boss, ee on ne ochen harasho gavarit pah-rooski," Sergei replies. (Rough translation: He's the boss, but his Russian stinks.)

We are headed to Yaroslavky Vokzal, or Rail Station—one of a dozen major train stations in Moscow. They are generally named for the city most trains depart for (trains to St. Petersburg leave from Leningradsky Voksal, for example). Many of the Trans-Siberian trains depart from Yaroslavsky—at all hours of the day and night.

The traffic on this night is surprisingly light, so after four minutes, the quickest thirteen-dollar cab ride in history comes to an end. Sergei and I are pulling our bags inside Yaroslavky Voksal, which is a fistful of humanity. In other countries—say, the United States—there is some unwritten rule that people generally don't like being active in wee hours of the night. Russians don't follow that. Flights leave airports at all hours of the night. Trains depart at all hours of the night. And restaurants and bars that stay open all night tend to be full—all night.

"David, we should stop at the ticket office."

Sergei has already purchased our tickets for tonight's leg from Moscow to Yaroslavl. But we had planned to buy tickets at this station for the next few legs, from Yaroslavl to Nizhny Novgorod, and from there to Izhevsk.

Now the fun begins: a Russian train-ticket window.

Here are a few facts. You *can* search Russian trains online. But the prices and availability that come up mean next to nothing. Even the times displayed can be meaningless, because often they are listed using Moscow's time zone, or they may use the local time zone of the city you're going to. There's just really no telling.

Basically the best option is to visit a ticket window at a train station itself, rarely a smooth experience, but at least you can go over each and every detail with a human being before you plunk down wads of money. Even then, the chances of everything on the ticket being clear and correct are fair at best. And there is usually a lot of yelling and stress in the exchange with the ticket agent, not to mention angry passengers in line behind you, hogging your space and giving every hint that you're taking too long. And there's the slight chance someone from the government is amid the chaos, listening in to learn where a Western journalist such as myself happens to be traveling—something I experienced in neighboring Belarus, a former Soviet republic so addicted to Soviet living it's as if news of the 1992 collapse never reached there.

As with many experiences around here, I typically approach a Russian ticket window with a great deal of anxiety. Over time, I have learned to treat this affliction prophylactically, taking deep breaths and distracting myself by imagining pleasant scenes of sailboats and seashells. Sergei and I walk up to the ticket area, and it's chaos as always. Some windows are closed, some are open, most are ambiguous, with a person staffing the window, a crowd of passengers milling about, but nothing apparently happening. We approach one window with just one customer—a woman in a sleek black overcoat, in my imagination an employee of one of Moscow's posh law firms or energy companies, yelling at the top of her lungs at the agent on the other side of the glass. She steps aside, stewing, clearing a path for us.

Deep breaths, deep breaths . . .

"Zdrads-vui-tyeh," Sergei says to the ticket agent, who just stares back. She has cropped hair that's dyed a color popular among many Russian women—it's an unnatural red, slightly less orange than a carrot, and clashing dramatically with her apple-red Russian Railways vest. Her name tag identifies her as Anna Nikitenko. I see Anna's mouth move and am fairly certain I hear something, but it's barely audible. There is a speaker on our side and a microphone on Anna's, but the system is not accomplishing much.

Sergei yells the details of the tickets we want—third-class tickets in a few days from Yaroslavl to Nizhny Novgorod, then a few days later to Izhevsk. This seems to have done something productive, because Anna begins slamming keys on her keyboard.

ANNA: [something totally inaudible]
SERGEI: "Shto?"["What?"]
ANNA: [something totally inaudible]
SERGEI: "David, she wants to know if we want insurance."
ME: "For what?"
SERGEI: "I don't know, and it would be confusing to ask."
ME: "Okay, no."
ANNA: [Something that sounds vaguely like "sblum" to me.]
SERGEI: "Shto? Shto?"
ANNA: [inaudible]
SERGEI: "Bedsheets?"
ME: "Yes, please."
SERGEI: "Da, da."

Sailboats, seashells . . .

ANNA: "Tri tysyachi pyatsot devyanosto rublei."
ME: "'3,590 rubles!' I understood that."
SERGEI: "Nice. Got the money?"

We pay—around one hundred and twenty dollars total for two third-class seats on these legs of our journey—and receive beautifully printed pink tickets with the gold seal of the Russian Railways, the reward for all our troubles. As we walk away, the woman in black returns to the window and begins screaming at Anna. Misery loves company, and just for fun I decide to linger. Sergei translates what the woman in black is yelling at Anna about.

"You didn't tell me when you sold me this ticket that I was in an upper berth! Do I look twenty years old? I have high blood pressure. I can't travel like that."

Sergei explains that this outburst is likely more about status than this woman's health. To many Russian travelers, third class alone isn't quite as low as it gets—third class with an upper berth is rock bottom. It brings the indignity of having to climb up, like a monkey, anytime you want to reach your sleeping space. To Russians, it's like being spotted driving a bad car.

"David, a Russian may work in agriculture and have a job digging mud," Sergei tells me, as we both lean against a wall near the ticket counters. "But if it makes him enough money to buy a fancy car he is happy to boast about, so be it. It's not about what business you're in. It's about whether the business makes you the money you need to drive the car you want."

Status is everything, a reality that often becomes comical. I recall once marveling at it inside a wine bar in Austria. Rose and I were on vacation and told the bartender we were living in Russia. He told us he just had a table full of Russian businessmen who asked for his most expensive bottle of Austrian wine.

"I told these guys that my favorite bottle is actually cheaper—the pricey one is really not a good year," the bartender said. "But they almost sounded angry, and cut me off. They said just bring us your most *expensive* bottle."

Arrogant as this behavior seems, there's also something melancholy about it. Russians spent so many years in a rigid Communist state with no personal wealth and little freedom to make decisions on their own. Now, people who have money are adjusting to the experience, flexing muscles for the first time. In fact my father, a physician, told me he wonders whether Russians in post-Soviet times are like patients emerging from a coma. "When you wake up," he said, "it's not like you can use all your limbs again immediately. It takes time to relearn how to move your arms, your legs." It's a metaphor that could apply to more than money. As Shishkin writes, Russians for generations looked for direction from leaders in an "unconscious slavery" that was "bitter for the body but life-sustaining for the spirit." As some Russians experience an awakening, in a society that's evolving, their behavior can seem erratic and unfamiliar to outsiders. I repeatedly reminded myself of this during my time in Russia: Culture and history matter. They've shaped people here, including Sergei.

I ACTUALLY FELT Sergei and I would have grown even closer as friends had culture and history not stood in the way of our truly understanding one another. We traveled everywhere together—to cover violence in Dagestan and Kyrgyzstan, discrimination in Estonia, environmental and political disputes in Siberia. Our friendship was cemented several years before any Trans-Siberian trip. It happened in Ukraine, the place that taught me that vodka and journalism don't mix well.

Rose and I had begun settling into our new life, and it was time to get to work. Getting over the initial shock of moving to Russia? Check. I no longer considered calling an ambulance when the cold froze my nostrils shut and eliminated air flow there. Russian language training? Check. After three intensive months, I could now ask for the check at a restaurant (*shchyot*), buy tickets for the subway (*bilety*), and offer my tea preference (*chyorny s limonom*— "black with lemon"). It was time for my first reporting assignment as NPR's Moscow bureau chief: to cover a presidential election in Ukraine, Russia's neighbor to the west. I have a personal obsession with Ukraine. My Jewish family has roots in the western part of the country: the city of L'viv, a place with cafés and cobblestones that feels as European as nearby Poland and Hungary. People speak mostly Ukrainian, and Russia feels distant on the map and in the mind. In contrast, eastern Ukraine feels bleak and industrial, and most people speak Russian. Western Ukrainians want their country in the European Union. Eastern Ukrainians have more complicated emotions. They generally feel estranged from the ethnic nationalism preached in the western part of the country. And their harsh existence and wariness about Western-style democracy make you think they would be soul mates with the Russians just across the border. And yet there's no comfort level or sense of connection with Moscow either. Nevertheless, if you imagine Eastern Europe engaged in an ideological tug-of-war between Western values and Russian thinking, it's hard not to see Ukraine as the rope, always stretched to the breaking point.

It was the first time Sergei and I would work together, and we decided to spend some time in eastern Ukraine, where voters were widely expected to back a presidential candidate who was viewed as a stooge of Moscow and an enemy of the West. We were about to witness a former Soviet republic turn back the clock, erasing years of progress that Ukraine had made toward joining the European family.

Sergei and I flew to the capital, Kiev, and took an overnight train eastward to the industrial city of Donetsk. It's a place famous for its coal mines. I grew up in Pittsburgh in the 1980s, seeing old photos of men covered in soot walking home from the steel plants. You don't have to search for grainy old photos in Donetsk—the dirty and cruel coal industry hasn't changed much. The air smells and tastes of coal. Men leave their shifts at the mines with faces smeared with soot like some primitive tribal war paint, straggling home stoically, side by side in exhausted silence, their empty lunch pails swinging rhythmically at their sides. The scene is repeated several times a day when shifts end and men return to their families too tired to talk, too dirty for a hug.

After a twelve-hour train ride, Sergei and I rolled into town at 7:00 a.m., as the overnight shifts at the mines were ending. We planned to begin interviewing people about the upcoming election by late morning. It was going to be a day when we took advantage of Sergei's local knowledge. Sergei is ethnically Russian, nearing fifty years old. He reluctantly acknowledges that he bears a striking resemblance to Vladimir Putin—receding hair, dark mesmerizing eyes, thin lips, and a face that narrows down to the chin. He is short and unassuming when you first meet him, but get to know him and you're treated to his biting sense of humor and infectious laugh. Sergei grew up in this hardscrabble Ukrainian mining region during Soviet times. After completing his compulsory military service as a border guard and graduating from college in Moscow, he became a Russian teacher for foreigners and a translator, including for Western news organizations.

Sergei's loyalty to me and NPR is impregnable. If he is given a work-related assignment or piece of equipment, he guards it zealously. Once I bought him a roller suitcase on the company dime so he could more easily carry his radio gear. He read the instructions carefully, and every time he reached a flight of stairs—even just two steps—he would stop, push down the metal handle, carry the suitcase up the stairs, then extend the handle back out. As a long-time owner of roller bags, I told Sergei it was fine to lift his up by using the outstretched handle. "David—the instructions," he said in his thick Russian accent. "They say it can damage the handle." That black bag came with us to every corner of the former Soviet Union and always reminded me that Sergei, as much as he is a part of my family, is also Russian—fearful of breaking a rule, mindful of authority. And I was his authority. I would often say, "Sergei, we are colleagues—we both work for the NPR foreign editor back in Washington." He would smile and say, "But you are the boss." Russians can't imagine life without a boss, without hierarchy. In the workplace they crave structure, predictability, and a pecking order. These touchstones offer comfort in a world that is otherwise chaotic and unpredictable. Doing anything—getting a new driver's license, scheduling a doctor's appointment, getting a document notarized—might require hours of delays and unanticipated bribes. The weather can get extreme at any moment. Traffic in the cities can become so bad, with no warning, that a trip you expected would take twenty minutes might take four hours. So Russians find their order and consistency at work.

Sergei, like most of his countrymen, loved regular hours. He appreciated the ability to arrive at work at a particular hour and leave at 5:30 p.m. Those hours, of course, didn't work for an American journalist responsible for covering news at any time of day. Sergei's devotion to me and the company outweighed his Russian instincts, and he was willing to work whenever assignments came knocking. We had a favorite phrase we repeated countless times—"we can do everything"—meaning if we keep working, beyond what we may have expected that day, perhaps long into the night, we really can accomplish whatever is demanded. Poor Sergei lived in Moscow's suburbs, a two-hour train ride from our office, and he spent many nights sleeping in a small bed in our office.

ON THE FRIGID Ukrainian morning when we arrived by train in his homeland, Sergei had one request: that we drop by his father's home on the outskirts of town for breakfast. He did not have to ask twice; I was thrilled to meet his dad.

The streets of his neighborhood were cold and depressing: dilapidated shacks lined uneven streets blanketed by dirty snow. The dwellings were not built of wood—a material beyond most families' means—but of slag, the waste matter from coal production, mixed with cement. The smell and essence of coal seemed to linger everywhere. We trudged through the snow, up to one home, and approached the door as a dog let out a headache-inducing string of barks. Greeting us was Nikolai Sotnikov, a seventy-five-year-old coal miner whose face and hands were leathery, covered in beat-up scars from years underground. The warmth poured out as Sergei and I entered his childhood home. Nikolai welcomed me with a hug, slippers, and the question I feared most: "Vodka ili cognac?"

Vodka or cognac? Sergei shot me a glance suggesting that no was not an option. Sergei, Nikolai, and I did a shot of cognac to toast our inaugural meeting. Then we did a shot of vodka to celebrate sitting down at the table, and another to celebrate that Sergei and I had begun working together. How could I remain a bystander? I led a toast thanking Nikolai for his hospitality. This time, we went back to cognac. Nikolai poured. I raised my glass first. "Spasibo, ochen priatno paznakamitsa!" ("Thank you, it is great to meet you.") Down went the cognac.

Like so many Russians, Nikolai uses alcohol to soothe himself on hard workdays. He has battled alcoholism for years but has never won. He lives in a home with no plumbing. Every time he uses the toilet he has to replace his slippers with sturdy boots and venture into the cold to a wooden outhouse. His home is heated by coal, which he gets for free as part of his pension from the mines, and he cooks on a metal slab that's heated by that coal. And here he was, fussing over making breakfast for me: delicious *pelmeni*, small Russian dumplings in broth, and a spread of Russian salads. As we finished, Nikolai stared at me from across the table and waited to speak until he had my full attention. Sergei finished slurping a spoonful of *pelmeni*, swallowed, and was ready to translate.

"People are poor and hungry in this part of Ukraine," Nikolai said.

He stopped, allowing me to digest that fully. It wasn't a complaint so much as a statement. He didn't seem eager to expand, and I hesitated to push. This was Sergei's family, and I wanted to keep personal and work relations separate. His words just hung there.

Nikolai moved on, saying something to Sergei in Russian far too fast for me to understand. Sergei turned to me and explained that he and his father were going to walk over to the cemetery to visit the grave of Sergei's mom. It happened to be the anniversary of her death.

Having lost my own mother when I was thirty, I felt strongly that Sergei should have whatever time and space he needed. I told him that he and his dad should take their walk. I would be just fine sitting (let's be honest, detoxing) in the living room. This many shots—I believe I counted ten—would be obscene for a night of intentional drinking at a bar. This was well before noon on a day when we were supposed to be practicing journalism. But Russian welcomes are often measured in vodka, and resisting could risk insult.

Sergei's father insisted I come along to the cemetery. As we bundled up in our hats, gloves and coats, Nikolai put a bottle of vodka and four shot glasses in a plastic grocery bag. After a frigid ten-minute walk, we arrived at the local cemetery, where only the tops of gravestones emerged from a thick layer of snow. Beside each gravestone—including the one belonging to Sergei's mom—were a small stone table and bench. Sergei, Nikolai, and I sat down on the bench, and Nikolai said what sounded like a few prayers in Russian. Then he noisily opened his plastic grocery bag, arranged four glasses, and poured shots of vodka, placing one on top of the gravestone.

"It's for my mother. It's Russian tradition to leave a shot for the deceased," Sergei explained. Nikolai's eyes filled with tears, and he and Sergei sat quietly for several minutes. Then we raised our glasses, motioning to the glass sitting atop the gravestone, and drank.

Russian traditions are ubiquitous. In her 2002 book *Russian Myths*, British scholar Elizabeth Warner described how for centuries, Russians believed so strongly in pagan customs—some of them peculiar—that they blended them with Christian Orthodoxy into what Warner called a "dual faith." The Soviet government suppressed religion any way it could—a 1976 article in the *London Telegraph* detailed the aggressive campaign to convince citizens that religion was "useless superstition." Russians still yearned for spiritual encouragement, and one way to find it was to adhere to actual superstitions. You'll find a mirror right by the front door of many Russian homes. It's bad luck to forget something after you've left the house. If you do, when you return home to retrieve the item, you have to look in the mirror on your way out to make sure your image is still there. Another superstition: never shake a Russian's hand across a doorway or your friendship will be severed. Whenever this rule slips my mind at someone's front door, the host will generally yank me back across the threshold to complete the handshake.

One final tradition that Nikolai passed on to me was one we Americans share: Na pososhok—"one for the road." This was one final good-luck shot before Nikolai hugged me good-bye and sent Sergei and me on our way.

In the following hours I wandered the streets of Donetsk with Sergei, chatting with voters in conversations I frankly don't remember. It was late afternoon when the ten or so shots of vodka began to wear off and Sergei and I began meaningful interviews. We spent hours in the break room at one of Donetsk's mines, an aging brick building where the walls were sprinkled with Russian Orthodox icons—small pieces of religious art that Russians often display, especially when they are doing something dangerous. The room was dark, the smell of coal oppressive. We were surrounded by various hunks of equipment, too old and dirty even to guess what purpose they served or when they were last used. The workers sat on wooden stools, still wearing grimy helmets outfitted with flashlights. One man at a time would speak to us. The others occasionally glanced up but mostly chain-smoked and paged through photos of naked women in Russian-language *Maxim* magazines.

Ukraine had gone through political upheaval in recent years. A Western-backed leader, Viktor Yuschenko, had become president in the 2005 Orange Revolution, an event hailed by U.S. president George W. Bush as a watershed moment in democracy's march to new corners of the world. (At the time, I was covering the White House for NPR and saw on television somewhere close to a million people filling the streets of Kiev, declaring victory for democracy.) Five years later many Ukrainians—especially here in the east— looked at the Orange Revolution as a failed experiment with democracy that delivered nothing. The miners of Donetsk saw their wages shrink and struggled harder to feed their families.

Now a Russian-speaking candidate, Viktor Yanukovych, was promising to end the experiment for good and make sure miners got good wages. Forget that Yanukovych was viewed by the West as corrupt and little more than a thug, or that he had been convicted on robbery and assault charges as a teenager and spent a year and a half in prison. He talked tough, spoke Russian, and the miners saw him as something familiar, an authority figure whom they believed they could trust.

"Politicians are all bandits," the coal miner Roman Fyodorov told me, holding his left palm on his *Maxim* so he didn't lose his place. "Yanukovych is just our bandit."

Several days after I interviewed the coal miners in Donetsk, I followed Viktor Yanukovych on the campaign trail. During my days as NPR White House correspondent I had the fortune of traveling in the luxury press cabin on *Air Force One*. Now I was aboard a sputtering Soviet propeller plane, built in 1969 and apparently not updated since. The seat cushions on the Yanukovych press charter were threadbare. A piece of metal pushed into my thigh with every

bump and the engines whined from age and overuse. Food and beverage service amounted to bottles of cheap vodka, which Sergei and
I made good use of as our plane violently lurched back and forth at
twenty thousand feet.

At one stop I interviewed Yanukovych and got my first close-up
look at the man who was about to win an election and lead Ukraine.
He was tall and imposing with broad shoulders that made him
appear brutish. More confident than smart, he was someone you'd
expect to see on a soccer pitch or rugby field rather than on a campaign trail. He was just the right bandit for his people and said what
ethnic Russians—who would turn out in large numbers for him—
wanted to hear. "In the last five years, Ukraine has lost so much,"
he told me, speaking Russian. "These have been lost years in the
development of Ukraine."

He was ready to begin a new era. The Orange Revolution was
over. And he was about to take office and fulfill his promise, moving
Ukraine further away from democracy.

After boarding our plane to head to the next stop, Sergei and I
spoke about the morning we spent with his father.

"Your dad was a coal miner, too," I said. "He's clearly struggling.
Who is he voting for?"

Sergei took a long pause, then sighed. "Yanukovych."

I've covered my share of politics back home. I've done scores of
interviews with Republicans, Democrats, independents. Sometimes
I connect with the point of view I'm hearing, sometimes not. But
I try to put that consideration aside. There can be no personal bias
in the business of journalism. Hearing Sergei say that name—
Yanokovych—was my first powerful reminder that I had to remain
true to that philosophy in this new chapter of my career. Covering

American politics, I meet people who disagree—sometimes fiercely. But in so many cases Americans agree fundamentally on the idea of democracy, the belief that people have the power to speak out and make change. Here, sitting in a creaky old airplane on a frigid tarmac in Ukraine, I realized I would have to take openmindedness to a whole different level. Yanukovych was open about wanting to roll back one of the most optimistic democratic movements in modern history. And the people supporting him were not just coal miners I interviewed on the job but also the father of my colleague and friend, the elderly man who fed me at his dining room table and took me to his wife's graveside. Even as I got close to people in this new job and entered their lives, I would have to be careful to try to see things through their eyes and to never make assumptions. Feeling a connection with a person would not mean they would necessarily have a world view anywhere close to my own.

The coal that heated Nikolai's home, over which he also cooked, came from a pension that was his lifeline. Nikolai needed every bit of that pension to stay alive, and feared it would dry up under capitalist rule. While talk of democracy and Western values sounded promising at one point to an old man like Nikolai, it was a Russian-backed, Russian-speaking leader who made him feel safe. He spent most of his lifetime valuing strong leadership and predictability, neither of which democracy can guarantee. To Nikolai, promises and talk of change were no match for the culture that built him and no match for the broad figure climbing the stairs of the plane next to ours, Ukraine's soon-to-be-president, Viktor Yanukovych.

"Na pososhok?" Sergei asked as he passed me a plastic cup filled with two fingers of vodka.

I smiled: "One for the road."

The two of us did love traveling together. I knew Sergei's idiosyncrasies, he knew mine. I knew he got stressed about money, wanting to make sure we had cash out to pay a cab driver when he asked, to avoid any delay or perceived impoliteness. He knew I got frustrated when we were trying to set up an interview and a person posed an endless stream of bureaucratic questions about our intentions, stealing valuable time from actual journalism. We knew how to calm each other down—but rarely was it necessary. We were always just itching for our next trip.

For Sergei, train travel is especially meaningful because it's where he met his wife. During his third year of college in Moscow, Sergei was invited by his sister on a short vacation to Leningrad (now St. Petersburg) with a group of employees from her factory, including several young single women. How could Sergei say no? Just before the trip, Sergei's sister bowed out—likely strategically, to lessen the distraction, because she wanted Sergei to get to know her friend Maria.

Sergei didn't like Maria much. The two other women in the cabin were Olga and Tania, his future wife. "And Olga liked me more than Tania," Sergei once told me.

"Wait! Your sister stuck you on vacation in a train cabin with three girls who all had a thing for you?"

"You could say that," Sergei said. "Nice ride!"

Sergei and Tania soon married and now have a twenty-four-year-old son named Anton, who's doing a medical residency in Moscow. As with so many families in Russia, the winds of change dictated their planning. Anton was born in the waning days of the Soviet Union, and with so much uncertainty ahead, Sergei and Tania decided to stop with one child at that point. Many of their friends decided a decade later—when Putin first became president and there were hints of prosperity—to have a second child. But Sergei and Tania decided it felt too late.

Now Sergei and I are beginning our latest journey together, aboard the Trans-Siberian. And for the next month or so he and I will be one another's family.

IT IS NEARING midnight in Moscow, and Sergei and I have escaped the ticket office and are sitting in the waiting hall on the second floor at Yaroslavsky station. At a plastic bench nearby, a police officer has paused, menacingly. He reaches down and jostles a young man from his slumber, angrily demanding to see some documents.

"Passport, passport," he says, using a word that's equivalent in Russian and English.

The sleeping man, dressed in black pants, holding the leather jacket that was his pillow, wearily reaches into the jacket pocket to find his passport and dutifully presents it. With black hair and a darker complexion, the man appears to be from the Caucasus— which means he is sadly accustomed to visits like this. After a string of terrorist attacks in recent years, Russia's uniformly unpleasant police spend much of their time interrogating people, mostly men, who have darker skin, suspecting they come from the North Caucasus region, a hotbed of Islamist radicalism. In the United States this kind of profiling is illegal, or in the rarest cases allowed but hugely controversial. In Russia, it carries on unencumbered by laws or debate.

A crackly march begins to blare from the station's old speakers. This moment of ceremony seems lost on the majority of people in the vast station—many of whom are asleep on benches. But this is an important ritual: the most famous Trans-Siberian train, the No. 2 Rossiya, is boarding to begin its six-day journey to Vladivostok. Russian train stations play music to mark the departure and arrival of the most famous trains. The Red Arrow, the best-known overnight train between Moscow and St. Petersburg, pulls out of St. Petersburg to the tune of "The Hymn to the Great City." That train is also known for its departure *time*. It leaves both cities moments before midnight. That allowed businessmen during Soviet times to claim an extra full day of work during a business trip—which they would not have been able to do if their tickets showed a departure at 12:01 a.m.

Our own train is leaving in about an hour. That means one thing: chai (Russian for tea). Having lived in this country for a few years, I can honestly say that the United States missed a golden opportunity to win the Cold War. Forget nuclear negotiations. Depriving this place of its tea would have brought an immediate cry for mercy from the Kremlin. Russians love tea and can't live without it. Hell, within months of moving to the country, *I* loved tea and couldn't live without it. I don't know if it's the cold chaos of the place that makes you crave a warm soothing drink, or if it's an old-fashioned follow-the-crowd syndrome that stuck, but the manic scene at the ticket office has left me in need of . . . tea.

"Chai?" I say.

"Chai," Sergei says, clearly already thinking the same thing.

We find the best Yaroslavsky Voksal has to offer at this hour—a woman at a kiosk with Lipton tea bags, small brown plastic cups, a rusty electric tea kettle and a bowl full of sugar cubes.

Sergei and I inspect the spread and have the same reaction: "Perfect."

3 · BORIS

THE TRANS-SIBERIAN RAILWAY is intertwined in Russian history. After years of struggle, mismanagement, and vicious battles with the land and elements, the railroad—at first, from St. Petersburg to Vladivostok—was completed in 1916 and quickly became a symbol of Russian ingenuity. Russians marveled at how they were able to build a six-thousand-mile-long railroad that held the vast country together and opened up the Asian frontier. The railroad crossed forbidden landscapes and required complicated bridges—one of which shared a prize with the Eiffel Tower for world-class design. Today, "Trans-Siberian" is a catchword for a number of routes. If you travel from St. Petersburg or Moscow to Vladivostok, or from Moscow to Beijing, you are definitely on a "Trans-Siberian" journey. But long trips between cities that are far apart, and that take you a good distance from west to east or east to west, can also safely be called "Trans-Siberian."

There is a haunting past. The rails were constructed largely by migrant workers and prison laborers, many of whom, in the words of American Paul E. Richardson, who writes about Russian culture, died "from exposure and from infectious disease, from typhoid to the bubonic plague." The railroad, once built, was also convenient for Joseph Stalin, who used it to transport exiles to Siberia. By the hundreds of thousands, the Kremlin could send government critics, lawyers, doctors, religious leaders—really anyone it chose—to the dreaded gulags in some of the harshest conditions on earth. Stanley Kowalski was a gulag survivor. His daughter described the tortures of the train her father experienced in her 2009 book, *No Place to Call Home*. The Polish army officer was captured by the Soviets in 1939, and transported by train between prisons several times—one journey took him across nearly all of Russia on the Trans-Siberian, in a red boxcar with little light:

> *The train . . . made unscheduled stops in deserted stations or empty fields where, if lucky, [prisoners] might be allotted their daily ration of food: a piece of bread and fish. Water, on the other hand, was becoming a rare commodity. At some stations, the inmates would pound upon the barred doors, demanding something to quench their thirst, but often their pleading was to no avail. Amidst these surroundings, the weak had little chance of survival.*

Especially striking was how in the midst of all this cruelty, Kowalski remembered peeking out cracks in the wooden walls of the boxcar to marvel at Russia's landscape. Lake Baikal in eastern Siberia, he recalled, "could take one's breath away. At first glance, all one noticed was the unadulterated beauty of the blue-green water reflecting the majesty of the mountain peaks beyond. The scent of pines completed the exhilarating experience."

Even as Stalin used the Trans-Siberian as a veritable death train, he was hard at work punishing other people by making them construct new railroads. In 2012 Lucy Ash, a reporter for Britain's *Guard-*

ian newspaper, unearthed remnants of Stalin's "deadly railway to nowhere," a thousand-mile Arctic route connecting western and eastern Siberia. "The labor force was almost entirely made up of 'enemies of the people'—prisoners convicted of 'political' offenses." Gulags were created every six to eight miles solely to house construction crews. "Prisoners built their own wooden barracks but the unlucky ones in the front units had to take shelter in canvas tents." Ash estimated three hundred thousand people were "enslaved" to build the project and nearly a third of them died doing it. Many of the slave laborers thought that by building a railroad they were contributing to something important, thus experiencing that elevated sense of purpose Shishkin wrote about. Therefore the cruelest part? The project was abandoned. The Russian woman showing the *Guardian* reporter around the remnants of the rail line put it this way:

> *Of course it was wrong to build the railway with slave labor. But once they'd started it and there were so many victims, I think abandoning the project was also criminal. I lead excursions and tell people about what happened. One man, a former prisoner, made a special trip up here and he just started crying when he saw the rusty engines and old tracks. Many of the prisoners believed they were fulfilling a useful and necessary deed, and all of it was just destroyed. It's heartbreaking.*

Amazingly, the Trans-Siberian route that saw so much hardship and death is now traversed by some of the world's best-off people. One of the trains that speeds along the track is the Golden Eagle, a luxury liner offering the best caviar and cabins outfitted with flat-screen TVs and heated floors. A one-way ticket from Moscow to the eastern port of Vladivostok costs close to twenty thousand dollars. And there are Russians who can afford that. This is a country with some of the wealthiest people in the world, the so-called oligarchs. They are often shrewd, politically connected individuals who swooped in and grabbed ownership of state enterprises as Soviet times ended. When those state-run businesses—mining, oil, and natural gas companies among them—privatized seemingly overnight, the people in charge became instant tycoons. And yet, fortunes under this new regime can be taken away as quickly as they are made. Just ask Mikhail Khodorkovsky, who once owned a giant energy company, Yukos, and was the richest man in Russia. After he began funding and supporting political parties in opposition to Vladimir Putin, Khodorkovsky was arrested in 2003 on charges of tax evasion and sent to a Siberian prison camp. I interviewed Khodorkovsky, by way of letters from prison, in 2010, and he urged Westerners to see Russia "beyond the window dressing." Russia is a country, he said, "where a political opponent can be sent to prison for many years and have his property taken from him. You have to see Russia as a country where society views all this with indifference, where the elite keep silent." Khodorkovsky speaks to Russia's modern-day identity crisis. The "window dressing"—a nation with elections and foreign investment that's eager to welcome tourists—hides a nation with all the repression of Soviet times, made even worse by corruption and a race for money.

IT'S COMPLICATED to consider the Trans-Siberian's impact on Russia's economy. In the early days critics saw building the railroad as wasteful. But closer to completion, others thought pouring money into the project was driving economic growth. What's more, it made it easier for the Soviet government to transport people and resources and industrialize Siberia. But that may now be part of Russia's problem. In their 2003 book, *The Siberian Curse*, scholars Fiona Hill and Clifford Gaddy describe how many remote cities are all but cut off: "They have no railways or major highways linking them to the rest of the country, while airline tickets remain prohibitively expensive." Riding the Trans-Siberian, you meet passengers who need to reach isolated places—for work, or to see family or friends—and the Trans-Siberian is their only option. They may get off the train in a large city, then drive hundreds of miles to reach their destination. But the question Hill and Gaddy ask: Should so many people be living in these places? They argue that the Soviet government, by relocating people and industries to some of the coldest, harshest, and most remote places on the planet, made "monumental errors" that now explain many of Russia's economic struggles. In a way, traveling the railway can feel as if you are riding down Russia's spine, seeing the link that connects so many disparate places. Deeper considerations notwithstanding, today a Trans-Siberian train adventure is a dream destination for travelers all over the world, mentioned in the same breath as the Orient Express and the *Queen Elizabeth II.*

Sergei and I are headed for Vladivostok—but not on a famous Trans-Siberian train. We chose train No. 240 because it makes a stop in Yaroslavl, a hockey-obsessed city several hours east of Moscow. Midnight has passed, but our train doesn't board for another forty minutes. Holding his plastic cup of tea, Sergei is a bit nervous. He purchased our tickets for this first leg from NPR's travel agent, and for the first time, she offered "electronic" tickets. We have no formal tickets—just a printed-out itinerary. Elsewhere in the world, this would be a welcome, modern convenience. Russia being Russia, the thought of a train attendant happily welcoming us onto a train without a fancy ticket with a pretty stamp—an official *document* she can review, contemplate, massage in her hands—seems inconceivable. The intense love of documents is a thoroughly annoying relic of Soviet bureaucracy. Russians themselves will complain about it and laugh at it, even as they keep on producing and signing more documents. In an essay called "Political History of Russian Bureaucracy and Roots of Its Power," Maryanne Ozernoy and Tatiana Samsonova explain how ingrained bureaucracy is in Russian culture. For one thing, a massive bureaucracy provided jobs—a ton of them—and gave people a sense of "stability and predictability," the feeling they had found "their positions in the political system." As much as various Soviet leaders abused the bureaucracy, the institution was also respected, in its most ideal incarnation, as a check on autocratic power. The thinking was, if all these agencies are in place, and documents are signed and delivered to record everything that's done, how could a single leader at the top manipulate society? Belief in bureaucracy goes back centuries, Ozernoy and Samsonova say. And "national mentalities and psychological stereotypes" have become as "fully integrated" in Russian culture as the bureaucratic institutions themselves. But this can play out in truly absurd ways. A friend and fellow American journalist who was based in Moscow, Miriam Elder, once wrote an account of her experience at a Russian dry-cleaning business:

> *You put your six items of clothing on the counter. Oksana Alexandrovna lets out a sigh. This would be the point where you would normally get your receipt and go. But this is Rus-*

sia. It's time to get to work. A huge stack of forms emerges. Oksana Alexandrovna takes a cursory look at your clothes. Then the examination—and the detailed documentation— begins. This black H&M sweater is not a black H&M sweater. It is, in her detailed notes on a paper titled "Receipt-Contract Series KA for the Services of Dry and Wet Cleaning" a "black women's sweater with quarter sleeves made by H&M in Cambodia." Next, there are 20 boxes that could be ticked. Is the sweater soiled? Is it mildly soiled? Very soiled? Perhaps it is corroded? Yellowed? Marred by catches in the thread? All this, and more, is possible. The appropriate boxes are ticked. But that is not all—a further line leaves room for "Other Defects and Notes." By now, you have spent less time wearing the sweater than Oksana Alexandrovna has spent examining it.

I wish Miriam were exaggerating. She's not. And so without physical tickets, Sergei wants to leave extra time to navigate any potential inconvenience, which was impressive foresight. We walk outside, onto a train platform that's a sea of chaos and smoke, as Russians are dragging roll-aboard suitcases with one hand and using the other to take desperate final puffs of cigarettes before boarding. We find car No. 8. The train conductor—or *provodnik*—for our car is standing outside, dressed neatly in her Russian Railways uniform, which includes white gloves and a fur *shapka*, or hat. Russians take their trains seriously, and those who operate them are always dressed impeccably. *Provodniks* stand almost at attention, waiting for passengers to arrive. Our *provodnik* is a woman in her thirties. Her hat and overcoat are emblazoned with three Cyrillic letters that—to an eye accustomed to Latin letters—most closely resemble

PZD. In Russian, they are the acronym for "Rossiiskie Zheleznye Dorogi," or Russian Railways, the massive government conglomerate that operates the rails. The woman is holding a flashlight, ready to inspect tickets. *Tickets.* Not itineraries. Sergei hands over our printout, reaching out gingerly, expecting rejection.

"Electronnye bilety, nyet." (Electronic tickets. No.)

Sergei and I are immediately directed to a place where three other passengers are standing—after-school detention for people who dared purchase electronic tickets. The *provodnik* addresses our failing in greater detail.

"We can't accept these types of tickets until we verify your names on the passenger list. Someone is bringing it over soon. It won't be long. And anyway, the air is fresh." With this, she inhales through her nose, quite dramatically, almost mocking our weakness if we are somehow intimidated by the cold. She smiles.

"Breath it in. Enjoy. Wait."

The temperature has dipped to nineteen degrees Fahrenheit. And the air, whatever she thinks, is actually a blend of smoke from cigarettes and smoke from the train's burning coal. After ten minutes, another *provodnik* brings our *provodnik* a list that seems to satisfy her and exonerate us, and we're waved onto the train. Immediately we walk from the frigid outside into a train car doing double duty as a sauna.

Russian trains tend to be cramped, sweaty, and chaotic. Most, like ours tonight, have fading carpeting and matching fading curtains. We walk into our car and enter a long hallway, with a clock at each end displaying the date and time. The clocks are modern and digital. But the list showing the various cities we'll pass through is on yellowed paper and looks like it was printed in Gorbachev's time.

Many of the engines pulling cars across the Trans-Siberian route are powered by electricity. But trains on long journeys are often heated by coal, and each time the train stops, conductors shovel fresh coal into a hole, an arrangement that causes temperatures to rise and fall unpredictably—usually they rise, leaving passengers sweating profusely. It's an astonishing paradox that you can be traversing a forbidding landscape with howling winds, horizontal snow, and unimaginable cold and yet be inclined to force the window of your train compartment open for relief from the sweltering heat inside.

The train's lavatories, located at the end of each train car, contain metal toilets, and flushing involves pushing down on a pedal that opens a metal flap, revealing the tracks—the receptacle area for whatever you're flushing. Walk past the lavatory, out a door, and you find yourself in a loud, semi-outdoor space equipped with metal cups that serve as ashtrays for smokers—in Russia, that's just about every passenger. The rules of the train govern that smoking must be done in these spaces between cars—but that rule seems to change with the weather. When it's too cold to smoke outside, many Russians hang in the indoor corridors puffing away. In the evenings, Russian passengers seem too desperate for a cigarette to care much about appearance, and you routinely find people lingering with cigarettes in the hallway wearing nightgowns or, in the case of men, boxer shorts and tank tops.

None of this seems, on its face, all that pleasant. Yet, I would take it over a ride on Amtrak any day of the week. There's nothing boring about riding the Trans-Siberian. It's hard yet poetic, perplexing yet entertaining. And you develop a routine. Morning, wake up, attempt to wash off in the cramped lavatory with the metal sink and toilet bowl. Use the hot water canister at the front of the train car to make instant coffee and instant oatmeal. Return for more hot water at lunchtime to make tea and instant noodles. Read, chat with passengers. In the evening, venture to the dining car for borscht or make more instant noodles. Visit a neighbor in his or her compartment and wash the night away with vodka.

Many Russians pass the time reading. In the budget-class cars, where there are no separate compartments—just bunks and tables, creating the feel of a wall-less hostel—younger Russians are reading tattered books. In the second- and first-class cabins, passengers are reading literature on Kindles and iPads. Seeing passengers dressed in little more than their underwear, smoking obsessively into the night, drinking vodka until they pass out, makes it easy to dismiss them as backward. But this is a mistake. Russia remains one of the most educated and literate societies on earth. I can see that in the Kindles being read, and sense it in the conversations.

Tonight, Sergei and I have a second-class compartment for four people. The doors to the compartments are lining the hallway to our left. Recalling the urgency with which our fellow passenger begged for lower beds back at the ticket office, Sergei and I feel fortunate to have the two lower beds on this trip. We enter our compartment, store our suitcases beneath the two lower berths, and sit down, knowing two strangers should be arriving soon.

SHARING CLOSE QUARTERS is second nature to many Russians, something I learned from Boris. He, Sergei, and I were once having dinner at a restaurant called Delicatessen, not far from NPR's office in central Moscow. Conversation among the three of us can be difficult—hardest on Sergei, because as much as he wants to engage in casual chatter, he's also translating. Boris knew enough English and I knew enough Russian for the two of us to get by—often with the help of hand gestures, noises, and second and third chances—but when we were all together we leaned on Sergei.

Delicatessen is a casual café. Like so many restaurants in Moscow, it's hidden underground. This struck Rose and me as odd when we first moved here. As if the city were not cold and imposing enough, there is no outward sense of life or energy on many streets. At first it was easy to conclude that this gigantic capital somehow lacked nightlife. But as you spend more time here, you realize there is an underground world—many bars and restaurants are, on the outside, just a metal door, often unmarked. When you know the right door and come inside, you often enter a welcoming (and usually smoke-filled) place, a warm, cozy respite. Now, when a pack of Western journalists and diplomats gather in any café for a boisterous night of conversation—especially speaking English—there are the occasional glances and stares from other tables. There's always the chance it's a security agent eavesdropping—a fear that becomes more acute when you travel, by train or otherwise, to the more remote parts of the country. But the odds are that any glances or stares are coming our way because, well, we're a boisterous bunch of revelers speaking a foreign language and interrupting another table's peaceful dinner.

Some of my fondest memories of Moscow were from places such as Delicatessen. The café epitomizes both what's right and wrong in the new Russia. On the one hand it's encouraging that this bustling capital has shed its Soviet armor and joined other international cities in being welcoming to outsiders. The café is a gathering spot for expatriates and has an English menu and a pleasant staff. At the same time the café is also a nighttime playground for Russia's young elite—an unavoidable reminder that central Moscow has grown wealthier and more posh in the post-Soviet years, as many villages and communities elsewhere have struggled.

Once you find a cozy spot in a place such as Delicatessen, it's tempting to spend the entire night there, because who wants to go outside in the cold more often than you need to? Rose and I would sit with expat friends—other journalists, diplomats, or English-speaking lawyers or bankers—and talk over wine or vodka for hours, chatting about politics or relationships or the frenetic way of life in Moscow.

Boris, Sergei, and I decided to order a bowl of pasta each and share a bottle of Chilean merlot. "You know, that was one of the first secrets I learned, moving here," I told my two colleagues. "In Russia, French and Italian wines are so overpriced. There's a feeling they must be the best, because they are French. And Italian. But South American wines? South African wines? You can get them here so cheaply because Russian wine drinkers haven't figured out that those are good wines, too."

Rose and I saw wine preferences as a meaningful measure of how far Russia has come since Soviet times (they drink and appreciate good French wines!) and how far it hasn't (they still undervalue more obscure wines highly respected in the West).

My observations about Russian life often resonated with Boris and Sergei, who would add their own thoughts. Occasionally they just politely nodded, which I took as a sign that I was trying too hard to see deeper meaning in every experience in Russia. I seemed to be trying too hard here. The three of us smiled and took a swig of the underpriced Chilean merlot.

"Boris, didn't you tell me you like Georgian wine?"

We had discussed wine from Georgia, the former Soviet repub-lic to the south, which claims to be the birthplace of wine. Ancient vineyards there fell into disrepair in Soviet times but have made a comeback since.

"You had a Georgian friend who liked giving toasts and over-serving you, right?"

"It's a big story." Boris smiled. "Eto istoria druga, Gia."

"The story of my friend, Gia," Sergei said, translating through a mouthful of spaghetti.

The warning from Boris that this was quite a story had Sergei a tad on edge because it meant so much unanticipated translation. But he was also eager to listen.

"Gia and I—and both our families—lived in the same commu-nal apartment in Moscow until I was in the fifth grade. There were ten families. In one flat."

In a way Boris was lucky. His family was Jewish but didn't advertise it. As Jews, not anywhere near the top of the hierarchy in Soviet times, Boris and his family could have been assigned to live somewhere far less pleasant than Moscow. Having the government offer a job and an apartment in Moscow, or any big city, was consid-ered a luxury. Of course, everything is relative.

"My parents, my aunt and me, shared a single room, eighteen square meters."

"How did everyone fit?" I wondered aloud.

Boris took his two index fingers and put them flat against each other, pointing in opposite directions, representing two beds, touching like Tetris blocks. "Don't worry about me. I'm not sure how my parents survived. But David, they were the best years of my life. I had my friends and family, all in one place. There was a babushka from another family who loved to cook. I can still taste her veal cutlets."

Sitting with Boris and Sergei in this basement café, I began to appreciate why Boris cherished those times. The world outside—frightening and dark and complicated. The world inside—cramped, yes, difficult, absolutely, but simple. I wouldn't wish for his life. No doubt, I'll never understand it. But I was understanding why Boris has happy memories of youth.

"When we were both in fifth grade, Gia moved away to Georgia. And things got worse. Families just weren't getting along anymore. One woman spat in other families' food."

Sadly, that was reality for too many Russians. In her 1999 book, *Everyday Stalinism*, Australian-American historian Sheila Fitzpatrick described Soviet communal apartments as cauldrons of jealousy and paranoia. "Private property, including pots, pans and plates . . . had to be stored in the kitchen, a public area . . . jealously guarded by each individual family. Demarcation lines were strictly laid down. Envy and covetousness flourished in the closed world of the *kommunalka*, where space and family size were often mismatched and families with large rooms were often deeply resented by families with small ones." She told the story—not uncommon—of a Moscow apartment where one family essentially spied on another, "writing denunciations to various local authorities. The result was [that] the family was successively disenfranchised, refused passports and finally, after the father's arrest, evicted." But "against the horror stories," she added, "must be put the recollections of a minority whose neighbors in communal apartments were mutually supportive and came to constitute a kind of extended family." Many of those positive memories came from Russians who, like Boris, lived in these environments as children. They had "less developed private-property instincts than their parents, often liked having other children to play with and found it interesting to observe so many varieties of adult behavior."

SERGEI AND BORIS had different Soviet upbringings. Sergei, in that ramshackle house outside Donetsk, Ukraine, is the son of a coal miner. And Boris was the urban kid in Moscow's over-packed communal apartments. Neither experience was easy. Both experiences shaped who these men are.

Boris lost touch with Gia and thought he'd never see him again. But then a decade later, as a teenager, Boris was in a hotel lobby in Moscow, and felt a tap on his shoulder.

"I didn't recognize him until he started speaking. But it was Gia. I can't explain how exciting this was."

Gia and his mother had come to Moscow from Georgia for a soccer game. They ended up skipping the game and drinking all night with Boris.

"When I got home, my dad was furious at me for being drunk. Until I told him I was with Gia and his mom. He was so very happy."

Boris calls Gia his "pervy droog"—first friend. After the unexpected reunion, they stayed in touch. But once the Soviet Union fell, things got complicated. Boris and Gia lived in different countries— Boris in Russia, Gia in Georgia. Boris did take a few trips to Georgia. The first time he visited Gia, though, Boris never *saw* any of Georgia, even though it was his first time in the country.

"We just spent three days straight in Gia's house, eating Georgian food, drinking wine, and talking about everything." Boris had
to promise his wife that on their next trip, they would be tourists
and see more of Georgia than a dining room table and the bottoms
of wine glasses. "Gia died of cancer several years ago," Boris said.
He paused in thought, perhaps chronicling the relationship through
the years in his mind. Whatever memory he settled on brought his
big lips into a smile.

Hearing him describe this friendship was powerful. Sure, I
have a "first friend." Her name is Marissa Goldstein. We grew up
together, our parents were best friends, and we remain close to this
day. We sign off e-mails to each other, "ff."

But something here was different. Boris and Gia and their families were forced into a tiny urban space. Their friendship was built
on mutual survival, on sharing a hiding place away from the uncertainty outside. To me, this makes the intimacy deeper. And then it
was taken away, not because Gia's family decided to move of their
own will. Few families moved from one Soviet republic to another
of their own will. They were forced to move. And then the next
chapter of history intervened—Russia and Georgia became two different countries, making it even harder for two friends to remain
close. Theirs was not a unique friendship, strained by distance and
circumstance. But somehow, I understood why Boris looks back on
his boyhood as a simpler time. After years of upheaval that split the
two friends apart—not to mention disrupted Russian families' lives
in so many other ways—Boris, as Western-leaning and cosmopoli-
tan as he may be today, looks back nostalgically on his Soviet childhood as the happiest time of his life.

. . .

THINKING BACK TO Boris' story, I feel a mix of curiosity and anticipation as Sergei and I wait for the strangers who will share our cramped space on the train tonight.

For now, it's just the two of us sitting in the four-bed compartment. Our *provodnik* ducks in from the hallway to deliver glasses for tea. They are icons of a Russian rail journey—simple glasses that fit neatly into decorated silver holders that are emblazoned with PZD. Our *provodnik*, now that we are all warm inside the train, is becoming warmer herself. She asks if we would like her to bring us some tea bags. Tea is free. Packets of sugar cost three rubles (ten cents). Sergei and I say yes to both. The train lurches forward and backward a few times, acting like an aging person revving up the momentum to crawl out of bed. And finally, train No. 240 settles on to her path out of Moscow, picking up speed. It seems like Sergei and I will be alone in the compartment tonight. Sure, it means more space and more privacy. And yet I'm disappointed.

4 · ANOTHER SERGEI

As THE TRAIN moves away from the station, a younger woman, perhaps in her late twenties, and a man around Sergei's age appear outside the door to our compartment. They are lurking quietly—as it turns out, waiting for me and Sergei to move. They boarded at the last minute and are just now making it to their compartment—*our* compartment.

Following a custom Sergei taught me, we lower-bed dwellers politely move out of the compartment, allowing our roommates space to spread out their linens and make their upper beds. This requires using our lower beds as footspace while reaching above to arrange things. The four of us finally make our beds and get situated, and all seem exhausted. We chat enough for me to learn that the young woman is Ilona. Her long blond hair is pulled back in a ponytail, with a Russian Orthodox cross dangling down over her brown sweater. Travel fatigue is evident in her eyes. "I live in two places right now." She is speaking Russian, Sergei is translating, and I am keeping my questions to a minimum as we are way past bedtime. "My boyfriend lives in Moscow. I was visiting him. Now I'm heading home to central Russia." Traveling so often, Ilona sees the train as a third home.

The Russian rails carry nearly a billion riders per year. Ilona is in second class on a ten-hour trip, a ticket that likely cost her in the neighborhood of three thousand rubles (about one hundred dollars). Had she chosen third class, she could have made the trip for perhaps half that. Our ticket for the four-hour journey to Yaroslavl was 1,200 rubles per person (forty dollars). Much depends on the quality of the particular train, but it's possible to get a third-class seat from Moscow to Vladivostok—six days, six thousand miles—for as little as two hundred dollars one way. More well-off Russians use the train to see family whenever they wish, or to travel to somewhere like Moscow or St. Petersburg for vacation. Russians with less money, especially in remote villages, might spend months or even years scraping together enough money for one third-class ticket to see a family member in a place that takes a few days to reach.

Rounding out our foursome tonight is Viktor, whom I recognize as a fellow member of the team admonished for using electronic ticketing.

Outside our window, everything is masked by darkness. But I know what's out there, since I left Moscow for Vladivostok in daylight last time. The landscape is whizzing by. Vast, sprawling Moscow first: endless blocks of bland Soviet-style apartment buildings, colorful mega-malls with IKEA furniture stores, flower shops, and *produktys*, or minimarts. Then the city will give way to snowy forests and the occasional crumbling village, with smoke rising from a few chimneys. By far, Russia takes up more of the earth than any other country. I knew this. But the earlier Trans-Siberian trip I did back in 2011 made me *feel* it. Four, five, six hours would pass, and all we would see outside was empty, white wilderness. Then a forest. Then a small city, with some decaying buildings—often an empty Soviet factory. Then hours more of nothing. The map would show that these hours barely made a dent in the trip across the country.

Last time I did this leg from Moscow to Yaroslavl, I wandered into the adjacent compartment and sat down for a while with a man named Sergei Yovlev, an employee of Russian Railways. He's in his fifties and often travels by train back and forth between Moscow and his hometown of Yaroslavl. Sergei is a midlevel bureaucrat, and I got the feeling his nicely pressed pinstriped blue suit, which he wears every day, is a symbol of pride, the uniform that reminds his family that he's working hard on these trips that take him away for days at a time.

I was sitting beside Sergei Yovlev, and Sergei my translator was facing us. (This seems an appropriate moment to point out that Russia's limited supply of first names makes storytelling a special challenge.) Our conversation turned to a tragedy in Yovlev's hometown, Yaroslavl, an awful story that made the news worldwide. The industrial city, in 2011, lost its entire professional hockey team in a fiery plane crash. It was an accident eerily reminiscent of the tragedy in 1970 in which Marshall University in West Virginia lost its football team when the team plane went down. I remember the scenes of carnage described in the news stories from Yaroslavl—the plane took off and quickly crashed to the ground near the Volga River in "flames as high as a nine-story building," one police officer told the BBC. A resident said she "saw them pulling bodies to the shore, some still in their seats with seatbelts on."

Yovlev was a fan—*is* a fan—of the team. He sat in his train compartment, looking at me, speaking in a hushed tone.

"Vashichek."

One by one, he named the dead players. To honor them. And to show me how deep his love for the team ran.

"Marek."

He paused.

"Demitra."

Painful as the memories remain, Yovlev has no doubt that the city's hockey tradition will come back because, he said, surviving tragedy is "the way the soul of a Russian person is built." His deep stare as he said those words was briefly hypnotizing and sent a powerful message: I was not supposed to feel sad for him. In a country where today there is little to be proud of or believe in, hockey had become Sergei's faith. And disappointment had made his belief even stronger.

Our conversation brought to mind a 2011 suicide bombing at Moscow's Domodedevo Airport that I covered. The Islamist insurgency had been growing ever bolder in Russia's North Caucasus, and terrorist leaders vowed to redouble their efforts to carry out attacks on Russian soil. It's the same simmering radicalism that some believe influenced Tamerlan Tsarnayev, the older of the two brothers who carried out the bombing of the Boston Marathon in 2013. Tamerlan is ethnically from Chechnya and spent time in Dagestan—both regions in the North Caucasus. On January 24, 2011, a twenty-year-old from another region, Ingushetia, set off an explosion in the international arrivals hall at the airport in Moscow, killing several dozen people. The attack set off an old debate over Putin's antiterrorism tactics. Putin supporters said the deadly airport attack was a reminder of why the Russian government must aggressively target anyone suspected of terrorist ties in the North Caucasus. Putin's critics said he has led a fierce campaign—often to score political points at home—that has backfired. Their thinking is Putin has been too aggressive, ordering Russian forces to round up young Muslim men in droves, which has actually helped the Islamist insurgency recruit in larger numbers.

Covering the aftermath of the airport attack stunned me. Even as body bags were still being removed from the international terminal, the airport was up and running again. Check-in desks were open for business. Newsstands were selling magazines and gum. Planes were taking off and landing. The cab driver who drove me back into the city after my night of reporting told me that his jacket, laid out in the back of his station wagon behind my seat, was covered with blood and pieces of flesh. He had been in the room when the explosion detonated. "One man, he fell down. His leg was torn off," he said in Russian to Sergei, who was sitting shotgun and translating.

"There were all these pieces of flesh," the driver said. "I am in shock. I still can't get myself together." I could not understand how this man was back to work, driving a cab, hours after witnessing such a scene. His explanation was matter-of-fact: "I have a schedule that I have to keep to. There's no way I can call my boss and say I'm not working anymore today." Duty called, a job called, and neither chaos nor anger nor pain was going to be a disruption. It was simply about moving on, fighting through.

It's the way the soul of a Russian person is built.

The historian Orlando Figes captured this in his 2007 book *The Whisperers: Private Life in Stalin's Russia.* After tragedy, he wrote, Russians have long sought out a "different type of consolation." Even gulag laborers, he found, believed they "had made a contribution to the Soviet economy. Many of these people later looked back with enormous pride at the factories, dams and cities they had built. This pride stemmed in part from their continued belief in the Soviet system and its ideology, despite the injustices they had been dealt and in part, perhaps, from their need to find a larger meaning in their suffering." Steven Lee Meyers of the *New York Times* wrote in 2005 that "it would be wrong to stereotype, to say that Russians are fatalistic or heartless. They are, however, not only resigned to tragedy but inured to it in a way that to many raises alarms about the country's future. They are not just helpless in the face of disaster; they could be called complicit, ever beckoning the next one by their actions or lack of action." His point was that if you believe tragedies will just happen, you don't work as hard to prevent them.

After pulling into Yaroslavl on our first train trip, Sergei and I took a daylong excursion to find a haunted village named Mologa. It's under water—Russia's own bizarre Atlantis. For years, occasionally, when the water level of a sprawling reservoir dips low enough, the dome of an Orthodox church peeks out of the water: a stunning reminder of an awful time. In 1939, Stalin demanded more hydroelectric power as he prepared the country for World War II. He ordered that the Volga River be dammed near the city of Rybinsk, creating a massive reservoir. He was undeterred by the fact that dozens of communities—including the village of Mologa—would be flooded and destroyed. Nikolai Novotelnov was a boy at the time. He and his mother watched their home taken apart, log by log, by prisoners and loaded onto a wooden raft to be shipped downriver. Novotelnov and his mother were homeless for a year and alone because his father was in one of Stalin's gulags—having been accused of telling a joke about the Kremlin in public. "They took him on September 10, 1936," Novotelnov remembered. "He was sentenced to six years." He died before he had served his time.

Novotelnov, now in his late eighties, recounted all this, sitting proudly upright in the living room of his home—the same one that was deconstructed to get out of the way of Stalin's floodwaters six decades ago. The home was rebuilt in 1940 and has been situated since in Rybinsk, not far from Yaroslavl. These days Novotelnov is angry. He's ashamed of Russia. "This county is divided between rich and poor," he said, "and money has become the most important thing." He also hates Vladimir Putin. To feel proud, he looks to the past: "Nothing good has happened in Russia during Putin's time. I am his opponent because if we look at our life before 1991, it was more quiet, more measured. Labor and people were valued." Novotelnov seems to say a great deal about Russia today. Here is a man who harbors so much anger at both Stalin and Putin. Yet he would never take his complaints to the streets—that would be beneath him. It would feel to Novotelnov like an act of weakness rather than one of survival. Grit and survival are the emotions he wants and likes to feel, because they give all his sacrifice a purpose. He has nothing to hold on to but a vague nostalgia for later Soviet times when—hard as things were—basic survival seemed more assured than it does today.

I began to think about how some Americans see Russians as weak, because they don't *fight* harder for democracy. In fact, Russians don't seem sold on democracy yet. Like Ukraine's democratic experiment from 2005 to 2010, Russia's experience with democracy under Boris Yeltsin in the 1990s was miserable—the economy collapsed and people went hungry. Russians take pride in enduring—certainly until they believe, without any doubt, that there is something worth fighting for. When I watch Russians go through the motions of daily life, the question I always imagine on their minds is, "Why take the risk?" Hardship, upheaval, and a feeling of having no control over anything combine to shape the Russian soul. And the latest difficulty just girds many Russians to endure the next.

IN FOUR HOURS, Sergei and I will be back in Yaroslavl. We are seated, sharing one lower berth, facing our roommates, Ilona and Viktor. Ilona is by the window peering outside quietly, I imagine, already missing her boyfriend back in Moscow. Viktor is returning from vacation in Thailand, but he seems melancholy about the trip. As a Russian on the beaches of Thailand, he felt like an outcast. At one point he had to exchange some Russian money, but the Thai clerk spoke only Thai and English. He asked several fellow Russian tourists if they knew English to help, and none did. "Young Russians today have to start learning English and other foreign languages," he says. He bemoans how, for decades during Soviet times, Russia was locked away from the world. Two decades after the Soviet collapse, Russians are just beginning to travel. But it is taking some adjusting—both for Russians and for fellow tourists who are often turned off by the Russians they meet. Speaking to Viktor reminds me of when the antigovernment riots broke out in Egypt, in the early days of the Arab Spring. Tourists fled from Egypt—except for Russians. Interviewed on the beaches of Sharm-el-Sheikh, they asked reporters why anyone in their right minds would pick up and evacuate. They paid for a vacation, desperate for some sunshine. You think just an outbreak of *violence* would cause them to change their plans? Russians *are* a different breed. But speaking with Viktor was the first time I realized that maybe some don't want to be and are feeling some discomfort and shame as they try to fit in.

Ilona uses the ladder to climb up onto her bed above Viktor. She reaches to remove her sweater. Without having to be asked, we men look away—awkwardly and politely—to give her an ounce of privacy. She curls up beneath the covers. This was the opening we all needed to politely disengage. Viktor climbs up and prepares himself for bed above me. I turn the lights off, shut the door, and lock it securely. I am the last to crawl under my sheets. I tell Sergei, "Spokoynoi nochi," or good night. He says the same back. The two of us fall silent. As my eyes begin to close, I see Ilona's face above, caught in the glow of her cell-phone screen, staring across at Viktor. They begin to whisper to each other quietly in Russian. I have no idea what they're saying. But these strangers, brought together in close quarters by fate, are enjoying one another's company.

5 · LIUBOV

I'M NOT SURE if our train has slammed into something on the tracks, but a loud bang wakes me up. Then another. And another. Half asleep, I realize our *provodnik* is waking us up as we are approaching our stop. *"Yaroslavl, tridtsat minut* [Yaroslavl in thirty minutes]." Sergei and I rustle ourselves out of bed as quietly as possible, as Viktor and Ilona are fast asleep, heading farther east. Neither of them wakes up amid our fuss—or at least they show no outward sign. I grab my toothbrush and deodorant and navigate the dark hallway to the lavatory. Hesitant to use the notoriously dirty train water, I use a bottle of mineral water to wet my toothbrush, quickly brush my teeth and wipe my face with the towel provided with my linens—it's smaller then an average washcloth, and not nearly as plush. As I return to the compartment, Sergei has already bundled up in his black winter coat, winter hat, and gloves, and he's ready to disembark. I quickly follow with my preparations, finishing as our train pulls into Yaroslavl. Sergei and I barely have time to drag our luggage and ourselves off the train and onto the platform as the train begins to pull away. At the last moment I catch the eye of our *provodnik,* who is smiling through a window, waving good-bye. So stern on first impression, as she refused our electronic-ticket itinerary, but with time I see her true warmth. I can't say the same about Yaroslavl's weather. Sergei and I are standing on a near-empty train platform in the bitter cold just after four in the morning. I am not sure why I had forgotten this would be our reality when we put together our itinerary: Overnight train from Moscow to Yaroslavl. Arrive 4:00 a.m. Wait three hours. Take local commuter train to the nearby smaller city of Rybinsk to meet the parents of a young hockey player killed in the team plane crash in 2011. I still stand by the plan. But the pressing question is what the hell to do with ourselves for the next three hours.

We wander into the station and are forced to walk through a metal detector. Both Sergei and I set it off, but no one is manning it, raising the question of its usefulness. The machine bursts to life with loud beeps that echo through an otherwise quiet station, where five or six tired passengers are—were—sleeping soundly in a waiting area. Sergei and I sit on a bench, and he brings out his laptop and begins to surf the Internet. I am too fidgety for this, and tell him I am going to wander outside to explore. There are about three feet of snow on the ground, and the cold is so bitter you can't keep your gloves off for more than a few seconds. But as I walk away from the front doors of the station, there is a familiar beacon of light beckoning: Bright . . . yellow . . . *arches.*

I travel. A lot. And as a rule, I avoid McDonald's. Why in the world would I choose an American cheeseburger or "Happy Meal" over local cuisine, which, whether tasty or not, is worth sampling if you want to understand a new place. But in the middle of the night in Yaroslavl, I offer myself excuses for making an exception. It is the only business that appears open for a mile in either direction, I am cold and hungry, and the waiting area in the train station was doing nothing for me. What's more, McDonald's experiences *are* a window into life in this country (or I'm telling myself that to rationalize my yearning for a McDonald's "Big Breaksfast").

In Russia there's nothing casual about restaurants. Dining out was so rare in Soviet times that when it happened, families took the experience very seriously. That seriousness remains part of the culture. Russian families will peruse a menu for minutes upon minutes—even if the server is just standing there waiting—as if menu reading is truly a rare treat. I recall my first experience with this. Sergei and I went out to report a story in Moscow shortly after I arrived on the new job, and I suggested we grab tea in a café near our bureau before heading off to the subway—like a quick Starbucks or Dunkin' Donuts stop on the way to work in the United States. We walked into the coffeehouse, and Sergei immediately told the hostess, "Table for two." Before I knew what was happening we were seated, and Sergei was looking over the menu, about to order a pot of tea and some food to go with it. Grabbing a quick tea—or quick anything—is just not the drill.

The rigidity of the typical restaurant experience can be mind-boggling. Once, Rose, Sergei, and I were out for lunch and Rose wanted some butter for her bread. Sergei kindly asked the server if they had butter. The answer: yes. So, Sergei asked, could she bring Rose a pat or two of butter?

"Nyet."

Butter, the server explained, is for cooking. There is no established price on the menu for butter "to serve." So Rose was out of luck.

As astonished as I was by the server's response, Sergei translated it to us without cracking a smile or noticing anything odd—at the end of the day this was just part of his culture.

Some Russians crave a more relaxed experience—which explains why McDonald's has become a stunningly popular dining option for Russians of all ages and socioeconomic classes. My Russian tutor, an educated language professor at Moscow State University, told me how she and her family would take monthly trips into the center of Moscow to attend the ballet or opera—and one of her favorite parts of the experience was stopping at McCafe, the coffee shop attached to McDonald's. It's the best coffee she's ever tasted, and she very much looks forward to her monthly taste. I was at first flabbergasted—an educated college professor sounding as excited about McDonald's coffee as she was about the ballet? But her exuberance makes sense. It's not a tidy narrative of Russians taking a liking to Western culture, as American media have reported. It's about desperately wanting a quick, casual bite and some coffee instead of an hours-long sit-down meal that, in the case of my tutor, would make her late for the ballet. The first McDonald's in the Soviet Union opened in central Moscow in 1990. The grand opening came after American teams were sent in to train newly hired Russian cashiers to smile when taking orders (sadly, not kidding). And here's a statistic: That McDonald's, off Pushkin Square, remains today the busiest in the world.

I am not late for any ballet, but I am damn hungry, and I could not be happier as I walk up to the counter and order eggs, pancakes, and coffee. Sitting here, in a booth at the McDonald's in Yaroslavl, I won't argue that I'm learning anything deep about local culture. The place is empty. The booths, tables, and menu above the registers look like those in any McDonald's from Boston to Bakersfield. The eggs taste like eggs. And I'm the only customer—no real chance for sociological research. But I don't regret this. Not for a second.

I trek back across the street to the train station, and find Sergei fighting off a nap. He and I decide to take turns snoozing, the person awake being responsible for keeping watch of our belongings. Finally, 7:00 a.m. comes and we board a local train to Rybinsk, arriving just as the sun is coming up. We take a five-minute taxi ride to the Hotel Rybinsk, a pink cement-block structure that hasn't seen a fresh coat of paint in the post-Soviet era. In Russia there are hotels—especially Western chains like Radisson and Marriott—that are beginning to shed the old Soviet "charm." The Hotel Rybinsk is only shedding old paint.

Sergei and I walk into the building. The floor is bland, gray concrete. To the right there is a tiny elevator, and in front of that, a desk, where a man in uniform is seated, watching an old television with a rabbit-ear antenna. He pays no attention to us. Sergei and I turn to the left and enter a slightly more welcoming space, a room with threadbare red carpeting, a plant perched on an old coffee table, and a woman seated at a desk where a small sign says *Registratsiya*, or "Registration." Just in case Sergei and I have some other purpose for being here, the woman looks at us sternly and says, "Registratsiya?"

"Da," Sergei and I say in unison.

"Dokumenty, pasporta," she says.

Sergei hands over his passport, and she glances at it quickly and hands it back. My U.S. passport is a different story, requiring a far more serious level of registratsiya. She takes my passport, walks briskly to a photocopy machine, copies far more pages than she should really have to (is she interested in my Belarus visa and Estonian entry stamps?), returns to the desk, searches page after page for my current Russian visa, shakes her head when I offer to help her find it, looks for it for a while longer, finds it, runs back to the photocopier to copy that page, returns, asks for my immigration card, grunts when I politely point out that it's inside the passport, back to photocopier, back to desk. Now she asks me to fill out a card with my passport information—details already in her possession, but I'm not about to remind her of that. "Tysyacha shestsot rublei," she announces. That's our bill—sixteen hundred rubles, or fifty-four dollars—for two rooms for one night. And we are not getting any keys until we pay. I pay in cash. Then we still don't get keys but documents—little cards that evidently give us eventual access to keys. This is where the guard at the elevator comes in. We walk back into the lobby and hand these small cards to the guard, who is not all that happy about being distracted from his movie but nevertheless puts the cards in two wooden slots behind him, and removes from those slots two keys. "Lift," he says, motioning to the elevator and returning as quickly as he can to the TV. Sergei and I arrive on the third floor and agree to meet in an hour, after freshening up. My room is roughly eight feet by eight feet, with a narrow bed, single window, and scarred wooden floor partially covered by a fraying Afghan rug. The tiny bathroom is minimalist—a long faucet protrudes out over a yellowing tub, and the faucet is dual-use, able to swing to the left on demand and serve as the water supply for the tiny sink. I make use of the amenities to shower and change, and meet Sergei to begin our day—or resume one that began hours ago in Moscow. We have a late-morning appointment with the parents of Nikita Klyukin, who fulfilled his dream of playing professional hockey as a member of Yaroslavl Lokomotiv. He died in the team's plane crash, at age twenty-one. Nikita was born and raised in Rybinsk, and his parents still live there.

THIS ENTIRE REGION of Russia—the city of Yaroslavl, outer cities like Rybinsk—is still mourning the loss of the hockey team but trying to move on. During our three-day stop in this area, Sergei and I wanted to attend a Lokomotiv game. The team obviously has all new faces but is competitive again. The Kontinental Hockey League—Russia's equivalent of the NHL—helped by asking other teams in the league to send a great player or two from their rosters to play in Yaroslavl, which the teams were happy to do. Some local fans did not support that, wishing instead that Yaroslavl would take just a break from competition for a few years, develop new talent, honor the dead, and ponder the future more slowly. But, like after the airport bombing, there was a rush to just cover up the tragedy and get back to it.

The evening hockey game, we were told, was sold out, and we had no idea how we would get tickets. We figured we would grab a taxi to the arena and keep our fingers crossed. As soon as we got into the cab, we knew we had found a man who could help. Our driver, a chatty Russian in his late forties with trimmed brown hair, had a little doll hanging from his rearview mirror. It was a hockey player in a Lokomotiv uniform, No. 79, with "Orlov" written across the back. Sergei was in the front seat, listening as the driver explained that Dima Orlov was his son, who plays for the Lokomotiv youth team, the cauldron of talent expected one day to play with the big guys. The next twenty minutes were a rush. Our driver was excited to have an American journalist on board, and he frantically called his son, Dima, who was already at the arena. He unloaded a mouthful of Russian into his cell phone, and the only words I could pick up were *"Amerikanets . . . journaleest . . . nuzhno . . . bilety? . . . davaite!"* which translates roughly into "Got some American journalists here and they want tickets to the game—let's help them!" And help this generous man did. We pulled up to the arena, and his son, Dima, ran up to the car to greet us. The tall, well-built teenager was soft-spoken, but there was little time to say anything anyway. We were in a rush to get inside. Dima told Sergei that we had no physical tickets—nothing but ominous, I had learned—but that if anyone asked, we should just say, "We are with Yuri Vladimirovich." I never did find out who Yuri was. But boy, was his name well-known at the arena! Sergei and I rushed behind Dima, passing throngs of people waiting to go through security. At the metal detectors Sergei yelled out "Yuri Vladimirovich!" and we were waved through like dignitaries. Turnstyles where people were collecting tickets? We strolled right on through, as Sergei kept saying, to anyone willing to listen, "Yuri Vladimirovich." Here, I thought, was a window into the shadier side of Russian life—know the right people and the sky is the limit. Ethical quandary—yes—but I comforted myself because Dima seemed to be doing something so very generous for us.

In many ways the arena was familiar to me. I love professional hockey. My team is the Pittsburgh Penguins, and I go to as many games as I can. There was a concession stand, where I bought a beer. Same as at home. What was different were some of the food offerings. To go with beer? The best-selling option was bags of dried, salted fish strips that resembled worms but tasted far better. I washed some down with beer; then Dima, Sergei, and I settled into seats, never having shown a physical ticket to anyone (victory!). We were behind one of the goals. The ice, nets, general vibe—same as at home. A difference, however: cheerleaders. The Pittsburgh Penguins have no cheerleaders. Here, in the aisle next to me, cheerleaders, one on each step, in orange tops and silver miniskirts. The young Russian women did not look older than teenagers, twenty-one at most. And this was just the beginning. Across the arena, on a huge platform situated above fans below, were more young women, dancers dressed in tight-fitting outfits with black and white stripes. The theme of their attire seemed, at least vaguely, to be related to the railroad. As unfair a comparison as it may be, I could not help but think of the book and movie *The Hunger Games*, where each region of an oppressed, postapocalyptic country represents a different industry, and where the young "tributes" are dressed in costumes representing the industry of their homeland. In Soviet times Russian sports teams were sponsored by different industries—and Yaroslavl's team, Lokomotiv, was and still is sponsored by the Russian Railway. As dance music blared, the girls danced in front of a sign that read, translated, "Russian Rails: main sponsor for Lokomotiv." All over the arena was the familiar acronym "pzd." On the scoreboard, ad after ad: "Russian Railways: We're making our future."

But then the past took center stage. Players from both teams—Yaroslavl Lokomotiv and the visiting Magnitigorsk Metallurg (this team, sponsored by Russia's steel industry, makes a Pittsburgh Steelers fan like me proud)—began skating around the ice as the arena fell silent. This quiet "skate" took place at the beginning of every Lokomotiv home game, to honor the fallen team. Then a ballad began to play, and images of the dead players flashed across the Jumbotron with a message: "The team that will always be in our hearts."

. . .

THE CIRCUMSTANCES surrounding that 2011 plane crash remain murky. The season was just beginning, and Lokomotiv was ready to fly out of town for its first game of the season. Shortly after take-off in Yaroslavl, the plane went down, killing all but one aboard. Officially pilot error was blamed. But the timing was odd. There was an international economic summit taking place in the city, and Russian prime minister (now president) Vladimir Putin was in town. Many local residents refuse to believe that his presence was not somehow related. Was Putin actually the target of a terrorist plot that somehow went awry? Did Putin actually order the crash to bring the nation together after a tragedy, just as he was running to become president again? These seem like far-fetched conspiracy theories, but they do point to the deep suspicions many Russians have about their leadership—and in particular, Putin.

More than twenty thousand fans were silent during the emotional tribute. Then came the cue that it was okay to start cheering. A loud train whistle blasted in the arena, and the new Lokomotiv team took the ice, to the delight of their wild fans. The game was close and intense, as fans urged the hometown team on, yelling, "*Shaibu! Shaibu!*" which translates literally as "Puck! Puck!" but translates among hockey devotees as "Goal! Goal!"

Lokomotiv lost in the end, but that may have been because they had already clinched a spot in the upcoming playoffs and weren't playing their hardest.

After the game Sergei and I caught up with Dima, who agreed to chat for a few minutes before going to meet his girlfriend—who, it turns out, was one of the cheerleaders dancing near our seats.

Dima, Sergei, and I stood near one of the concession stands as fans streamed out of the arena behind us. He explained that the plane crash was especially hard for him, since he knew all the players. "I trained with them. I grew up and lived with them." He dismissed all the theories about how the crash was anything but an accident. "Only God decided that something like that would happen." Dima spoke quietly, thinking about every question I asked. Sergei somberly translated for me. I asked Dima about his plans for the future, and he revealed an inner conflict I found in many younger, more educated Russians with enough money to consider their options. "I live in this city, and I love this city," he explained. "But I want to play in the NHL. It's my dream. Because life is better in countries like the USA and Canada. My girlfriend, she is twenty-one. I am twenty-one. And we will be married in two months. The laws are better in those other countries. People are more helpful. Everything is more comfortable. Why can't we have that here?"

For many young Russians like Dima, there is a desire to leave and see the world, but it comes with guilt and a nagging sense that a Russian should stay and endure rather than escape. This view of the world was summed up perfectly by a woman named Ella Stroganova, the curator of the Yaroslavl City Museum, whom I met on my first train trip across the country. I had asked her why Russians responded to harsh experiences with determined fortitude and a feeling of inevitability, rather than being spurred into action to find solutions and make things better. Looking for answers, or *doing* something, she explained, was simply un-Russian. It was an admission of vulnerability that Russians see elsewhere in the world. "Progress makes a person absolutely weak," she told me. "He loses his strength because he no longer needs to think how to survive." Some in Russia's younger generation, like Dima, are escaping this thinking and dreaming of new things and different places. But as I would learn on this trip, not all young people feel as Dima does.

Sergei and I walked out of the arena, into a light snow. I looked back at the arena, where a huge portrait of the fallen players hung on the outside wall. I had not seen it going in, since we were in such a rush. Under the portraits were the words "Our team. Forever." One of those portraits was of a young fallen star, Nikita Klyukin.

SERGEI AND I leave our indulgent digs at the Hotel Rybinsk and find a taxi to go visit Nikita's parents. Like many Russian cities Rybinsk is a factory town, built around its industrial fortress—an aging behemoth that for years has produced jet engines. The buildings lining the city's boulevards are beige or gray, the snow is abundant but not fresh, so it's turned gray, and all this paints a depressing backdrop interrupted every so often by flower kiosks bursting with color. Bland, dark, and cold as Russia can feel, no society has a deeper love of flowers, or *tsvety*. At the end of a workday, on the streets or on the subway, in any Russian city, you will find men and women carrying bouquets. For any occasion—birthdays, retirements, office parties—flowers are nothing short of a requirement. And so without even mentioning it to each other, Sergei and I know that visiting Nikita's parents means bringing flowers. We ask our driver to stop by a kiosk near our destination.

"Maybe a half-dozen roses for Nikita's mom?" I say to Sergei.

"No," he says, almost sternly. "Even numbers of flowers are only for funerals, for mourning a death."

After several years in Russia, this is the first I've heard of this particular tradition. (And it is no small realization, having brought Rose even numbers of roses on many occasions. Oops?)

"Sergei, they lost their son a little more than a year ago. Are they *still* in mourning?"

The two of us are perplexed. When does a parent close the door on such a tragedy? Never, of course. But when it is time to move on? More to the point, when does a person not want to be reminded of a tragedy anymore? I lost my own mother in 2006. Her sudden and unexpected death, from a blood clot, was easily the hardest day of my life. Not a day goes by when I don't think about her. But within months I began the hard process of moving forward, unshackling myself from that awful day in the past. I want to believe Nikita's parents are well on their way down that road.

"Odd. Let's go odd. Five roses." Sergei thinks about this for a moment, then nods his head approvingly. "I think this is the right decision."

Our decision reached, the woman at the flower kiosk delicately pulls five roses—three red and two yellow—from her gorgeous stash, dresses them with white baby's breath, trims the stems with scissors, wraps it all in plastic, and ties the bouquet neatly with yellow ribbon. I hand her seven hundred rubles (twenty-three dollars), and we are on our way up the street.

Nikita's parents live upstairs in a tan-brick apartment complex that's as drab and uninteresting as so many buildings in Russia. But I learned a rule very quickly in this country: Don't judge a building by its structure. Many a time I have trudged through a trash-strewn courtyard, opened a rusting metal door, climbed a dark, cracked-concrete staircase only to find a person's apartment beautifully decorated and welcoming. Many landlords could care less about the outside. Tenants care deeply about what's inside.

Nikita's mom, Liubov, opens the door of her *kvartira*, or "apartment," and waves her right arm in a sweeping motion for us to come in. I hand her the flowers. She nods and quietly says "*Spasibo*," thank you. She looks down at them for a moment, perhaps counting, and smiles, the only hint that we made the right call. Following another tradition, I remove my snow-covered boots, since we are in someone's home. Liubov points to a pile of slippers, which families always have on hand for guests, but Sergei and I both just stay in our socks— one of two acceptable options. Nikita's mom is a short, tough-looking woman with cropped dark hair, a square-ish face, and a gap between her two front teeth. At first the tension is difficult to endure. She isn't sure whether to detour into small talk or go right into talking about her son. Sergei and I aren't sure where to go either.

She quietly walks us into a room that I immediately identify as Nikita's old bedroom.

"This is my museum," she says.

It's full of medals, photos, hockey sticks, and other memorabilia. The centerpiece on the wall is a photo of Nikita, in his red-and-white Lokomotiv uniform and red helmet. He looks as if he belonged in the NHL, with long black hair, stubble on his face, and a cool, confident stare that could say to a defender, I'm ready to finesse around you for a goal, or maybe instead I'll body-check you into the boards. Nikita's hockey gloves are sitting on a ledge beneath the photo, facing outward from the wall, arranged perfectly so you see this young man's face above, then you look down to see two hands that could be part of the same body.

"He was born a big baby," Liubov tells us. We have now moved to the living room, Sergei and I on a couch, with her to my left. "It was written on his birth that he would be a famous person."

There is a sudden crash from the other room. "Ah, the vase, the vase, excuse me!" The flowers were too big for whatever vase she had placed them in, and our gift had fallen over. She is back within moments, and picks up where she left off. She's told this story before.

"Nikita started studying hockey when he was six. He worked hard. But we never saw tears. I had a rule: If we ever see tears or bad grades, you come home. It was hard on him. But he never complained."

By age twelve, he was at a boarding school in Yaroslavl, a couple of hours away. Nikita's parents thought about moving to be close to him, but his dad has a reliable job at the jet engine factory in Rybinsk.

"At age twelve he's captain of his youth team. At fourteen he's selected to the national team. At age eighteen, he has a bronze medal in the hockey world championships. And he became the youngest player ever in the KHL."

"Can you tell me when you last spoke to him?"

"Ten minutes before the plane crashed. He called me to say he was ready for the season. In a very good mood, but as always, he was a little afraid to fly. I said good-bye, and he made that sound of a kiss. And we said good-bye."

A door opens and closes out in the hallway, and Nikita's dad walks into the room. "Sergei," he says, introducing himself, before shaking my hand and the other Sergei's hand. Now I know where Nikita got his size. Sergei is broad and tall, with thinning blond hair and his son's eyes. He quietly sits down, sensing that his wife was in the middle of answering my questions.

"So when did you learn about the crash?"

"An hour later," Liubov says. "My mother called and said, 'Where is Nikita?' She had seen the news on television. I had to tell her he was on the plane."

She and Sergei drove as quickly as they could to Yaroslavl. "The team didn't call. No one called. We didn't know whom to ask. And there was security everywhere. Finally they told us to go to the——"

Sergei, translating as quickly as he can, now pauses, looking for the right word in English. "Morgue," he says.

Liubov continues.

"And so we were at the morgue, for almost a day until . . . we recognized him."

We sit for a few moments in silence. And then I ask the couple if there is anything, perhaps a lesson, I can learn from this tragedy.

"We live in a very dangerous country." And it's not just one thing, Liubov says. Infrastructure is simply not safe. There are plane crashes, ferryboat accidents, fatal collisions on the roads, all far more often than in other countries as developed as Russia. Life is even dangerous just walking from one place to another. Each year in Moscow there are as many as a dozen deaths caused when an oversize icicle falls like a dagger from a building and impales a pedestrian. Because of this threat Rose and I spent much of our time in the winter looking up, while walking on sidewalks.

But what strikes Liubov most is the uncanny attitude of public officials, and other people in power, when tragedy strikes.

"When it comes to ordinary people, we felt support from everywhere. The entire community. We felt everyone was with us, and shared this with us. But as for the other category? The government?

Team management? The attitude from their side to those who suffered—it is a situation impossible to find in any other country. No one from the team ever called us to ask how we were doing."

I wonder if some part of that is a sense that tragedy is just part of life—a way to make people stronger. Liubov nods.

"There is this belief in our country that tragedy is a test for people who are supposed to be strong. And Sergei and I are strong. That is why we will get through this. I still have both my parents alive. Sergei has his parents. Nikita loved his grandparents very much. So we can't be weak. We have our old people to take care of. They need our support."

"We've always needed revolutions and wars," says Nikita's dad, "because after each of those tragedies, we rise and are reborn again."

"But why do people in Russia believe that?"

Liubov thinks for a moment. "We probably don't know how to live any other way."

This couple has suspicions. They've never accepted the determination that the plane crash was simply pilot error. Maybe it's a conspiracy theory born in anger and loss, but Sergei Klyukin says Putin was gearing up for an election run, and certainly needed something, anything, to turn citizens' attention away from their living conditions.

"Tragedies distract people from their other struggles," Sergei says.

"Are you saying this plane crash was planned?"

"I don't think this was human error. This was ordered not by God but by our leaders. But we have the ability to forgive. That's how we live on."

His wife agrees.

"Love exists in this country. And it is impossible to be without it."

I am not sure what to make of this couple's range of emotions. Sergei's allegations seem far-fetched. But this *is* Russia. This is the country where a former KGB spy, Aleksandr Litvinenko, said allies of Putin indeed carried out terrorist plots in the country to rally support behind him. He also accused Putin of arranging for a well-known journalist, Anna Politkovskaya, to be assassinated. Shortly after making that claim in 2006, Litvinenko was fatally poisoned in Britain.

I am not convinced that Russian officials planned to crash that plane. I do think Sergei and Liubov Klyukin speak for many in their country. They view their leaders with great suspicion. But they feel a sense of duty to endure, and believe that every difficulty makes you stronger. And in times of hardship the impulse is not to turn your anger into action, but to turn inside, protect the people close to you, and feel the warmth and strength from the people you *do* trust.

Sergei and I walk to the door and begin putting our shoes back on. "David, this is for you." Nikita's father has a red scarf in his hand. It says, in Russian, "Lokomotiv. Our team, forever." The names of all the players are there. Sergei begins to cry as he points to his son's name. "Thank you," I tell him, putting my hand on his right shoulder. "I will treasure this and display it proudly in America."

After leaving this apartment, there is one more stop I want to make in Rybinsk. It is not in any guidebook, but there is a small memorial just outside town, honoring victims of one of Stalin's gulags. The infamous labor camps were primarily located farther east, in remote Siberia. But a few were here in western Russia, including the Volgolag camp near Rybinsk. It was first opened in

1935 and housed one hundred thousand prisoners at a time, many of them convicted of political crimes. That's according to Dmitri Macmillen, who recently did a student research project called, "In Search of the Rybinsk Gulag." The camp apparently provided laborers to build the dam that flooded Mologa. Nearly nine hundred thousand prisoners died from "hunger, hard labor, abuse and failed escapes" over eighteen years, Macmillen wrote. "The production of a mere megawatt of power in the first years of the camp's existence came at the expense of forty human lives, a futile sacrifice, only exacerbated by the realization that the hydroelectric station achieved a minimal level of electric production."

Sergei and I wave down a taxi. Our driver, a young guy in a black leather jacket, has never heard of this place. "Gulag," Sergei keeps saying. My colleague finally makes a phone call to a local museum, hands the phone to our driver to hear the directions, and we are on our way.

The driver is blasting techno music, with English lyrics that in no way align with my mood. "I like sexy, sexy. I like to roll in king-sized beds." Neither Sergei nor I are speaking. I am in the backseat, watching Rybinsk pass by. There is the jet engine factory where Nikita's dad works, a sprawling, dirty complex that probably hasn't changed much since Soviet times. We continue through the center of town, past a snow statue of Russia's Santa Claus—Ded Moroz. Weeks after Orthodox Christmas, it's probably time for Santa to be relieved of his duties—the red paint from his hat is bleeding into the muddy snow—but no one has taken him down yet. And just outside town we pull over, and our driver points across a field to what appears to be nothing more than a clump of snow. Sergei and I tromp about fifty yards, and as we approach, we see that the mound of snow is actually covering a rock. There is a plaque on the front of the rock that Sergei translates for me.

"This is the beginning of remembering victims of the Volga camps."

"It says 'beginning,'" Sergei points out. I can see his breath in the frigid cold. "Because, David, we could not talk about this for many, many years. We could not see monuments like this. We could not see anything."

In other words, in this country some tragedies happened long ago. But there is a reality that outsiders may struggle to understand. Since public displays of emotion were frowned upon for years, many Russians are just now coming to terms with their history, and the pain. They are only now beginning to mourn what was lost. In the snow, beside the rock, just below and to the left of the plaque, there is a bunch of flowers. They're red roses, fresh, as if put here within the past day or so. And I can't help but count the number.

Six.

6 · NINA

ROSE AND I had a rule in Russia: Never ask why.

Asking why in daily life (*Why* do train-ticket agents' microphones never work? *Why* don't the authorities do something about those fatal icicle incidents in Moscow? *Why* can't I order some of the butter you *told* me you have in your kitchen?) gets frustrating. And *why* would you want that?

In the daily humdrum of life here, it's advisable to avoid the question and move on or your blood will remain at a boil (sailboats, seashells . . .).

We left Rybinsk, caught a two-hour ride into Yaroslavl, and are arriving at the central train station to resume our eastward journey. There is a line outside the main doors. We wait in it for five minutes and eventually make our way inside the station, to the front of the line, where it becomes clear what created the line in the first place: an upright metal detector and bag scanner that appeared to be out of use the other night when Sergei and I whizzed through. But now, even though no security officer appears anywhere in view, people have formed a line and are approaching the security area, placing purses, backpacks, luggage, wallets, belts, and jewelry on the conveyor belt, walking through the metal detector, retrieving their belongings on the other side, getting themselves organized, and moving on. All of this takes time.

I am generally a fan of these devices, willing to sacrifice time and convenience for safety. But not a single police officer or railway employee or *vokzal* staff member is manning this security post. It strikes me that perhaps there is someone hidden in an office somewhere monitoring the passenger entry point by remote video. But this hypothesis is blown up by the fact that more than half the people passing through this security checkpoint are setting off the alarm at the metal detector—and nobody is emerging from some obscured monitoring station to stop them. The scene is annoying and comical. Someone passes: *Bleep, bleep.* Next person passes: *Bleep, bleep.* I pass through: *Bleep, bleep.* Now I would literally offer myself up for a pat-down, were anyone around to perform it. But so it goes. One by one, people wait in line in the cold, arrive at security, go through the motions dutifully, all for no apparent reason, all with a headache-inducing soundtrack: *Bleep, bleep.*

Okey, I'll do it just this one time. *Why?*

Rose and I always figured that things like this were remnants of Soviet bureaucracy, with layers of institutions and agencies that don't communicate with one another. In this case there is likely a domestic security agency responsible for maintaining security checkpoints at many if not all of the country's train stations. After the recent acts of terrorism in the country, the Kremlin has promised beefed-up security at transportation hubs. But then there is the staffing, which may fall to another institution that never got the memo about providing personnel to actually monitor the results of these security checks.

Yet, just as mind-boggling as the scene here is the fact that everyone—Sergei and myself included—is simply going through the process without questioning it, walking through the line, sending baggage along the conveyor belt. This would get Rose worked up. "Why is this thing here?" I remember her once saying, as we waited in a useless security line at a train station. "I'm not doing it. I'm not." She then walked around the security checkpoint, ducked under a rope and stood on the other side with a satisfied smile. I am more of a wimp about these things and fully expected Rose to get tackled by a Russian security official. It's a risk Rose nodded to when she told me she would probably get into a lot more trouble if she was fluent in Russian and could engage more easily in "why" debates with authorities.

"I'd probably be arrested in this country if I knew the language," she once told me.

I laughed. Nervously. "That's not funny, dear."

But Rose had a point. In the United States, when things don't make sense, we ask questions. Rose has been furious at taxicabs in Washington, D.C. We and our friends have been overcharged and hit with imaginary fees, our female friends have been verbally abused by male drivers, and the city's taxi system was for a long time an unregulated free-for-all. Rose began an online campaign to drum up support for change, and she attended city council meetings to make her case. Things have changed, slowly. Recently NPR moved to a new building in Washington. And one of our beloved colleagues on the facilities staff was not offered a job in our new digs and was about to be unemployed. I banded together with several other journalists, and we met with one of our top executives, pleading that the man should be treated better and given his job in the new building. It happened.

Not everyone is a fighter. But there is a sense at home that if something seems unfair in life, there are places to turn—at work, or in a community. Maybe you won't get your way. Maybe a boss will tell you to shut up, and you'll be in the uncomfortable position of having to listen to him or her, for fear of losing your job. Our system is far from perfect, and people are mistreated. But the overall spirit, the sense of possibility, the sense that you can raise your voice and have a chance to bring change, is something that exists at home, but not so much in Russia. And I wanted to understand—yes—why.

AROUND THE TIME of my first train trip, in late 2011, the largest antigovernment protests since the Soviet collapse were taking place in Moscow. Thousands of Russians filled the streets, expressing their fury over a flawed election and demanding an end to Vladimir Putin's rule. Putin, a tough-talking leader beloved by many for his bravado—a man who happily went shirtless to show off his muscles on Russian television—long enjoyed broad support in his country. But in Moscow, Russians were on the streets, voicing opposition to his anticipated return as the nation's president.

I remember the enthusiasm well. I boarded a creaky Soviet-era trolleybus and traveled to one protest with Russians of all ages—students carrying protest banners, pensioners chatting with one another about how big the crowd might be. Yet for all the anger and passion, no one in the crowd could explain what they actually wanted. Putin gone? Sure. Then again there was no viable opposition leader, no one proven to replace him. Stay on the streets and fight until the government is gone, as in Egypt and Libya? No, people said they feared chaos like that. The protests allowed Russians to use muscles they were rarely allowed to flex during Soviet times and in the period since, and it felt good. And yet Russians there had trouble communicating what they were fighting for. Translating anger and frustration into action, and a message, was unfamiliar territory. And the lack of a message was one reason the fight never really caught on elsewhere in Russia. I recall heading off to the east on that first train trip, finding many Russians perplexed by what was unfolding in Moscow and feeling little desire to become part of it.

In reality the December 2011 protests were a political statement by Russia's urban elite, Moscow dwellers with white-collar jobs who largely benefited from Putin's economic policies but who grew tired of his political heavy-handedness and war on civil liberties. "The demonstrators were the relatively privileged in economic and social status, not the economically disaffected and disadvantaged," wrote Fiona Hill and Clifford Gaddy in their 2013 book *Mr. Putin.* It would be foolish to dismiss what happened on the streets of Moscow. Two of the most respected economists who follow Russia, Sergei Guriev and Aleh Tsyvinski, have written that "sufficient prosperity has arrived, calling forth a middle class solid enough to demand government accountability, the rule of law and a genuine fight against corruption." They believe that in Russia "the political mobilization of the middle class will eventually lead to democratization." And yet there was an inherent contradiction in the fact that the very people enjoying the most economic success under Putin were those taking to the streets. That made this movement in 2011 incomparable to revolutions elsewhere in the world, driven by economic hardship. What about the *other* Russia—"popular Russia," as Tucker at Princeton called it—the people, the masses elsewhere in the country? Without an investment from them, it's hard to imagine a revolution bringing fundamental, long-lasting change. And they have never been part of a political movement. The novelist Mikhail Shishkin also holds a view of "two Russias." In the nineteenth century, aside from the educated city dwellers, Russia had "millions and millions strong" living in the provinces—"poor, uneducated, slowly drinking themselves to death and mentally still residing in the Middle Ages." That's a harsh and unfair characterization today. And it's worth mentioning that Moscow may be a wealthier and more educated place—but we found far more warmth, generosity, and personality everywhere else in the country. Still, the division that has always been there, the feeling of two countries—rich and urban versus rural and poor—still exists.

HAVING SET OFF the alarm at the security checkpoint—and avoided any further scrutiny—Sergei and I are boarding an overnight train to Nizhny Novgorod, where we will spend two nights with Sergei's family, at Aunt Nina's place. I am excited to meet more of his family, to get a better sense of his roots. Thus far I just know Sergei's wife and son in Moscow and his dad in Ukraine. Tania, his wife, is a tough woman who works, often overnight shifts, at a sock factory. She is, as Sergei likes to say, his true "boss"—a view on marriage he and I share. Sergei's son, Anton, is an eager young man, twenty-four years old, who attended medical school in Moscow. He often slept on the couch in NPR's office to make his early classes or overnight shifts at the hospital in Moscow, avoiding his two-hour commute from the city out to his parents' house in the suburbs. Anton has arrived at a risky time in his life. He is in between medical school and residency, a moment when the Russian government could intervene and demand he perform his mandatory year of military service, a requirement for all young men. This could mean awful things—perhaps an assignment to the volatile North Caucasus, where Russian militiamen are often targeted by Islamist radicals. Whenever Sergei speaks of Anton, he always tries to stay optimistic, hoping that a residency program accepts him and the authorities delay his service to allow him to complete his medical training.

Sergei and I are climbing aboard our next train, and I am bracing myself for my first experience with third class. To control cost, Sergei and I decided to go under this option for most of the remainder of the trip.

Third-class cars are arranged more like open dormitory rooms. There is a narrow aisle that passes through areas that each sleep six people. In each area, to the right, there is a table with two seats that becomes a bed, or berth. There is a second berth above. To the left there is a table with two benches, perpendicular to the window. The two benches double as berths, and there is a berth above each of them. If Russians can seem selfish, heartless, and disinterested in public, they are often warm and considerate in intimate quarters like this.

The unspoken ground rules are not unlike those in second class: If you have one of the upper berths by the window, it's entirely okay to spend time sitting on one of the lower berths—call it a communal couch. If someone in a lower berth is sleeping and you need to climb to your upper berth, it's fine that you may need to step on your neighbor's bed—perhaps his or her feet or legs—to reach yours. The difference is, in third class there's a larger audience to see whatever you're doing—like trying to elevate. At the edge of the lower berths there is a small metal stepladder designed, in theory, to assist upper-berthers. But the ladder is at the end of the lower berth, next to the aisle, which fully exposes you to the spectators. I prefer moving away from the aisle, closer to the window, to leap up, attracting somewhat less attention. The best method I've found is to put your two feet on the side edges of each of the lower berths (desperately avoiding stepping on the occupants), then put your elbows on the two upper berths, using all the forearm and shoulder strength you can muster to lift your body up. While thus elevated, you thrust your buttocks onto your berth. Next challenge: avoiding slamming your head into the roof of the train in midthrust. Ducking your head can avoid a collision, but ducking while thrusting can be more than the mind—and body—can handle, and often you lose focus and tumble to the floor, which amuses other passengers. Fear of this embarrassment can be consuming, worse than fear of hangovers and frostbite, which in Russia says a lot.

It's all about finding a comfort zone aboard a train, so you can begin to appreciate the poetry of the experience. My first evening aboard a Russian train, Sergei, Rose, and I ventured to the dining car. American dance music from the 1980s blared from an old television. We sat in a booth, and a server ambled over and presented a voluminous menu—fourteen pages describing some delicious dishes.

I ordered stewed chicken with vegetables. The server shook her head.

"Nyet."

Pork loin?

"Nyet."

Finally I asked her what she *did* have.

"Borscht yest [Borscht we have]."

I finally confronted the reality: Menus around here are for show. About the only hot item they had was borscht, that ubiquitous and timeless Russian dish. I like homemade borscht. I just don't always trust it coming from a Russian train kitchen. Pacing my train car, hungry, led me to stop and say hello to my neighbors, travelers in the compartment next to mine. One of them was Zhanna Rutskaya, an effervescent forty-five-year-old woman who worked as a hotel receptionist and was returning home from seeing family in Belarus. I greeted her with a smile and a *spasibo*—thank you—for inviting me in. Zhanna greeted me with a link of Belarusian sausage, using it like a baton to wave me into the seat beside her. Then came the jar of homemade horseradish-and-mayonnaise, a concoction that I was instructed to spread onto toast and devour. Whether this strikes you as appetizing or not, trust me: It beats the borscht in the dining car. The only unpleasant development was realizing how little I had to offer Zhanna in return. Food sharing is a Trans-Siberian Railway tradition for which I was embarrassingly unprepared. Here was Zhanna, bringing out sausage, delicately prepared at her family's home in Belarus, the meat pushed into its casing by Zhanna's relatives. Her mother used an old family recipe to mix the horseradish and mayonnaise, sealing it in a jar, surely expecting Zhanna to share it with a worthy fellow passenger. All this warmth and generosity, and what was I able to gin up in my compartment? Luna bars. She was patient with the newcomer, politely declining my American snack but saying nothing more.

Sergei and I find our spots in the third-class car, one upper berth and one lower berth in the section of four by the window. As we are removing our heavy coats, a woman with short blond hair and glasses enters our space, greets us with a nod, then pushes her way past us to the window. Outside, on the snow-covered train platform, her family is scanning the windows of the train car until they spot her looking out. "Do svidaniya, do svidaniya!"—good-bye, good-bye—she yells, blowing kisses to her family, who jump and wave back.

Having learned the lesson on that first train trip, I have come somewhat more prepared to share food this time, opening a bag of chocolate croissants and motioning to our blond traveler that she should have some. "No, thank you—I brought my own food from home." She is friendly but clearly determined to prepare for bed, as it's approaching midnight. Our train begins slowly pulling out of Yaroslavl.

I'm a big fan of lower berths, and Sergei agrees to let me have it on this trip. After a quick stop in the lavatory, Sergei is ready for bed and, like a gold-medal gymnast, he puts his forearms in place, lifts himself up, smoothly transitions his body over toward his berth, and delicately lands. I half expect him to raise his arms for the judges and await his score. He simply smiles and says good night. I open the plastic packet of sheets, make my bed, and settle in. The lights are now off in the cabin. Sergei is asleep above, and our blond neighbor is asleep, facing me in the other lower bed. In the quiet darkness I am having trouble dozing, at which point the concert begins. The blond woman begins to snore, a lower tenor sound, smooth notes, perhaps one every two seconds. Then a lower baritone sound comes from a few sections away. These notes are deeper, louder, and more frequent. And finally, a brassy, higher-pitched, squeaky snore emerges from a bit farther down the aisle. No one around me seems to notice—perhaps more acclimated to life in such close quarters—but my own sleep on this eight-hour night train to Nizhny Novgorod is limited.

NIZHNY NOVGOROD IS a tree-lined city of a million people in central Russia, situated around two important rivers, the Volga and the Oka. The landscape reminds me of my hometown, Pittsburgh, with crisscrossing bridges, linking neighborhoods that are close in proximity but feel distinctly different because they're on opposite banks. Arriving in Nizhny, I feel like a real Russian traveler, because we have a family waiting excitedly to greet us. As soon as we descend the metal stairs of the train car, two women waiting on the platform leap at Sergei and bury him with hugs.

"David, this is my cousin Ira and her daughter, Zhenia."

"Ochen priatno paznakomnitsa [It's nice to meet you]," I say, shaking their hands.

Ira has short red hair and Sergei's facial features. Zhenia is twenty-three, with long, shiny black hair and is wearing the uniform of many young Russian women—skin-tight jeans and wedge-style shoes that extend her height by a good four inches. Rose liked to offer commentary on the clothing choices of Russian women, often focusing on their determination to wear high heels or uncomfortable wedges no matter how much ice or snow was impeding sidewalks. Zhenia leads us, uncomfortably, over chunks of ice and snow to her car, and we pile in and head for Aunt Nina's apartment. Again, on the outside, a gray, drab building. We go up a cramped, old elevator the size of a broom closet, enter the flat itself, and it could not be a warmer place.

While Sergei is saying hello to other family members, Aunt Nina and I are having one of those conversations with no speaking because of the language barrier. I hand her a box of chocolates, and say (motion, really), Thank you for having me. She takes my suitcase, motions for me to open it, and points to a small room with a shower. I now get the point. As her travel-weary foreign guest, I am meant to have the first crack at a shower, and who am I to refuse?

Aunt Nina and her late husband were given this flat during Soviet times. They lived modestly by Soviet standards. She was a schoolteacher who later worked a desk job at a local prison, where Sergei's late uncle Peter was a top official. Those jobs, along with other murky considerations the Soviet authorities never divulged, determined their status and living situation. The apartment has a tiny kitchen with a stove and fridge, a closetlike room with a sink, a bathroom with a toilet and shower, a small bedroom, a larger bedroom, and a spacious room that serves as living and dining room. For one or two people, the space would feel plentiful. But as with many Russian families, generations live under the same roof, trying to maximize whatever they can get from housing that was allocated for free during Soviet times. Aunt Nina sleeps on the couch in the small bedroom. She has given the master bedroom to Zhenia and her boyfriend, who are both out of school and beginning new careers that don't pay much.

When I emerge from the shower, it is late afternoon. Irresistible smells are already wafting from Aunt Nina's kitchen. She and other family members are arranging the dining room—pulling up the couch to provide seating on one side, adding chairs in other places. I can already tell we are going to spend some serious time here.

At five o'clock I am instructed to sit and ten family members join. Aunt Nina is bringing out dish after dish, one more delicious than the next—homemade borscht with a dollop of sour cream, stewed chicken, pickled vegetables, soft brown Russian bread (with as much butter as I want!), and—vodka.

"David, vodka. You like?" says Pavel, one of Sergei's cousins. I can't tell if my smile reveals the fear or not. But he takes it as yes. And so it begins. I *am* eager to get to know Sergei's family a bit before entering a drunken stupor.

This is Sergei's mother's side of the family. She died several years ago and is buried in the cemetery we visited in Ukraine. Sergei and I both lost our mothers when they were relatively young, and we often talk of that shared pain and about the positive influences our mothers had on us.

Sergei is not close to many people on his father's side. His grandfather died fighting with the Red Army in World War II. That was a reality faced by far too many families. Russia lost millions of men in that war, more than any other country. After his grandfather's death, Sergei's grandmother immediately remarried. "And my father never forgave her for that and never wanted to see her," Sergei once told me. This unwillingness to forgive always struck Sergei as odd, coming from a man who needed forgiveness himself. Like so many Russian men, Sergei's dad struggled with alcohol and abused his wife. "I once asked my mother if dad ever beat her. Twice, she told me. David, I can't relate to a man who does that. I have never raised an arm, or even raised my voice at Tania."

Sergei could not have been more excited to see his mother's family in Nizhny. He hadn't seen them in six years—even though it's only a six-hour train trip from Moscow, he and Tania have just been too busy. On his last visit he had not even begun working for NPR. On this visit, at the table, Sergei hands out his NPR business cards, and explains he works for an *Amerikanskaya radiokompaniya*. They pass the cards around the table, studying every detail, a moment that makes Sergei proud and me proud for him.

I am on my second bowl of borscht when Zhenia, trying her limited English, declares: "I am going to come to America and write a book!"

I ask if she's serious, and she says a stern "Nyet," then smiles. Zhenia is happy to have a job at a small automobile company, and her dream is to travel with her boyfriend, Albert, to some of the Russian cities near Nizhny, if they can save enough money. Life isn't easy—she and Albert are cramped living with Aunt Nina, and there's little extra money for travel. But the couple is happy, satisfied to live and eventually raise a family in Nizhny.

Meeting Zhenia makes me eager to meet more young people. In Moscow, people in their twenties and thirties are on average wealthier and more educated, often in well-paid jobs at energy companies or law firms. Many of them were part of the middle class that rose up in those December 2011 protests. The image the world saw was Russia's young generation rising up. It was an attractive narrative for Western journalists who spent years watching and waiting for Russia to see its own Arab Spring. In truth, though, Zhenia may better fit the mold of a more prevalent young Russian—struggling to get by, satisfied to be near family, educated and familiar with the West but not clamoring to see or be part of it.

Aunt Nina is to my left at the table, keeping constant watch over my plate to make sure it's never empty. Her insistence that I keep consuming food gives me ample time to pick her brain about the time she and Sergei's uncle spent working at the local prison colony in the 1970s. "And Peter had the rank of major," she says. "But he was never promoted, because of an incident at the camp." She explains that the camp dentist needed an assistant and designated a prisoner, who enjoyed the freedom that came with working for a prison staff member. He used that freedom to go on a killing spree, hanging a woman who worked in the prison pharmacy and fatally stabbing a prisoner.

"The man's name was Grom," Aunt Nina remembers. "He fled to the woods near the camp. The dogs found him. They wanted to take him alive, but Grom yelled there was no way they would get him. So they shot and killed him."

Uncle Peter was not directly involved, but he was in charge that day. The local Communist central committee investigated "and needed someone to blame. So they put a reprimand in Peter's file, and it stayed there forever."

"So, Aunt Nina," I say, pausing for a quick sip of tea *"Was* this one of the gulags we in the U.S. heard about?"

"No, I don't think so. There was respect here for prisoners. They had new uniforms that were replaced often. I do remember different classifications for prisoners, which determined their treatment: 5-A was the code for sick prisoners who needed food often and got better treatment; 9-A meant you received bread and broth once a day; 9-B meant you had violated a rule and received bread and broth every other day."

I ask if people died at the camp.

"There were death-penalty prisoners, but people were not killed there—at least I don't know of any."

"Were there people there for political crimes? Do you think anyone was innocent?"

"Well, Peter said he saw innocent people who were there. He tried to help them. He helped them prepare their appeals. He was an honest person."

GULAG is an acronym that essentially translates into English as the main department of labor camps. Sergei suggests that Western historians have used the term more broadly than Russians have. The colony where Aunt Nina worked was something different, a place for thieves and murderers—not for political prisoners. Aunt Nina tells me she knows little about the "gulag" system we in the West heard so much about, which seems revealing. Here was a system that under Stalin, and after his death, killed millions of people, often for political crimes. Aunt Nina and her husband did not work in a gulag—their prison colony was wholly separate. And yet I'm struck that she seems sincerely unfamiliar with the larger picture of violence—and not so eager to speculate about it. From what I know of Soviet times, it would make sense for a person to have his or her job, do it dutifully, and collect paychecks, with little curiosity about the broader picture in the country, no concept of Stalin's cruelty, unless a friend or family member was a victim of it. It's clear Aunt Nina doesn't talk much about this. Not many Russians do.

In my imagination, those six flowers at the gulag memorial near Yaroslavl were left by someone only now confronting the horror of the past. In many ways Russians were trained to put painful things out of their minds and just move on to the next day, and the next day's duties and tasks, without even asking "Why?"

. . .

I'LL NEVER FORGET a reporting trip I made to Kaliningrad, a seemingly misplaced chunk of Russia that is separated from the rest of the country, bordering Germany and Lithuania on the Baltic Sea. I went to visit a Holocaust memorial that had recently opened, revealing a long-kept secret.

In January 1945, days after Auschwitz was liberated and the Holocaust was nearly over, the Nazis, in one of their final cruel acts, marched seven thousand Jewish prisoners north from Poland to a beach in east Prussia. Scores of prisoners died on the march. Those who survived were slaughtered on the beach—according to some accounts, the Jewish prisoners were shot while standing ankle-deep in the ocean and facing the horizon.

After the war Germans who had memories of the atrocity were sent away and the region was repopulated by Russians and became known as Kaliningrad. For fifty-five years little was spoken about the mass killing. The Soviet government, meanwhile, didn't even single out Jews as special victims of the Holocaust—grouping them as "heroes" with everyone who died in the war. It was not the Communist way to single out certain religions or ethnicities for any reason. For people who live in this coastal village, Yantarny, in Kaliningrad, it was as if the atrocity never took place—until a small stone was placed in 2000, amid restaurants, to memorialize the victims. I spoke to the director of the Yantarny History Museum, Lyudmila Kirpinyova, when I visited in 2010.

"In those days everyone kept silent," she said of Soviet times. "They didn't reveal anything. Even nowadays my husband tells me if I had a shorter tongue, I would be of greater value. But since I couldn't speak much in the past, now it is my time to speak—a lot, at last."

In 2010—*2010*—her husband was *lecturing* her about being more "valuable" if she would just keep her mouth shut about the Holocaust!

This is a country where, for years, people were taught that if they had a mundane problem—the electricity or water service went out—they could call the local Soviet authorities and the problem might be promptly fixed. But if they saw something unjust or awful, the wisest choice could be to simply ignore it or move past it. People were not taught to raise questions—because doing so could be dangerous, and really there was nowhere to turn for answers anyway. A foundation of Communist ideology and Soviet power was keeping people convinced that they had to accept their fate as it was—and that, in the end, this would be better for everyone. But this philosophy remains in the DNA, passed from one generation to the next, including to a younger one that so far shows little sign of extinguishing it.

In Kaliningrad, in all but the rare case, it was reflected in years of knowing something terrible happened on that beach but not wanting to ask questions. For Aunt Nina, it was innocently passing on questions about Soviet gulags—even though she worked at a prison colony. At the Yaroslavl train station, it's accepting a bizarre and annoying security check, not asking any questions. This plays out in Russian life in ways large and small. What little tension there ever was between me and Sergei would come from me pushing to ask more questions than he felt comfortable with. Often he would call to set up an interview—perhaps with an official. I wanted to meet the official in a place with rich sound. (Yes, the stereotype is true. We in public radio do yearn for the sounds of street musicians, chirping birds, or church bells to spice up a scene.) The official's assistant may tell Sergei that his or her boss can meet in the office. Sergei would say okay and break the news to me. I would then say to Sergei, Do we have to accept this? Did you ask why? Did you tell them that I want—need—good sound for my piece, so could this person take ten minutes of the day to meet outside? Sergei says in those cases he knew he could have pushed harder—he just became convinced that the person likely felt too self-important and would not cave to any amount of persuasion. Truth be told, Sergei is more aggressive than most Russians. He prided himself on not doing what many Russians do—immediately declare a job impossible (*nevozmozhno!*). Still, he stops far short of where American journalists might stop—I don't blame him at all. It's just a different ethos. We come from different cultures.

Aunt Nina has brought out tea and dessert—delicious little chocolates. And Pavel is pouring the next shot of vodka. He passes a plate of pickles to me, and I grab one. He raises his glass, and dedicates the toast to me: "To our visitor from America."

"Spasibo," I say. We all hold up our glasses and down the shot. The rest of the evening is hazy.

After a few more shots here, Zhenia, who does not drink, agrees to take us on a drive. We end up at one of Sergei's cousins' homes. Everyone is friendly, offering plates of sausage . . . and cheese . . . fruit . . . and more vodka. Sergei is talking about the interview we have tomorrow (well, now it's later today). We are meeting a man named Alexei who, Sergei explains, was a former traffic cop, falsely accused of killing a woman, tortured to force a confession. Pavel, who has moved on with us to this next stop, gives me a don't-believe-what-you're-hearing glance. He has worked for the local police.

"And I will tell you—I have never, ever, heard of such a thing happening."

Around three in the morning Sergei and I stumble into Aunt Nina's flat. She is awake, watching TV, and says something sternly in Russian about too much vodka. I have been assigned Zhenia and Albert's bedroom (they generously agreed to stay elsewhere), where I immediately pass out. The last memory I have is Sergei and Aunt Nina on the couch out in the living room, chatting about . . . well, something.

7 · ALEXEI

THE RUSSIAN WORD for "hangover" is *pokhmelye*. To truly capture the strength of the word and the condition, say the first syllable as if you are clearing your throat. "Pokhkhkh. . . ."Put the major emphasis on the middle syllable, "MAY," then bring the word to a gentle end with a quiet "leh."

Now, imagine Sergei's family—each and every member who encountered me—looking at me and immediately saying this word in the form of a question: "Pokhmelye?"

It becomes the running joke of the day. Sergei, joining Aunt Nina to deliver water to my bedroom: "Pokhmelye?"

Pavel, more of a statement of fact than a question: *"Pokhmelye. Ya tozhe* [Me, too]."

By late in the day, say 6:00 p.m., the joke extends to how long my *pokhmelye* seems to be lasting. "Yeah, evening is not so much pokhmelye time, huh?" I say, which Sergei translates, sending Zhenia and her mother into convulsive laughter.

I have emerged from my therapeutic shower, consumed a good dozen of Aunt Nina's pancakes, gulped down several cups of water and coffee, and informed Sergei that I am now human enough to get on with our day.

Zhenia drives us to a bland-looking brick apartment building about ten minutes from Aunt Nina's place and tells us to call whenever we wrap up our meeting.

Sergei and I enter the building, climb four flights of stairs, and locate the home of Alexei Mikheyev and his mother, Lyudmila.

She opens the door and eagerly says "Zdrastvuyte, zakhodite [Hello, come in]." I already have the sense that a visit from a journalist offers some glimmer of hope that she and her son rarely see.

Lyudmila has a round, haggard-looking face. Her age and fatigue are not disguised much by the bright red she's used to color her chin-length hair. Sergei and I remove our shoes, and Lyudmila guides us through a door to the right and into a bedroom where her son is lying flat on a queen-size bed, his head propped on a pillow. "Dobry den [Good day]," he says quietly.

Lyudmila pulls up a few chairs around the bed, and we all sit to chat. Alexia is thirty-seven. From head to waist he's built like a wrestler—shaved head, broad square shoulders, muscular arms. Then you notice his legs, stretching out on the bed toward me. They're thin, frail, and useless.

"I do my best for my son," Lyudmila says, almost apologetically. She points to the wheelchair in the corner of the room. "He can't walk. The doorways in our flat are too narrow for the wheelchair. It doesn't fit in the bathroom, so I lift him up and put him on the toilet. It's not easy." She's smiling. "He's a big guy."

We are sitting in awkward silence. "Alexei, may I hear your story?"

He's told it before and is happy to tell it again, grateful for as many people in the world as possible to know what happened— because, he says, too many in Russia just look the other way.

"I used to be a traffic cop. One night in 1998 I was off duty, driving home with a friend, and two girls on the side of the road needed a ride."

As we know, it's fairly common in this country for strangers to pick up people who want a lift.

"One of the girls asked to be dropped off at one spot. Then I dropped my friend off. Then I drove the other girl a bit farther and dropped her off. The next day I got a call from a colleague who said there was a girl missing in the city. He asked if I would come in to the office to give any information I could. Turns out it was one of the girls, and the other girl remembered my car and told the police about the ride. I put on my uniform and went to the office to help in any way I could."

He could tell immediately something was wrong: "An officer said I was being charged with a crime. He said that fact that I gave this girl a ride meant I must have kidnapped her. They said the fact that I asked the girls to fasten their seat belts was evidence that I was restricting their freedom."

Alexei was detained, and then things only got worse: "Soon, they charged me with rape and murder."

Lyudmila is giving her son a look of proud determination, hoping his strength grows each time he recounts this. Alexei uses his powerful forearms to lift himself higher up, so his back is more upright and he can look more easily at me and Sergei. He is now sitting up, in a gray T-shirt, the wall behind him covered by an oversize Afghan-style rug.

Alexei says his friend in the car with him, Ilya, was interrogated about the night: "We were questioned separately. And they brought me a written statement from Ilya detailing how I raped and murdered this girl. There were details about how I tied up her hands, and where I dumped her body."

Ilya was Alexei's best friend growing up, and as an adult.

"Why do you think he said these things about you?"

"I have no idea. He was probably scared about what the police would accuse him of."

Alexei says they were determined to convict a fellow cop: "This was 1998, in the middle of an anticorruption campaign in Russia. I'm sure this seemed like an ideal case. They could convict, and everyone involved would get promoted. I was told later that the missing girl's uncle was in the federal correctional service—a colonel. He ordered everyone to pay close attention to this case. So very high-ranking officials from the region got involved. The uncle ordered that they wrap this case up in ten days."

I ask what happened next.

"I was held for several days. They kept saying, 'This is your friend. He is telling us everything. And you are lying. They tried to get me to confess. I refused. And they began torturing me. They beat me up. They attached metal things to my ears and electrocuted me. They kept increasing the intensity. I couldn't take it. So I confessed. I said, 'Yes, give me the papers, I'll sign them. I raped and killed this girl.'"

But Alexei tried to roll that back.

"After I confessed, two other people came in—some top officials—and started asking me for more details about what I did. I told them, 'I didn't kill anybody.' I thought maybe *they* could help me. The deputy prosecutor was there. I thought maybe he would help. But I finally realized there was nobody to complain to. I was brought back to the room and handcuffed. Then they started torturing me again. The electricity. They threatened to attach the things to my testicles. I thought I would die, honestly. And they would just tell everyone I had suffered a heart attack in prison. I don't know how I did it—I thought my handcuffs had me attached to the chair—but I just jumped as hard as I could. There was a window two meters away. I crashed through the glass."

Alexei fell three stories, landing on top of a motorcycle in an internal courtyard of the police station. "I felt my body just draped over the bike, with glass everywhere."

His spine was shattered.

"An ambulance came and drove me to a hospital. But nobody treated me for days. I think doctors were told not to approach me because I was a maniac. Five days after I got there, the guards suddenly left my room. They took me in and operated on my spine. I was told that the charges were all dropped. The missing girl had been found."

Lyudmila came to the hospital and saw her son for the first time. She did not know yet that he would never walk again, that she would become his full-time nurse.

For fifteen years mother and son have been largely shunned in the community. It is as if they were responsible for causing some dust-up with the authorities that people prefer to ignore—as if mentioning it, or asking questions, or being in any way associated with this mother and son, might somehow get them into trouble.

"To this day," Alexei says, "not a single person has apologized to me."

Nearly a dozen investigations were opened into the case, but all were quickly closed. Finally a local group called the Committee Against Torture took up Alexei's case and brought it before the European Court of Human Rights in the Hague. In 2006 the international body, ordered the Russian government to pay Alexei 250,000 euros ($400,000).

Two other things happened, seemingly as a result of the European court taking on the case. Two local police officers were sentenced to four years in jail for their treatment of Alexei. And the Russian domestic security services began pressuring the Committee Against Torture in Nizhny Novgorod, suggesting they might be receiving money from British intelligence.

Alexei leans his head back against the rug on the wall behind him. His mother is smiling at him but also quietly sobbing. The money from the European court was drained quickly by medical bills—Alexei once traveled to Norway to see a spine injury specialist. Now he and his mother live on a small government pension that barely covers their living costs. There is no money to upgrade to an apartment that's wheelchair accessible. Here there is no elevator, so Alexei must crawl down four flights of stairs to go outdoors. Lyudmila says they have asked local agencies if there's public money to help a disabled person, and have been told there's just nothing available.

"You know, in Soviet times, people helped each other," Lyudmila says.

Many Russians say this—that in Soviet times perhaps strangers didn't help strangers on the streets, perhaps people generally looked the other way when others were treated unfairly, but among family, friends, and trusted close neighbors there was a sense of shared sacrifice and survival.

Today feels colder and more lonely to people. In Soviet times people did not ask questions or challenge the authorities, but if something went wrong, you could turn to your small community for warmth and safety. Boris had Gia in the communal apartment, and it felt like the best time in his life. Lyudmila once felt that same closeness and believes neighbors or local officials would have helped her and her son in the past.

Maybe in those days she could have persuaded those in charge of communal housing to move her to a first-floor flat.

ACROSS RUSSIA TODAY there are countless stories of people being falsely accused, beaten in prison, blamed and convicted for something they never did because the person opposing them in the case had more money or better connections in the local courts. I did some reporting on Russia's justice system during my assignment in Moscow, focusing on statistics for the first nine months of the year 2010. During that time eight hundred thousand criminal defendants faced charges in the nation's federal court system. Of them, 99.3 percent were found guilty, according to the Russian Supreme Court.

That's mind-boggling. There is no way nearly every person charged with a crime and brought into federal court is guilty, unless the system itself makes that assumption. And a former federal judge I interviewed, Aleksandr Melikov, told me that's just it. There is a "mind-set that a court is a law-enforcement body," he told me, "not an institution there to protect citizens." Melikov lost his job after his superiors began complaining that he was being too lenient with defendants.

There are victims of this system everywhere. I met one,

Andrei Grigoryev, in 2011. He was forty-three, married with an eleven-year-old daughter, and worked as a forest ranger in a rural area a few hours east of Moscow.

He once went after some hunters who were illegally shooting fox and deer in a wildlife preserve. When he gave chase, they came after the officer on their snowmobiles. Grigoryev told me he was knocked down as he fired his rifle in the air.

One of the hunters was a powerful local politician. Not coincidentally, Grigoryev was quickly charged with abuse of power, facing up to ten years in prison—basically for doing his job.

Russia's justice system allows for Grigoryev to be wrongly accused. It allows Alexei to be beaten and tortured. It allows high-profile figures like Mikhail Khodokorsky, the former oil tycoon, to serve time in a Russian penal colony for crimes that still remain unproved.

It is easy to blame Russia's leaders. I also struggle over why Russia's citizens aren't *demanding* something better. Whatever is holding them back may well be the same thing that keeps Sergei from asking tougher questions when he's setting up an interview. It could be why that man in Kaliningrad lectures his wife for being too vocal about the Holocaust and why Russian train passengers go through the motions at the security checkpoint—assuming it just has to be this way.

Sergei and I have been sitting with Alexei and Lyudmila for two hours. I have one more question: "Did you ever see or talk to Ilya again?"

"Never. And we were best friends. But I never want to see him again after what he did to me."

"You want to know how sad it is?" asks Lyudmila. "When Alexei was growing up there were maybe thirty or so boys in the neighborhood who were friends. So many of them have died—of drugs. Or serving in the wars in Chechnya. Really there were only two left, Ilya and Alexei. And now they never speak."

Sergei and I begin to get our equipment together. "Thank you for your time, Alexei. Good luck to you. I will be thinking of you a lot."

"Spasibo," he says, before resting his head back on his pillow.

Lyudmila walks me and Sergei to the door. We are putting our shoes back on. "Please, if there is any way you can find a doctor who can treat him, will you let me know? We are always looking."

"Konechno [of course]," Sergei says.

As we walk out into the hall and begin walking down, I imagine Alexei on these very stairs, in a sitting position, his mom helping him down each step, one by one. I look back up, and Lyudmila, with her dyed red hair and watery eyes, is watching our every step as we walk away. She doesn't want to close that door just yet, because it will once again seal off that desperate world within.

8 · VASILY

Now I get to enjoy the Russian tradition.

During our trip so far, I've seen so many made-for-the-movies scenes of families dropping loved ones off to catch a train, or greeting them with hugs and love as they arrive. It happens everywhere, at every stop the train makes. It's hard to find that kind of poetry on Amtrak.

I got a small taste when Zhenia and Ira picked us up two days ago. But this evening I am getting the full treatment.

Zhenia and her friend drove to the station separately, just to make sure they're able to say good-bye.

"David, this is for you," Zhenia says. She hands me a magnet, with an artist's rendering of Nizhny's rivers and landscape. I'll cherish it—this city that looks so much like my home, Pittsburgh.

We hug, as Pavel reaches behind me and grabs my roll-aboard suitcase from my hands. "David, let's go, we have to board."

Yes, *we.*

Pavel walks, dragging my suitcase along, boards the train with us, finds our seats with us, and gets us settled until it becomes clear our departure is imminent. He and Sergei share an extended hug, and Pavel kisses Sergei on the cheek: "Sergei, you come back soon. David, very nice to meet you."

He gets off the train and positions himself on the platform, with the entire family, waving and waving as our train begins to move. I still have a photo of the scene on my iPhone—the flash off the window distorts it some, but there is Pavel, in his black leather hat in the cold, pressing his face against our window, and Ira, bundled in a black jacket and hood, smiling warmly at me and Sergei, posing as I snap the shot.

Russia can be so maddening. The day before, I listened to Alexei describe the horror of being tortured at a police station, then ignored after being fully exonerated, living his life without the use of his legs and with no one seeming to care but his sweet mother. This country's system of justice—this *country*—is so deeply flawed.

And then there are these poetic moments—a poetry that grabs you and touches your heart in ways I rarely experience at home, or in any other country.

"Russia giveth. Then so quickly, she taketh away." That's how my best friend and college roommate, Chandler Arnold, summed up his vacation when he came to visit me and Rose during our time in Moscow. Each day, each hour, seemed to bring dramatic emotional swings.

I remember one day in Moscow that especially struck me. I waited for a city bus outside my office in the bitter cold. The bus arrived and creaked to a stop. The door opened, I boarded, and reached into my pocket for rubles to pay the driver. He was in an angry mood and kept speaking to me sternly in Russian. I used the little Russian I knew at the time—"Ne ponimayu [I don't understand]." He was cold and mean and aggravated with my lack of Russian, or my being American, or both. I finally found the change, but he refused to give me a ticket, which you need to scan in order to pass through a turnstile and reach the seats. I was trapped there, with him, at the front of the bus. He pulled to the next stop and opened the door, fully expecting me to surrender and disembark. That's when a voice came from the back of the bus. "Malchik!" (I had just been addressed as a "young boy.") A large woman, bundled up in a maroon overcoat and maroon fur hat, was approaching me holding up a card with a bar code. I saw two other older women, babushkas, in their seats, also holding up cards. They were monthly bus passes. The first woman handed me her card. I scanned it at the turnstile and walked through as the driver grunted. The woman then yelled at the driver in Russian (I don't know what she said, but I liked it). Her generosity, and the generosity of the other women who were ready to lend me their passes, filled my eyes with tears. I returned the pass and held out the change from my pocket, but the woman refused to take it. "Nyet, sadeet-yuh [No, just sit down]!"

It's just my own small taste of how Russians live their lives. Difficult things happen, and you pray for the moment or day when things turn brighter. It's as if Russians can't appreciate something beautiful without first experiencing something hideous. This is where Russians seem to find their strength. Our train is now heading from Nizhny Novgorod to Izhevsk, in the Ural Mountains, so we can visit some babushkas who define finding strength in tragedy.

When we were planning the trip, Sergei called to set up an interview with Mikhail Kalashnikov. Yes, *that* Kalashnikov. He's ninety-three years old, lives in Izhevsk, and invented one of the world deadliest weapons. To reach Kalashnikov, Sergei had to go through the public affairs department of the Kalashnikov factory and museum. That's where our trouble may have begun. "I'll need passport information for you and the American correspondent," the woman told Sergei on the phone. "Well, this is not for journalism, it's for a book," Sergei said. "Well," the woman said, "the FSB may still want it—I need it in case they ask." The FSB is Russia's modern-day domestic security service—today's KGB. The new agency is still based at Lubyanka, a menacing building in central Moscow that long housed the KGB—it has a small clock on the top floor that the British novelist Tom Robb Smith once described as gazing over the city like a beady eye.

Any inconvenience seemed worth it, as I did want to meet Kalashnikov if possible (The inventor died following this trip at age ninety-four). And in any case the authorities were sure to find out at some point that I was poking around the country. But after Sergei's phone call, I had a sinking feeling Izhevsk would be the spot where I'd encounter "friends"—my code word for the thuggish guys who would occasionally follow us.

MY FIRST EXPERIENCE with Russia's shadowy security services came shortly after I arrived in Moscow. I hadn't even begun reporting yet, and was taking three intensive months of Russian-language training. I was sitting at a coffee shop in central Moscow, sipping tea while studying Russian verbs of motion, when I noticed that I didn't feel my briefcase touching my leg anymore. Sure enough, it was gone. I asked the security guard at the café if he saw anything, and he said no, but that he was willing to call the police. I then called Sergei and Boris, who urged me not to call the police—it would only mean paperwork, hassle, hours at a police station. In Russia, often, involving the police is far more trouble than it's worth—especially for an American journalist who may have just been had by one of their sister agencies.

"David, is there anything important in there?" Sergei said over the phone.

"Not really—my iPod, my digital recorder for work, and two Russian-language books."

"Boris and I both feel you should just let it be."

That evening, the phone rang in our apartment. Rose picked it up. It was a woman, speaking broken English.

"My father. He found a bag on street. Maybe your husband's?"

I was delighted. Rose and I told the woman that we would meet her father the next day in front of the puppet theater, across the street from our apartment building. The man, in his fifties with a mustache, pulled up in a silver car right on time and handed me my briefcase. I handed him flowers and a box of chocolates, as a thank-you.

"Gde, gde? [Where, where]?"I said, pointing to the bag, wondering where he found it.

"Na ulitse [On the street]," he said. He hastily waved good-bye, returned to his car, and drove off with the flowers and chocolates.

I inspected the bag. Everything was there—that is, except for anything electronic. No iPod, no recorder. Rose and I returned to our building and both went upstairs to tell Boris and Sergei what had happened. Boris looked at me, shaking his head back and forth. Sergei looked suspicious as well.

"David, did you have any identification in the bag—ID, business cards?"

"No."

"How do you think they found the number to call your apartment?"

I felt queasy. I had just gotten my little reminder from the FSB that their beady eye was watching me. I didn't want to be paranoid. But a friend who worked for the U.S. Embassy in Moscow said many Western journalists and diplomats get just such a nudge. A fellow American radio reporter in Moscow described how after she arrived in Russia and received her press credential, she returned to her apartment—which she had locked and closed up in the morning—and found her bedroom light on, her computer turned on, and her e-mail open.

Luke Harding, a correspondent with the *Guardian*, was hounded more than any other Western journalist, even briefly expelled from the country. He described a break-in in his apartment that left the window to his son's room open:

> *Nothing had been stolen; nothing damaged. The intruders' apparent aim had been merely to demonstrate that they had been there, and presumably to show that they could come back. The dark symbolism of the open window in the child's bedroom was not hard to decipher: take care, or your kids might just fall out. The men—I assume it was men—had vanished like ghosts.*

Alas, all the work of "friends."

ON SEVERAL reporting assignments, Sergei and I were obviously trailed by a car. In the volatile region of Dagestan—where the FSB often targets and rounds up people they suspect of having ties to radical groups—we were almost happy to be followed. Better to be fully transparent about who we are and what we're doing if it reduces the risk of the authorities mistaking our identity and doing something stupid.

In Minsk, Belarus, Rose was with me when we spotted a thuggish-looking dude—dressed in black, hair slicked back—watching us at a café, then trailing us on the sidewalks, following us into our hotel, even joining us on the elevator. Rose, never hesitant to push buttons, waved good night down the hall to the man as we entered our room to turn in.

These memories weigh on my mind as our train pulls into the station in Izhevsk. At the ticket window, as we're paying for our next two legs, to Perm and then Ekaterinburg, I catch the eye of a young man at the adjacent window. He is acting as though he's in a dialogue with the agent, but is paying way too much attention to the details we're providing about our travel plans. The young man has a shaved head and is wearing a red, blue, and white athletic warm-up suit. When we're done at our window, he cuts his conversation off—never buying a ticket to go anywhere—and abruptly walks away.

"Our friend," I mutter under my breath.

Sure enough, as we walk out of the station, we see that young man and another look at us, then quickly look away, then get into a car and wait. Sergei and I find a taxi and are on our way, and we can spot the guys in the car following a good distance behind us.

We try to ignore them as best we can and enjoy the drive out of Izhevsk and into rural Udmurtia. Russia is predominantly Slavic, but there is a dizzying mix of clans and ethnicities, large and small. The Udmurts are a people who live in this leafy part of southern-central Russia, on the western edge of the Ural Mountains, which divide European from Asian Russia. The Udmurts are known for their red hair and round faces, their own distinct language, and their traditional clothing that, for women, often includes colorful patterned head scarves.

We are en route to Uva, a resort town of sorts in the forest. There is a famous *sanatoriy*, a health complex that probably compares best, though not perfectly, to the old resorts in the Catskills beloved by Jewish families from New York and immortalized in the movie *Dirty Dancing.* We heard that the "babushkas of Buranovo," an inspiring female singing group, were on a five-day vacation here, and they agreed to let us drop by the next morning.

Being followed by people can get into your head and make you paranoid. Sergei and I find a hotel a short walk from the *sanatoriy* and check in. The place is small, wooden, and drab, with just six small rooms. It seems entirely empty, but as we walk across the creaky wooden floors and back toward our rooms, a man walks out of another room and immediately introduces himself.

"My name Vasily," he says in broken English.

I extend a hand to shake.

"Ochen priatno, menia sovut David [Nice to meet you, my name is David]."

We carry on a simple conversation in a mix of basic Russian and English. Vasily learns that I am a journalist from America working on a book. I learn that Vasily is a doctor on business in Uva. Vasily says we are the only people staying at the hotel.

"Banya!" he suddenly says, motioning outside. There is evidently a *banya*, a traditional Russian bathhouse, attached to the hotel. Vasily is proposing we join him there.

"Sevodgnia vecherom [Tonight]?" he says. I give a nod that I hope agrees to nothing more than maybe.

Here is a moment when I want to believe this is Russia giveth but fear it's taketh, and I am caught in between.

Vasily seems as unthreatening as you can imagine—a short, unassuming friendly guy in his fifties with thinning hair and a bushy little mustache. He probably just wants a few friends to drink and steam the night away with. Then again, isn't it odd that he is the only other person staying in this hotel with us?

Isn't it odd that he happened to be coming out of his room just as we checked in?

Could he actually be working with the FSB?

I wrestle with whether I should let my paranoia and suspicion stand in the way of meeting a fellow traveler. I want to go to the *banya*—but feel like precautions are in order. Maybe its going overboard, but I decide that we should be on guard, especially so if there is food or drink presented by Vasily (I prefer that Sergei and I never both consume the same item) in case he's laced it with poison and intends to rob us.

The *banya* is a truly Russian experience, and Vasily does it up. We meet him after dinnertime in the small wooden building next to the hotel. He has brought beers, a bottle of vodka, glasses for both, pickles and homemade horse sausage (right, horse sausage) from his hometown, a few hours away. All this is spread out over a wooden table. Vasily is *banya*-ready in a green tank top and shorts. We have agreed that I'll partake of the bathing itself. Unlike most Russian men, Sergei isn't all that fond of the *banya* anyway, and he can stand guard over all our things.

Vasily tells us he is in fact the chairman of his local *banya* society, so I'm presumably in good hands. He instructs me to remove my clothing—as much as I would like. Some men go full monty. I typically hang onto the boxer shorts. I'm pretty happy when Vasily does the same.

I've been to a *banya* a half dozen times, and while I always feel cleansed and rejuvenated afterward, I can't totally disagree with Daniel Rancour-Laferriere who, in his book *The Slave Soul of Russia* drew a parallel between the bathhouse and the pride Russians feel from enduring something difficult. The author called the *banya* a "favorite theater of pain" for Russians.

> *The idea may seem strange to the Westerner who is accustomed to the lonely pleasure of a tepid bathtub, or the bracing spray of a shower. A proper Russian bath, however, is not just relaxing, or bracing. It truly hurts. The Russian does not merely soap up and rinse off, but endures additional quotas of suffering. The water . . . thrown onto the stones or bricks atop a special bathhouse stove . . . produces steam which is so hot as to bring out a profuse sweat in the bathers. The eyes and nostrils sting from the heat. Moreover, the naked bathers flail one another (or themselves) with a bundle of leafy birch twigs (termed a venik). This mild flagellation supposedly assists the steam in flushing out the pores of the skin, and leaves behind the pleasant fragrance of the birch. Sometimes the hot portion of the bath is followed up with a roll in the snow, or a dip in a nearby river or lake, or a cold shower.*

"Sergei, you good?" I say, looking at my colleague seated before a spread of horsemeat and beer. "I'm good, David, enjoy."

Vasily walks me through a thick wooden door into the next chamber, where he tends to some mechanics. He opens the metal door to a compartment and ensures that a burning fire has the pile of stones good and hot. We then move to the third room of the wooden cabin, the bathhouse itself. There are wooden benches, and I sit comfortably on one as Vasily opens another metal door—accessing the same compartment but from this other room—and douses the hot stones with water. There is a sizzling sound, and the heat in the bathhouse goes immediately from really, really hot to unbearable.

I am sweating profusely. *"Aaarrrhhh."* Vasily is making an animal sound, suggesting he's enjoying the heat. I would not call it enjoyable, but I do feel and appreciate the therapeutic nature of all this. I take a deep breath—the air is hot and clean as it runs into my lungs.

"David."

He's trying to get my attention. This isn't my first rodeo, so I know what's about to happen. As per tradition, Vasily has taken a birch branch—the *venik*—out of a bucket where it was soaking, and he is motioning for me to lie down. I do, and he begins whacking me violently with the branch, while making that animal noise: *"Aaarrrhhh."*

I really can appreciate most *banya* traditions. But the idea that violent contact with birch somehow adds to the experience seems like a stretch. After a few whacks Vasily lies down, and I return the favor.

After ten minutes of this, we both return to the middle chamber, where the next tradition awaits. There is a bucket of ice-cold water, and I dump it over myself, screaming bloody murder but knowing this is somehow making me a healthier and happier person, because why would generations of Russian men have done it otherwise?

Vasily does his dunk. Both dripping wet and shivering, we return to Sergei and sit at the table.

"How was it?"

"Great, Sergei, thanks. You sure you don't want a turn?"

"Yes."

"Sausage?" Vasily is holding a chunk of horsemeat in his right hand, and a large sharp knife in his right. By this point Sergei and I have concluded that Vasily seems genuinely harmless—though Sergei still decides not to drink the beer or vodka (I take one for the team here).

Vasily and I are sharing a small bench in boxer shorts, our wet bodies all but touching.

"So you're a doctor," I ask, with Sergei generously translating.

"I'm a doctor of alternative medicine. For animals. I'm here to treat cattle around Uva. They've been having infections in their hooves." He then cuts two hunks of horse sausage. We both chew them and wash them down with beer.

"I have a special honey that I invented that treats ailments. I'll give you some when we go back to the hotel."

Vasily and I talk into the night about our jobs, our professions, our countries. "You know, David, if you and I ran the two countries, there would have been no Cold War!" We find this funnier than Sergei does, perhaps helped by the beer and vodka. When the three of us return to our rooms and say good night, I am happy that Sergei and I were careful with a stranger. I am also happy we kept that *banya* date, because the memory of that night remains special. (The same cannot be said for the photo Sergei snapped of me and Vasily, dripping on each other on that cramped bench.)

The next morning Sergei and I walk up a snow-covered dirt street to the entrance to the *sanatoriy*. It's a sprawling two-story tan-brick complex set in front of a frozen lake, with forest extending to the horizon behind it. Soft music is playing from a set of outdoor speakers, interrupted every few minutes by a woman's voice announcing the day's activities (Karaoke! Skiing! Excursion to a museum!), or meal hours at the cafeteria or just general messages of warmth ("Welcome to our *sanatoriy*. Have a nice trip, for those leaving. We wish everyone a cozy atmosphere, love, and happy days until our next meeting.")

Personally, this kind of place would be my worst nightmare as a vacation spot. But my favorite babushkas are here, and I'm anxious to reconnect with them.

9 · GALINA

THE BURANOVO BABUSHKAS live in the tiny Udmurt village of Buranovo, just outside Izhevsk. After many of them lost their husbands, they turned to music for comfort. Somehow a Beatles cover they performed at a local concert made it onto YouTube and went viral.

On my first visit to see them I was overwhelmed by their charm and courage—such big personalities in such tiny bodies. Most of them barely reach five feet. I sat at a dining room table next to the oldest member of the group, eighty-four-year-old Elizaveta Zarbatova, whose head barely reached above the table. But her high-pitched, crackly voice carried authority. She was widowed in 1957, when her husband was electrocuted. She was sitting next to a woman who lost her husband in 2004 to drinking and diabetes. Another fellow babushka lost her husband in 1984 to alcoholism, and shortly after his death, she lost her own right arm trying to use an electric saw. But Zarbatova, like her friends, was in no mood to complain.

"After I lost my husband, I received some kind of gift—the ability to compose music," she told me. "The music comes from the heart. The suffering comes right from my heart."

My story about the babushkas was produced in 2011 with support from the Kitchen Sisters, veteran independent radio producers who made the piece part of an on-air special called *The Hidden World of Girls*, hosted by the actress Tina Fey. I was honored and touched. But I never felt any sense of finality. I never felt as if I asked these women questions that truly got to their pain. I always wanted to revisit them.

In 2012 these tiny women—never having traveled much beyond their small village—represented Russia at Eurovision, the international music competition held that year in Azerbaijan. It's as if the babushkas of Buranovo—and greater Russia—were collectively sending a message to the world: We may seem like some relic dying off, but don't count us out yet. Maybe, somehow, that's Russia's message today: We may be misunderstood, we may seem like we don't know where we're going. But given our rich past, given where we've been, what we've endured, what we've accomplished, and how we've influenced the course of history for better and for worse, don't discount us. As Zarbatova testified, out of the darkness can come something beautiful.

Sergei and I walk into the lobby and tell a receptionist that we are here for a scheduled meeting with the *Buranovskiye babushki*. The man says we must see Marina. I did not yet realize the impact of his directive.

Marina is the exuberant, overhelpful activities director for the complex. Think annoying tour director whom you want desperately to scream at, but you can't because he or she so innocently thinks he or she is being sweet and helpful.

Thing is, there are a lot of Marinas in Russia. For so long, life here was bleak, days were monotonous, travel was restricted. There were few chances for vacations, or relaxation—a word that has a most-unpleasant translation in Russian: *Otdykh*. So when it actually happened, nothing about it was casual. It was a big moment. Families expected—at least hoped for—over-the-top treatment. What's more, the Soviet government kept a watchful eye on citizens' movements. So many tours were rigidly organized, in order to fit code. Take all that together, and a culture was born. When you arrive somewhere to see something—on vacation, or say as a journalist or writer innocently trying to do his work—nothing is casual. A tour, or a trip—an *"ekskursiia"*—must be arranged. And there must be a guide. In this case her name is Marina.

As a reminder, Sergei and I are here with a sole purpose—to reconnect with the Buranovo Babushkas. Marina is not allowing access to them at this moment.

"Mozhet byt ekskursiia?"

"Maybe a tour?" Marina says at her desk, with me and Sergei facing her in two chairs. Marina is in her forties, with jet-black hair, small eyes, big lips, and quite an outfit: A tight, long-sleeved leopard-print top that doesn't at all go well with her bright turquoise ski pants with suspenders.

She speaks very loudly, as if there is a tour group of hundreds gathered, not just Sergei and I sitting in her office.

"What is your purpose?"

Sergei explains our previously arranged interview with the babushkas. They have a producer who does their music and publicity. We'd talked to her. Said we'd meet them here. In and out. Nothing complicated. Or at least that is what I imagined Sergei telling Marina in Russian.

She yells back. Sergei translates.

"David, Marina would like an hour of your time to talk about the Udmurt people and give you a tour of the *sanatoriy.*"

"Okay," I say, smiling at Sergei with gritted teeth.

Sergei translates my okay. "Okay," he says.

Marina smiles. "Plan."

In Russia that word is as frightening as *ekskursiia,* or *vodka.* A *plan* is translated into English as "plan" but means so much more. It means that Maria has devised a schedule that will be hard to alter once it comes out of her mouth. She begins rattling off times to Sergei.

"Okay, David, Marina says now we have lunch in the cafeteria of the *sanatoriy.* At 3 p.m., you meet with Marina for an hour. She wants to spend time showing you around and talking about the *sanatoriy* complex and the Udmurt people. At 4:00 p.m. you may meet with the babushkas. After, you will have dinner in the cafeteria. Later, at 9:00 p.m., Marina will be available to answer any more questions you have."

My head is spinning. I can't help but notice we're spending a lot of time with Marina now, but this must be separately allocated time with her, not part of my additional hour in the afternoon. She's still yelling at Sergei.

"David, Marina would like to know if we want her help tomorrow."

Pangs of fear.

"Tell her—um—we'll see."

"She wants to know our plan."

"Okay, tell her our plan."

Sergei tells her we are trying to go to the Kalashnikov museum in Izhevsk. Quickly, Marina is on the phone, speaking to the Kalashnikov museum, working up our plan for tomorrow which now seems to include her.

With that, Sergei and I are dispatched to lunch in a sunny dining room that feels in every way like the cafeteria in an American hospital or nursing home. On the buffet line is borscht, warm noodles, stewed meat in gravy, and an array of Russian salads swimming in thick cream. I go for the noodles. Sergei and I finish up and return to Marina's office, where our *ekskursiia* commences.

"Come," says Marina, who has added blue pearls to her outfit, almost matching the snow pants. She takes us on a dizzying tour of the complex. We see mosaics of Udmurt cultural scenes. "You know," says Marina—the jewelry on her hands and wrists clanking whenever she points at something—"there is an old Russian tradition of welcoming someone into your home with bread and salt. For the Udmurt people it is honey instead of salt. Okay, come."

Now we've stopped in a room where you can rent skis, sleds, roller skates, guitars, movies—seems all purpose. The man behind the counter is standing, almost at attention, almost as if Marina had *told* him she would be bringing some folks by on an *ekskursiia*.

"David, Marina wants to know if you have any questions."

"I'm good, Sergei."

Marina is leading us on. "Come into this office. This is Tatiana. She is our psychologist."

It appears that Tatiana was also warned that we were coming. She is standing in front of a wall of little bottles, each containing a liquid of a different color. I am suddenly transfixed trying to find the exact tone of turquoise that matches Marina's snow pants. "We work with color correction—color therapy. Nontraditional methods. We can tell what a person lacks in his or her life based on color therapy."

We thank Tatiana and move on to the library; then it's another stop at the cafeteria to see it as tourists, not diners, then back to Marina's office.

"She's like a fast train," Sergei whispers to me. Marina is now putting her coat on with a jaunty smirk: "Let's go outside."

"Aren't we talking to the babushkas?"

"You can talk to them later. Let's go for a walk outside."

Then an idea arrives. Marina's eyes widen.

"Actually, I will go get them and see if they want to come!"

We arrived three hours ago with a single purpose, and it has not been achieved. But as much as I am done with touring, and really eager to interview the babushkas, a walk in the forest with them seems enticing. Marina asks if Sergei and I have snow pants. Mostly out of fear of her loaning me a pair, I say we will be okay, Sergei and I both really like the cold.

Minutes later we meet Marina outside the complex by the lake, and here are the babushkas, with all the warm memories. These half dozen women, ranging in height from maybe four foot seven to five foot four, are bundled up in coats and snow boots, with head scarves covering their gray hair.

Elizaveta Zarbatova, the eldest member of the group, has not made this trip. But there is Galina Koneva, who hosted me and Sergei in her home in Buranovo in 2011. I remember her as the toughest one, a seventy-four-year-old woman who squints her eyes and purses her lips when she's not pleased. She once told me she wasn't ready to be "interviewed" at the moment. "Right now I am hungry," she said, waving a finger at me. "And when I'm hungry, I might eat you."

She is standing in the snow next to seventy-four-year-old Valentina Pyatchenko, a woman whose smile is so broad and dramatic it forces her cheeks to balloon outward. That smile has overcome a lot. Her alcoholic husband died in 1984 and she mostly got along by herself—but lost her right arm using an electric saw to build a new porch. The prosthetic she has is heavy and uncomfortable, but she wears it whenever the babushkas perform—including when they were unlikely stars of that Eurovision contest in Azerbaijan in 2012.

As it stands, there is little chance to chat because Marina is strutting, leading the babushkas and us on a tour of the outdoor portions of the *sanatoriy* complex. We all walk together into the forest, and slowly the natural beauty of the scene melts away my impatience.

Loud as she is, Marina is so sweetly holding hands with the babushkas, pointing up at the tall trees, describing the nature around us. They are giggling, almost hopping along on the snowy path, as an old man passes by on cross-country skis and waves. The sun is getting low in the late afternoon, casting a warm glow through the giant evergreens lining our path. The snow is almost orange.

I don't know if my impatience with Marina was unwarranted and I'm now relaxing, or if I'm just blending into this mosaic that captures a culture so unfamiliar to the outside world.

I'm reminded of a New Year's Eve with Rose outside Moscow at a friend's *dacha*—or summer home. Nearly every family who lived in the city in Soviet times had a *dacha*—for some it was little more than a shack outside the city to spend time and plant a garden in the summer. More prominent people with higher positions in the Communist Party were given spacious vacation properties.

That New Year's Eve we spent hours inside a house cooking and chatting and drinking. Then, when midnight neared, we joined dozens of other local *dacha* owners in the forest, as a light snow fell. I was standing with a glass of champagne, looking at Rose, who was ten feet ahead with her back to me. Suddenly I saw what looked like a fiery rocket illuminate directly in front of Rose, then soar up in the air. I honestly thought for a split second that I had lost my wife in some fiery accident. She was okay—and watched, as I did, as this rocket reached the sky above us and exploded—it was industrial-scale fireworks, the kind you see at a baseball game, the kind where in the United States there are strict limits on how far a bystander must be from the launch site. On this night someone set it off within feet of my wife.

"I think I almost died," Rose said, a bit shaken but smiling. This place can be so crazy and loud and unregulated and dangerous. Any worry melted away quickly, though, as Rose and I stood in the forest and kissed at midnight. We agreed that snowy New Year's Eve in the Russian forest was one of the most poetic evenings either of us could remember.

So is this night, walking in the forest in Uva with the babush-kas. Marina is standing near a log in the snow—the babushkas are listening intently—explaining that it is a special piece of wood, that sitting on it can be good for men's "health."

"Health" is how Sergei translates, but I can tell by all the laughter there is more to it. "Sexual health," Sergei clarifies quietly. Everyone is still laughing.

"David and I are both fine," Sergei says amid chuckles. "We are both married men."

Galina suddenly grabs my right hand and looks at Sergei. They exchange words in Russian.

"Galina says you have no wedding ring. I explained to her that in America, you wear your wedding rings on your left hand, not your right."

I show her.

Galina offers a warm smile, then is back to finger waving.

"You promised when you visited us that you would bring your wife next time."

"Oh, Galina, I'm sorry. I will bring her the next time."

She gives a stiff nod that communicates You'd better.

We all walk quietly back up the path, and return to the *sanatoriy* building. Marina has set up a conference room for Sergei and me to meet with the babushkas. She won't be far, right outside in the auditorium, leading other guests in karaoke.

The babushkas have found seats around a long wooden table. We are all quiet at first. The subject I really want to talk about— how they survived losing husbands and found the strength to move on—is the one they were least happy to talk about last time. These women don't like to boast about survival skills.

Galina reminds me only half-jokingly that my leash is short: "I once drove away two journalists who asked the wrong questions. They said, 'We have a list of questions, and we'll get started.' The guy started reading to me his questions, as I sat with him, alone in my house. He says, 'So do you have "intrigues" when you travel? Do you fall in love with anyone when you travel?' I said, 'Get out of here now!'"

Everyone in the room is now laughing but me.

Galina reaches into a bag and pulls out two little babushkas— knitted versions of themselves. "We sit and knit these together," she says. "They are for good luck and happiness. Here is one for you and one for Rose."

This is incredibly sweet. I also get the feeling they are not expecting any of the more sensitive questions I danced around last time.

I ASK GALINA how construction on the church in Buranovo is going. Restoring the church is vitally important to these women. Their village, like so many across Russia, became a sad and barren place during Soviet times. Their Orthodox church was destroyed—along with thousands of others under a regime that eschewed organized religion. Roads are not paved. The women walk to each other's houses on mud paths. The money they have made performing around Russia has all gone to rebuilding their small Orthodox church.

"The brickwork is done," Galina says. "The bell tower is ready. Now we need to do the roof, but we don't have the money yet."

"Can I ask, how important is the friendship you all share?"

The Soviets got rid of religion—and also languages that were not Russian. The women of Buranovo could not legally speak their native Udmurt. So in 1990 they tried to do something about that. These women met in the village hall, knitted, and began singing Udmurt songs together.

"We are one family. One family. It is impossible to separate us. We've been together for a long time. More than twenty years."

I knew that part of their fellowship came from the pain of being alone. I am treading delicately: "I guess women need to find their strength, especially after losing husbands."

Galina and I are now in a stare-down.

"When there is a man, it is easier to live for a woman." She pauses. "We have all had different fates."

Many of these women had fathers who fought and died in World

War II, and watched their mothers make it alone: "There was a war, and the entire burden was laid upon women's shoulders," another babushka says. "And so we children had to work too, weeding the fields."

Galina: "I have this mark"—she's showing me her hand—"from a sickle. I wasn't even going to school at that time. I was a child, working in the field, and cut my finger with a sickle."

"May I hear more about your husbands?"

We had started the conversation in Buranovo several years ago but didn't get very far.

"I don't really want to talk about it," says Galina. "My life has been . . . interesting. But I don't want it in your book. Why write about it? All of it has passed. I will just tell you there's a saying in Russian, 'I am a mare, and I am a bull. I am a woman, and I am a man.'"

Many Russian women have had to be both in their older years. Until recently the life expectancy in Russia for men was barely fifty-nine. It has inched above sixty, while the average woman lives to be seventy-three. These numbers are alarmingly low for a country as developed as Russia. As my friend Kathy Lally wrote in the *Washington Post* in 2013, "Russia bears a staggering load of risk factors for disease, with 60 percent of men smoking and each citizen consuming, on average, more than four gallons of pure alcohol a year. Half the population is overweight." The Russian government has been taking steps—small ones—to improve the situation. In 2013 they finally classified beer as an alcoholic beverage, which brought new restrictions on its sale. Until then beer was considered a food in Russia.

This is a country where women in their older years know how to go it alone.

I turn to my left, to Valentina, the woman missing her right arm. She has a beautiful round face, and an infectious, youthful smile.

"Valentina, I remember you started telling me last time about how you lost your arm. May I hear the full story?"

"I came to Russia in 1984 from Turkmenistan. My husband had started drinking. A lot. So I went away. My children came with me. He died a long time ago. I had many friends in Turkmenistan. But after the Soviet Union broke apart, it was hard for them to come to Russia, because we are different countries now. So we stay in touch. And exchange letters. But we women, we had to do everything by ourselves. I was working on my porch. I could have waited. My son was at school. I could have waited for him to come home. But those boards, they were just standing there—standing there. So I decided I would try to work on the porch while he was gone. I forgot to take my sweater off. I didn't even notice when it happened. The circular saw just caught it together, the sweater and my arm. I guess we women deal with a lot."

Galina has an approving smile. "She was panicked, I remember. She said, 'How will I live without my arm?' I told her, 'You are not the first, and you won't be the last. People do everything without their hands. They embroider, they do everything. And *you* will learn to do everything.' Those words bucked her up. I gave her a scolding. I think it helped."

Valentina is nodding that it sure did.

"I can do everything. I dig with a shovel in the vegetable garden. I mow. I dig for potatoes. I plant vegetables. And you know, without the prosthetic, it's better. That thing disturbs me. It's rather long, not very good. If I could get rubber, maybe it would be better. But I do everything. I was sixty when I lost my arm. Now I'm seventy-five. These women—they don't leave me alone. Without their help I would have been weaker because of this. It's friendship, support, mutual help. We all live near one another."

The room is quiet again.

Sergei and I have always had an arrangement. If we are in an interview and things get uncomfortable, I have told him to dive in on his own, leaving me behind. Forget taking the time to translate if it makes things go more smoothly to speak in Russian. Sergei gives me a look, and I know what he is asking. I nod back. Sergei, who so often looks to me to take charge as the "boss," takes the reins impressively, pulls his chair a little closer to Galina, looks around at the other women, and begins a long, emotional conversation.

I am left in the dark, unable to focus on what these women are saying, but able to focus on how Sergei is growing as a journalist before my eyes. The Soviet legacy in work environments here is for everyone to accept his or her lot, do a day's work, look for cues from the "boss," never take charge, and never, ever make waves. I always encouraged Sergei to take charge whenever he felt the urge. And here, in this conference room in a health complex in rural Russia, I am watching Sergei leap the barriers put in front of him and other people in this country. I see a determined confidence I haven't seen before.

Sergei talks to each and every babushka about everything—including their husbands, based on the little Russian I can understand. He and Galina talk for maybe a half hour.

Sergei is respectful and compassionate, as Galina—this strong woman with an attitude—descends into tears. I run to find a Kleenex and some water.

. . .

ONLY LATER, WHEN Sergei translates for me, do I learn the stories.

Zoya Dorodova, seventy-two, lost her son to war—he died fighting for the Soviets in Afghanistan—and her husband in an accident that is all too common in Russia. "He drowned in the river. He was coming home from work. Maybe he was drunk. It was October, and the ice was thin. He walked straight over it and drowned. We looked for his body for a week until it was found down the river."

Natalia Pugachyoya, at seventy-seven the oldest and tiniest in this group, is the rare babushka with a living husband. "Soon it will be fifty-seven years together." Sergei asks if their marriage is happy. "You know, it's a husband and a wife. Things happen. We have been together a long time."

Ekaterina Shkliayeva says she was married for six years. "My husband got sick. He had epilepsy. It happened during the night. He just couldn't breathe. He was sleeping, didn't have enough air. He was lying on the pillow. I didn't notice until the morning because I was sleeping in another room, with our children."

Sergei asks exactly what I would have asked—if these experiences had formed the characters of these women.

"We work. We work the land," Galina says. "We work our vegetable gardens, so they are not neglected."

"Galina," Sergei says, "can you tell me a story that will help me understand your character?"

"I can't. I'll start crying."

Sergei is respectful, not pushing, talking to the other women. Then at one point, Galina turns to Sergei.

"Would you like to hear my story?"

Sergei says yes.

"My father went to the army when I was three. Thank God he wasn't killed. He was wounded twice but returned home alive and lived to sixty-four. He got sick with tuberculosis. I was the oldest of six children. We sawed and chopped firewood. We took care of the vegetable garden and milked cows. I went to school and became a kindergarten teacher and got married to a Russian guy. We had a baby. And somehow life changed. He started drinking."

Looking back at the transcript later, I believe this is when Galina is taking pauses and fighting tears.

"He got ill-tempered. Once, when I was pregnant with our second child, he shot at me with his rifle. Now, I was athletic. I skied and ran track in the summertime. So I was able to jump out of the way. But he had a serious rifle that was loaded to hunt wolves. Another time, he started coming at me with an ax. And . . . one time, he hit me on the ear and on my head. That is when I said 'I won't forgive you for this.' And I sent him out of the house. I said the world is too big for this. 'I'm pregnant with our second child—five months pregnant. I'm twenty-two years old.' I told him, 'You run. You'll run all over the Soviet Union, but one day, you will come back to me to die. You will crawl on your knees back to me.'"

And Galina was right. He returned thirty years later.

"He crawled back, with diabetes. He had been sick for a long time. I told him, 'My children might accept you, but not me.' My children kept saying, 'Mom, he doesn't drink anymore, he doesn't drink.' I did feel sorry for him. And you know, I guess a woman has long hair but a short wit. I took him back. He worked another four years, but then because of the diabetes, he lost his legs, went blind, and got weak. I was supposed to retire then, but I told him, 'You help as best you can, and I'll keep working.' I buried him nine years ago. I took care of him for thirteen years. That was my fate."

As Sergei finishes listening, he asks if there's anything more. I tell him this is his interview, he can decide. "I think we're good, David."

The babushkas are not sure when their next big concert will be. I tell them I hope they'll come to America at some point.

"When we went to Eurovision," says Valentina, "we had only one thought. Let's just not disgrace our little native land, Udmurtia. We will perform and do our best. We got first in the Russian qualifiers and got to Baku. Then we are thinking, let's not disgrace our Russia. This was our only thought."

"We just cry sometimes, onstage," Galina says. "When people stand up for us. At Eurovision, all of them stood up and greeted us and applauded for so long. We were just crying not even understanding what was happening."

She goes on.

"You know we have our land, our soil, our dreams, our goals. We have this goal, to build a church. This is our goal, and hopefully people will remember us for it. Our children, our grandchildren, our great-grandchildren will say, you see who built this? They have already laid a stone there that says this was initiated by the Buranovo Babushkas. And the stone will stay there forever. We sing about it in one of our songs—that we shouldn't praise ourselves. Let other people praise if they wish. Let our names stay with people. Now the time has come for us to sing. There was a time when we had to work. Right now? It's time for us to sing."

. . .

It's time for us to sing: Those words have stayed with me. These women are tired. So too is Russia. Decades of war, work, alcoholism, death, upheaval. These women are relishing what they have, and decided that it's just time to sing.

We all walk into the auditorium, where Marina is on stage, singing a karaoke song, and dozens of guests from the *sanatoriy* are clapping along. Sergei and I and the babushkas take seats in the back rows. In between songs Marina announces that the Buranovo Babushkas have come in, and the crowd applauds.

Sergei and I say farewell to the babushkas. I give Galina a kiss on the cheek and tell her I'll see her in America, when they come for their first U.S. concert.

Before heading to the hotel to sleep, I want to thank Marina for her help and to say good-bye. Then, tomorrow, Sergei and I will be on our way to Izhevsk for a quick stop at the Kalashnikov museum, then back to the train and east to Siberia.

We catch Marina by the side of the stage, in between karaoke songs. (It was karaoke night, but she didn't seem to be giving up the microphone).

"Zavtra? she says. [Tomorrow]." This was my fear.

Unbeknownst to us she has nailed down all of tomorrow's details. The *sanatoriy* driver—and herself, of course—will accompany us to Izhevsk for all our interviews. Had I heard this news earlier in the day, I might have cringed. But having spent that magical sunset in the forest with Marina and the babushkas, I am enjoying her company more—of course, with no idea what the morning may bring.

10 · MARINA

THE NEXT DAY, shortly after 8:00 a.m., Sergei and I are walking out of the hotel when his cell phone rings.

"Marina," he announces, seeing the number.

"Zdravstvuyte, Marina." After offering this greeting, Sergei doesn't contribute much more to the conversation, just listening to mouthfuls and offering brief responses. All I hear on our end is "Da . . . , Da . . . , Da, da . . . , okay."

Marina and her driver are already waiting for us at the entrance to the *sanatoriy*. We find her, not expecting such a cramped seating arrangement. It turns out that Marina is going to Izhevsk with us. And we are taking Tatiana, the color-therapy psychologist. The car is cozy. Sergei and I squeeze into the backseat with Tatiana. Sergei is in the middle, I am to his right, with my knees up against the back of Marina's seat.

First stop, an office in Uva that runs the hotel where we stayed. We have to return our keys and check out. The process is not so simple.

Inside, the desk clerk tells Sergei that she received a call from the local immigration authorities asking about me, and requesting that we call him back. Sergei and I are suddenly nervous. We return to the car, and Sergei calls the number, with Marina listening.

I hear him tell the person that we were interviewing the Buranovo Babushkas.

"Babushkas—hoorah!" Marina says, hearing this. I'm glad she is optimistic, as I am contemplating my imminent arrest.

Sergei speaks for a few more minutes, then hangs up. The man on the phone asked how long I was staying in the region, and when we were leaving. "I told him we were leaving from Izhevsk tonight," Sergei says.

"What was his name, Sergei?" says Marina.

"Dennis Alexandrovich."

Marina quickly calls her friend, who works in the region's immigration department.

"She's never heard of him. Maybe he called from a different department."

I'm convinced it is the FSB, or some related agency, just following our movements. My only worry is we have not been too careful in registering me each time we stop. It is an annoying and time-consuming process. But foreigners are supposed to register with the local immigration authorities whenever they arrive somewhere new. The most aggravating part is, it is never clear when you actually have to register—like so much in Russia, the law is ambiguous, often changing, and never available to read anywhere.

"Sergei, I guess my only worry is if we give them some lame excuse to come after me. We should make sure to have every hotel from here on out register me."

"I agree," Sergei says.

After an hour we are in Izhevsk, a pleasant city of just over a half

million people. The city center has a vast promenade, with a water-
fall and food stands, that slopes down a hill to a picturesque lake. I
always had a fond feeling for this city, having seen it the first time
in the summer when families were taking afternoon walks, teenagers were eating ice cream while walking their bikes along, and bar
hoppers were dancing. It all makes it so easy to forget that the place
is best known for producing a killing machine.

One heavily industrial section of the city is home to a weapons
factory that has produced more Kalashnikovs than any other factory
in the country.

Marina has a well-planned itinerary that involves a very quick stop
at the city's Kalashnikov museum. We enter, pay for tickets and are
confronted by a museum employee. "You must put these on," she says,
pointing to a box full of something resembling purple shower caps.

"They're for your feet," Marina says. I am aware of this—every
museum in Russia attempts to keep floors clean by making visitors wear shower caps on their feet—but I was hoping to avoid the
things just this once.

"We simply don't have time to see everything," Marina says,
rushing us into the museum.

This is one of those moments where we are all rushing—for no
apparent reason. Our train is not until 11:00 p.m. But Marina has a
plan. Sergei and I may not be abreast of the plan, but we are inex-
plicably held hostage to it. We spend about five minutes moving
briskly though exhibits dedicated to the history of the Kalashnikov.
Marina's high heels have pierced her shower caps. I have nearly
slipped and killed myself about a dozen times. Sergei, repeating his
gymnastic performance from the train, seems to be floating through
the museum unencumbered.

"You know, there is a special room where you can shoot," Marina says. *Shoot?*

She rushes us to the basement of the museum, where there is a high-tech shooting range. A woman is behind glass, aiming a deadly Kalashnikov semiautomatic weapon at a target—and firing. Multiple shots.

I can think of no museum like this at home.

Off to the side, there is a small gift shop selling T-shirts and model Kalashnikovs, which resemble the real thing to the naked eye but are presumably less lethal.

"These are . . . for sale?" I ask the clerk.

"Oh, yes. But if you are flying, it is not possible to carry them."

Oh, right. The whole thing about not carrying look-alike semi-automatic weapons on airplanes. I nod in appreciation for the tip.

Marina quickly rushes us out of the museum, tossing our shower caps in a box before going out the door. We jump in her car (more spacious now, as we dropped the psychologist off for a meeting) and take a ten-minute drive to a museum that is very similar, though attached to the gun factory itself.

We walk inside, and are directed to sit down in front of a glass case featuring different versions of the Kalashnikov and also some very menacing-looking knives. We come to learn that unfortunately Mikhail Kalashnikov is not available, but his seventy-year-old son, Viktor—also a gun designer—has joined us.

He's a quiet man wearing a gray sweater under a black suit that all but swallows his small frame—he's about as nonthreatening a guy you could find, but for the fact that he's designed some of the world's most lethal weapons.

Sergei seems a bit nervous by the high-profile nature of the interview. "David, let's do it this way. You ask questions. He answers. I translate. Okay?"

"Sure."

"Okay, your questions, please."

Sergei is all business.

I ask about how his father came to invent such a weapon.

"In 1941 my dad was wounded in the war," Viktor says. "In the hospital he spoke about the kinds of armaments he saw on the battlefield. The kinds of guns the Germans had, and the kinds of guns the Russians had."

While serving as director of the weapons factory in Izhevsk after the war, he set out to design an automatic rifle that could be produced en masse and match the automatic weapons the Germans had been deploying. And so the Kalashnikov, as it's also known, was born. The AK-47 has gone through many iterations and been used on battlefields and also by gangsters and terrorists around the world.

"My father's slogan was to create a weapon that could protect the motherland," Viktor tells me.

I ask if his father has any regrets, given how many people have been killed—including countless numbers at the hands of criminals.

"Sure, it has been used by criminals. It is a reliable weapon. But I would like to emphasize, the constructor is not guilty in that—politicians are." He says his father does tell himself that a lot, because there *are* moments when he thinks about the impact of what he invented. "Yes, Dad thinks about it and talks about it."

He sure should. The gun he invented is used by armies, child soldiers, criminals, terrorists. And it's available everywhere.

According to C. J. Chivers of the *New York Times*, who wrote a
book about the Kalashnikov called *The Gun*, so many of the guns
have been produced that there is one for every seventy humans
on earth. "The Kalashnikov is the most common weapon you will
see," he told my colleague Terry Gross on NPR's program *Fresh Air*,
suggesting that if you find yourself anywhere in the world that's
unstable or unsafe, chances are these weapons are not far away.
The AK-47 "gets used in those places in the commissions of crimes,
in the commission of human-rights violations. It is often used by
governments as a tool of repression. It's the weapon of the crack-
down and has been for more than half a century." But the market
has become so flooded with the guns that orders are beginning to
fall off—and that's bad for Izhevsk, Chivers said in another NPR
interview.

> *This is, in the simplest sense, a struggling factory town that's
> looking for more orders so it can keep more people at work.
> There's also sort of something psychological at work here. The
> Kalashnikov is, in many ways, Russia's Coca-Cola. It's their
> brand. It's the one thing that they made that we all know of
> and that has had global saturation. You know, we don't buy
> Russian pacemakers, or Russian watches, or Russian per-
> fumes, or Russian automobiles in any significant numbers.
> But the Kalashnikov is the thing.*

There's something melancholy about this—not exactly the fact
that gun orders are down, which is a good thing, but that Russia is
so desperate for its brand to be respected again. There was a time

when Russian citizens felt an enormous sense of pride—like when the cosmonaut Yuri Gagarin became the first man in space.

"America could not do that, okay?" Yuri Karash once told me. The Russian commentator often writes about the space industry. "Western Europe could not do it. No other country in the world could do it. But the Soviet state could."

That was then. Today, there's far less pride—even at moments when there should be more. When the U.S. Space Shuttle program ended, NASA began paying Russia to carry Americans into space for an undetermined period of years. Like many Russians I spoke with, Karash was less than impressed. He described the moment as similar to a Mercedes breaking down in the middle of the desert. "So you suddenly see a Bedouin riding a camel on the shoulder and you ask him, 'Hey, guy, do me a favor, give me a lift to someplace?' And he says, 'No problem. Pay me $63 million and I'll take you there.' Does it mean camel is better than Mercedes?"

For a country whose people are already prone to fatalism, you can imagine a loss of pride only piling on.

I THANK VIKTOR KALASHNIKOV for his time and bid him farewell. I can't stop thinking about how Russia is chock-full of characters. I just think about the babushkas and their tragic but inspiring stories, Marina in her over-the-top ski pants that fit her personality, Vasily serving up horse sausage in his *banya*-soaked boxer shorts and this quiet, peaceful soul in a black suit whose father invented the AK-47.

In the parking lot Sergei and I say a final good-bye to Marina.

I realize, in all the chaos and haste, I never asked about her story. I do, briefly, and she says very little other than that she lives alone—no husband—raised two daughters alone, and now has three grandchildren.

"I don't like to talk about myself much," she says. "But maybe you can find me a husband in America."

I'm suddenly overcome by warmth and guilt. She's loud, bossy, and quirky. Actually, I've never liked someone so much who annoyed me so much. I think about the babushkas, and somehow Marina makes more sense. She's lonely, looking for connections, and proud of the job she does. In her own way she saw it as her duty to go above and beyond for me and Sergei—as our tour guide during our stay here. And for that I am grateful.

"Thank you again, Marina."

"You're welcome." And then she drives off.

We have a few hours to kill, so Sergei and I find a nice table in a hotel restaurant to grab a bite and write some notes from the day.

And there they are. Our "friends."

The same guys who followed us out of the train station when we arrived in the city walk into the restaurant, pretend not to see us, but grab a table in our section. I am sure they'll trail us to the train station in a few hours. I just hope they are local and let us go on our way once we are off their turf.

Sergei and Liubov Klyukin lost their son at age twenty-one when a plane carrying Yaroslavl's pro hockey team went down in a fiery crash. The couple built a shrine to their son in his bedroom. "There is this belief in our country that tragedy is a test for people who are supposed to be strong," the mother told me. "And Sergei and I are strong. That is why we will get through this."

This stone, easy to miss fifty yards off a small road in the city of Rybinsk (outside of Yaroslavl), honors those who died in a Soviet gulag here. The fresher bouquet sitting in the snow had six roses—notable because in Russia an even number of flowers is given to people who are still grieving.

Third-class accommodations are not unlike a cramped college dormitory room. Sergei is on his bunk, researching our next stop on his tablet, jumping on faint cell signals that appear occasionally. There is a bunk across from Sergei, two upper bunks above, and two more across the aisle, where the man is peering out the window (his table converts into one.)

Sergei's family in Nizhny Novgorod could not have treated me more warmly. Aunt Nina is at the center, with Sergei to her left.

Alexei Mikheyev, with his mother, Lyudmila, in Nizhny Novgorod. Alexei was a police officer in the city. After top officials in the Russian government began a campaign to root out bad actors in the police forces, Alexei was falsely accused of kidnapping while off duty. During a horrific interrogation, he escaped and fell from a window, shattering his spine. He was quickly cleared of all charges but is now confined to a wheelchair.

Boarding a Russian train is no small thing—especially when passengers are saying good-bye to family they see rarely. Sergei had not seen his cousins in several years. As our visit ended, they followed tradition: They escorted us to the station, carried our luggage to the train, boarded with us to get us settled, then stood on the platform, blowing kisses as our train pulled out.

After leaving Moscow and traveling across the world's biggest country, to finally see Russia's Pacific coast gave me chills. I was searching for some poetic ending, so I went to this spit of land extending into the bay near Vladivostok. Quiet reflection was rudely interrupted by this gas-guzzling, four-car ferry that *put-put-putt*ed its way to the shore, slammed into a rock, piled cars on, then loudly made its way off into the bay again. (*David Gilkey/NPR*)

My wife, Rose, with Alexei Kamerzan at a café in Novosibirsk. Alexei's mom was among those who benefited financially from the Soviet collapse, filling the void when state companies broke up. She started a carpet empire that her son helps to run today. Alexei went to college in the United States and vacations abroad. He thinks Putin's last election victory was rigged, calling that "unpleasant, but not such a big deal."

Heading to the station at dusk in Novosibirsk, Siberia's largest city, to board an overnight train east to Krasnoyarsk.

The Siberian city of Krasnoyarsk, surrounded by gorges and snow-capped mountains, is Siberia's most gorgeous city, according to the great Russian writer Chekhov. I could not disagree.

A bride and groom posing for photos at a river overlook just outside Krasnoyarsk. The couple and their friends were all smiles, exuding a warmth that seemed to melt away the troubles faced by so many in this country—at least for this fleeting afternoon.

Men from Central Asia use the Trans-Siberian to travel deep into Russia, looking for construction work. Our seatmate is from Uzbekistan. In intimate third-class quarters, you are all but on top of fellow passengers. This photo was taken from Sergei's bunk. My bed is above Sergei's, and Rose's bed is just above where this man is sitting. We shared dessert, but the language barrier made conversation tough.

More often than not, this was dinner on the train. And honestly, I began to crave it. Boxes of instant noodles were on sale at every train station for as little as twenty rubles (sixty-seven cents) each. We kept a good supply at all times, so when hunger hit, you could carry the noodles and your tea cup to the hot water samovar at the end of each train car, fill up, and your meal was ready.

Walking on water: Lake Baikal freezes solid during winters, and Russians love to tempt fate by driving, biking, and taking strolls on the ice. Sergei and I opted for a hovercraft.

I wondered whether this would be the last photo ever taken of me and Sergei alive. To cross frozen Lake Baikal, we hired a hovercraft that seemed, shall we say, make-shift. It resembled a mini-van superglued on top of a pontoon with a steering wheel inside that was surely ripped off a Russian Lada automobile.

Sergei Sotnikov: proud husband and father, NPR producer, awesome travel mate, best friend in Russia.

Lenin, pointing toward the train station in Vladivostok on a snowy evening.

Russian train platforms are full of energy, chaos, and confusion, overwhelming the senses. The smell of cigarette smoke blends with the smell of coal and occasionally the smell of sweat from passengers who haven't showered for days. Everyone is in a hurry, dragging suitcases over the concrete. There's a nonstop stream of announcements blaring from speakers, occasionally clearly enough to understand. *(David Gilkey/NPR)*

In the dining car I often go with beer and pistachio nuts. They are reliably available, unlike most else. Menus will have dozens of offerings—seafood, meat dishes, soups—but the required ingredients are often not on board. The television doesn't appear to have worked for a decade. And even though we're several time zones east of Moscow, the clock is set to Moscow time, a quirk of Russian trains that was designed to avoid confusion but seems just to fuel it. *(David Gilkey/NPR)*

Something about this scene captures Russia for me. In the background, pristine Lake Baikal, a World Heritage site that the Russian government seems to neglect and underappreciate. Storm clouds impose themselves on what could be sunny skies. And an old Soviet Lada, symbolizing a previous generation's engineering ingenuity, sits unclaimed on a snowy shore. *(David Gilkey/NPR)*

Zhanna Rutskaya used a link of Belarusian sausage as a baton, waving me into her cabin. So began my education about life on the Russian rails: It's all about sharing food and conversation. Her cabinmate—they, too, had only just met— is Sergei Yovlev, a die-hard fan of Yaroslavl's pro hockey team. The 2011 team died in a plane crash. Yovlev said the ability to survive tragedy is "the way the soul of a Russian person is built." *(David Gilkey/NPR)*

Albina Ostrovskaya (right) lost her husband a decade ago. Like too many Russian men, he died before the age of fifty. Her sister-in-law, Tamara, often makes a three-day train journey to Moscow to keep her company. She likes to fit in some shopping. "Here, I have a rug, a small rug, my clothes, and some-thing to eat," Tamara told me, pointing at her overstuffed parcels. She doesn't mind the train at all. "Nice people in the cabins, so we have a good time." *(David Gilkey/NPR)*

Viktor Gorodilov is a Russian lumberjack. He lives and works in the timber-producing village of Sagra, where there are no paved roads and no reliable police response. When a criminal gang made its way there and the police didn't show, villagers fought them off using rifles and pitchforks. They were charged with hooliganism and faced potential jail time. But Viktor's son, Andrei, helped with a public relations campaign to fight the charges. "Publicity was our protection," Andrei told me. A lesson in democratic values? Maybe, Andrei said. "But our Russian mentality has to be protected, too." *(David Gilkey/NPR)*

Olga Granovskaya is a college professor in Vladivostok. She had just returned from teaching a semester at the University of California, Berkeley, but she has no interest in moving to the United States. She loves Russian culture and loves vacationing with her family on Russia's Pacific coast. She doesn't know where her country is headed and has come to a less-than-comfortable peace with that. "You get used to knowing nothing about your future here." *(David Gilkey/NPR)*

11 · ANGELINA

THE RUSSIAN VILLAGE of Sagra is where I nearly lost my wife.

When we stopped there on our Trans-Siberian trip in 2011, a man named Andrei Gorodilov took a liking to her. (Okay, that's at least the way I saw it at first). I had to stomach this, because Andrei, thirty-nine, and his family were people I was eager to get to know.

If anyplace in Russia seems to be experimenting with democracy, it is this tiny village in the Ural Mountains. I had read the colorful story of how villagers in Sagra, including Andrei's family, took up hunting rifles and pitchforks on a summer night in July 2011 and defended the community against an approaching criminal gang. As the story goes, the gang had been in skirmishes with residents of the poor village in the past, and on this night was approaching in cars just before midnight to terrorize the place. Residents clashed with the gang, and one of the intruders was killed. A *New York Times* story a month after the attack said villagers tried to alert authorities but got nowhere. "For nearly five minutes, by her count, a resident named Tatyana Gordeyeva tried to persuade a police dispatcher on the telephone to connect her to a station. When help finally came, she said, the battle had been over for two hours." At first local officials interrogated residents of Sagra and, according to villagers, charged some with hooliganism. That included Andrei's father, Viktor. In response, villagers did the unthinkable: They took to the Internet to fight the local authorities. They found a lawyer to fight for their rights against a local government that seemed to have decided the case before it began.

And they won.

Arriving in Sagra that first time, I immediately noticed (perceived, at least) Andrei's fascination with Rose. Perhaps this threw me off my game—or maybe Andrei used Russian voodoo to put a curse on me—because for whatever reason, I couldn't walk a block on Sagra's snowy streets without falling flat on my face. One fall was especially troublesome—I was carrying two bottles of vodka, gifts for a family we were to interview, and I slipped, saving myself but shattering the vodka bottles.

Unofficial Russian law says one never sacrifices vodka to save himself.

This event earned me the nickname *Lokh* (dope) among Andrei and his friends. But Rose, as she so often does, came to the rescue. After my brutal fall, she could tell I was humiliated and swung into action. Andrei and Viktor had brought us to a neighbor's house in Sagra for lunch—brown bread, homemade vegetable spread, and six jars, each containing a different variety of pickle. Rose befriended the woman hosting us, telling her she bore a striking resemblance to Angelina Jolie. Then she befriended Viktor and before I knew it, Viktor had Rose doing shots of pepper-flavored vodka with him. He had her convinced it was an elixir, as she had been battling a cold.

Andrei, seeing Rose hanging out with his dad as if they were old-time friends, seemed unthreatened by me and (mercifully) no longer called me *Lokh*.

Andrei, thirty-nine, has a graduate degree in economics. More than anyone else I somehow expected him to believe in democracy the same way I do, especially after the experience his village had just been through to protect its legal rights. But Andrei didn't draw a connection between the battle his village waged and some broader fight for a different future for Russia. He watched the news. He knew all about the Arab Spring. But what happened in Egypt and Libya only scared him. Andrei had lived through the Soviet collapse and then suffered as boasts of democracy were followed by economic crisis.

"I can see what's happening in Libya," he told me. "That was our path in 1991. The Libyan people will live much worse than they used to live. They had social programs, they got apartments for free. Now this will stop. I already lived through those kinds of changes."

What Andrei and the villagers of Sagra did was fight when they were pushed to the brink—they fought on the streets because they believed lives were at stake. They took to the Internet to fight because otherwise family members might have gone to jail. But there is no broader confidence in free expression and public activism. In fact there's still a fear that those things, when used too often, can make life worse.

Meeting Andrei gave a face to some polling that stunned me. The Pew Research Center polled Russians, Ukrainians, and Belarusians, and people in other neighboring countries. They asked questions like "would you prefer a strong leader or democratic values?" When they asked the question in 1991, majorities wanted democratic values. Today the opposite is true—people prefer a strong leader.

Those early poll results came amid the Soviet fall, when there was a desperate plea for a new system to restore order. But there has never been any deep or lasting commitment to democracy.

Sagra is in the Ural Mountains, the window onto Asian Russia and the vast region known as Siberia. Often late at night aboard the train, Russian passengers stand along the corridors, gazing out at the dark, empty landscape, often glancing at that list of stops to see when the train would next be pulling into a station. The stops often last fifteen or twenty minutes, just enough time to jump off on an icy platform and buy some potato chips or, when we are lucky, dried fish from women selling from baskets outside. The conductors shovel in more coal to heat the train cars, chop ice loudly from beneath them, and then call for us to board. And the train sets off again.

One night in 2011, I had my iPhone plugged into a wall socket in the hallway to charge it. As we pulled out of a city I saw the single bar of phone coverage disappear, and I didn't have service for hours. I just stood there, gazing out into this vast, white Siberian landscape that was lit by the moon at midnight. I felt melancholy, this feeling that Russians are living in some sad darkness, unable to see the future that could await them if they only fought harder. And yet something about the poetry of the place, the pain people have been through, the laughter and strength and kindness from so many I've met, all made me want to smile.

Before leaving Sagra back in 2011, Rose and I gave Andrei our phone numbers, and promised to stay in touch. I bought three new bottles of vodka and asked Andrei to give two of them to the neighbors (who were supposed to receive the ones I broke) and to keep one for his family. I told Sergei and Rose that I had to return to Sagra, to learn more.

. . .

WE FINISH UP dinner and tea at the hotel restaurant in the center of Izhevsk, and cab to the train station. Our FSB friends are still with us. We saw them ask for their check at the restaurant as soon as we did. We saw them leave the lobby of the hotel just after us. Now we see them on the platform. Since we have no family to bid us farewell here, this almost makes me feel special, that a couple of thuggish strangers are seeing us off!

To reach Izhevsk we had to detour off the Trans-Siberian main line. Tonight we are heading north to the Russian city of Perm, on the western edge of the Ural Mountains. We have to lay over there for a few hours, then rejoin the main line, cross the Ural Mountains, and reach Ekaterinburg where Andrei is picking us up for our trip to Sagra.

The trip has been grueling, frustrating, exciting, with unexpected twists at every step—but you fall into a routine that gets you by. Often I'm especially in the dark because I don't know the language. It strikes me—what a metaphor for how Russians approach their lives. In a way I feel that's how the Russian government keeps citizens in the dark—laws are never clear, courts are unreliable, punishments are arbitrary—it's like living in a place where the people in charge are speaking a language you never understand. And consider what that does to any impulse to speak up.

I remember on one Russian Trans-Siberian train a pleasant young woman with dyed blond hair stumbled into my compartment and seemed delighted to have found a foreigner. She was holding a plate of pirozhki, little stuffed pies—these had cabbage—and said in very broken English, "You get all, twelve hundred rubles. Deal good, very good." I wasn't understanding, so I asked if I could find my translator. "No, no. No. good deal. Pay, please." I wasn't inclined to fight with an employee with whom I would be sharing a train for days, so I handed over twelve hundred rubles—roughly forty dollars. The woman left the plate of cabbage pies and scurried away. They turned out to be stale and lacking in cabbage. Sergei came by, saw the plate, and burst out laughing. I had apparently fallen for the oldest trick in the book, handing over a fistful of money for day-old dough that was the end of the batch after the cook ran out of cabbage. Humorous as that was, in truth, I feel that Russians lead their lives in a chaotic and confused world, protecting themselves as best they can but with little incentive to make waves. I could have gone to find the vendor to get my money back—but I didn't.

Our train pulls out of Izhevsk, and I am already settled into the humdrum routine. I make some tea, make my bed, and smile at the woman in the berth across from me. She is already tucked under her blanket, reading.

My first solid night of sleep in a while ends with shouting. The *provodnik* is yelling "the bathroom will be closed in five minutes for cleaning. Thirty minutes to Perm!" I crawl out of bed, and run to the lavatory to brush my teeth and throw cold water at my face. Then Sergei and I gather our belongings and disembark in Perm, where we have a few hours to burn. This is by far the most ramshackle train station we've visited so far. In a dingy basement Sergei and I find a luggage storage room to leave our suitcases. Then we walk upstairs to a small café.

"Sergei, I'm starved—you want any food?"

"Just tea, David."

I walk up to a buffet line and take two hard-boiled eggs, some kasha, and two teas—all for a whopping sixty-nine rubles (two dollars). I am peeling my first egg when a thought occurs to me. Maybe total paranoia, maybe not, but I ponder one way our "friends" could bring an abrupt end to my trip: If they planted drugs or something else in my suitcase. I scarf down the food, and we return to the basement to grab our luggage from the storage room. Then we find a taxi.

One potential stop that interested me in Perm was the local office of Memorial, a nationwide organization that highlights the repressions of Soviet times and helps modern-day citizens fight for civil liberties. The group is often a thorn in the Kremlin's side, exposing how protesters are jailed and intimidated, hurting Russia's image abroad. Sergei had made a few calls and was told some of their leaders would be available today if we stopped by.

Our taxi pulls up on the side of a busy street, where there is no obvious sign of Memorial, just a gray cement block of apartment buildings, with storefronts on the ground floor. Then I see it— next to a manicure/pedicure shop, beneath an advertisement with a woman in a bikini is a small sign—"Memorial"—near a brown metal door. Sergei and I swing the creaky door open and walk into a dank cement corridor with signs for lawyers, travel agents, and business advice plastering the walls. On another metal door at the opposite end of the corridor, there's another sign for Memorial, mentioning "alternatives to military service and questions about human rights." We knock, and a pleasant young woman invites us inside. The floor is wooden, covered with dried mud. There are several wooden desks, an aging photocopier, a coffeemaker, an electric teakettle, and the telltale Memorial flag with a red flame draped on the wall.

"The people you want to see will be here shortly," the young woman says.

Sergei and I sit, and I can't help but think how this shabby office next door to a mani/pedi shop says a lot about the battle for civil rights here. The organization fights a lack of money and lots of government pressure to achieve a respected place in Russian society.

Several minutes pass, and an older woman walks through the door, gives us a look, and motions to a table in the corner, where the teakettle and cookies are located.

"Ochen priyatno—David," I say.

"Angelina."

She turns the switch on the teakettle, munches on a cookie, and waits for the water to heat. Sergei and I sit in the second and third wooden chairs at the table.

"What would you like to know?" she says. Sergei briefly tells her about my book, and how he was told that she had a painful story from Soviet times that caught Memorial's interest.

"You know they wrote a book about me?"

Angelina reaches into her bag and pulls it out. It's called *The Whisperers: Private Life in Stalin's Russia*. The book, which I mentioned earlier, is by British historian Orlando Figues. She pages through and finds a black-and-white photo of a baby girl. "That's me. That was the last photo my father took of me."

Angelina Bushueva has red-dyed hair tied in a pony tail. She's wearing a black blouse and purple scarf. She squints a bit through her glasses when she speaks.

"You're young," she says to me, smiling. "You don't know these stories."

She puts a tea bag into a cup and pours hot water in. She motions with her head to some other teacups. Sergei and I each take one, along with a tea bag, and we pour.

"My father was head of a technology bureau. One day, just like that, he was arrested on his lunch break. And after he was arrested we were evicted from our house. We were told we were 'enemies of the people.'" That was the fall of 1937. To this day she doesn't know why her father was taken. But in Stalinist times this was common. He ordered arrests and executions of people because they were academics, or in the sciences, or of certain religions, or because Stalin and his cohorts just acted on whims.

"My mother saw him in prison. This photo, she brought it to him. Then he was sent to be executed."

Angelina is speaking smoothly and quietly in Russian, with little outward emotion.

"It was impossible to talk about any of this. Only in 1986 did my mother begin telling us all the details. At eighty years old, my mother starts talking. You know, she was pregnant when my father was executed."

It was a baby boy. And after the birth, Angelina's mother and baby brother were sent to a gulag—a "camp for wives of betrayers of the motherland," Angelina recalls.

She was two and had a sister who was four. "My sister and I were sent to an orphanage. My grandmother found us when I was six."

Angelina and her sister went to live with her grandmother. Other families were there, including a man from Leningrad who ran a printing house. "And he is the reason I learned to read."

She and her sister started receiving letters from their mother, from a gulag in Kazakhstan. Finally the two girls were allowed to travel to be with their mother—and they attended school in the camp settlement.

I can't stop thinking about my morning—my anger at being followed by a few thugs, my worry about our luggage, my impatience and desire to just get through this layover in Perm so we could be on our way to Sagra. I never expected to meet this woman and get such a vivid portrait of tragedy.

After the Allies won World War II—"Victory Day," as it's remembered in Russia—Angelina and her family were freed from the gulag and returned to Russia. Her mother's movements were restricted. She wasn't allowed to live in big cities, and the work she could do was limited. But she took illegal jobs and got by.

"I came to Perm and started school," Angelina says. "When Stalin died in 1953, my mother came to Perm and was able to rent an apartment. She received papers confirming her 'rehabilitation'—she was no longer an enemy of the people."

She pauses here and shakes her head.

"There were no real crimes. Stalin wanted there to be enemies everywhere. You know my brother went to the army? He served west of Moscow and studied to work in the Interior Ministry. He died with a very high rank. What an irony, given that's the agency that arrested his family."

Angelina worked as an elementary school teacher, then moved to a factory for twenty-nine years. Then she settled at Memorial, trying to raise awareness about what happened in Soviet times. Trying to confront the past so Russia can move into a new future.

"For years people have been afraid. Worried about their children, worried that history could one day repeat itself. The way I talk now? It's difficult to get other people to do that. They are still afraid."

She looks directly at me: "There has never been an apology for Stalin's crimes. But the time will come. The time will come when they apologize."

It was no apology, but the Soviet leader Nikita Khrushchev did stun the world in 1956, famously denouncing Stalin in a speech. The general trend in modern Russia is a growing nostalgia for Stalin. Putin has spoken almost fondly—rarely critically—of him. And while there is no organized campaign of fear and terror in today's Russia, Putin's regime has increasingly clamped down on democracy, rounding up protesters and targeting human rights groups like Memorial. Not to mention, of course, the corrupt and flawed system of justice that sends innocent people to jail—maybe not at the hands of Stalin but at the hands of an overzealous judge under pressure to rack up convictions. Russians today live in some state of purgatory—told by their leaders that they live in a democracy, encouraged to go to the polls and vote. But meanwhile, Russians can never be sure when the authorities might act in a wholly undemocratic way—bringing terrifying memories of this country's past back to the surface.

Angelina finishes her tea, and we say good-bye.

As she puts on her coat, a young man walks swiftly into the office, hangs his coat on the coatrack, and positions himself at his desk.

"I'm Robert," he announces to us across the room.

"Ah, David," Sergei says quietly. "This is the gentleman we are supposed to talk to."

He's Memorial's local director.

We walk over to Robert's desk.

"Please. Please sit," he says.

I ask Robert about the situation for Memorial since Putin

returned to the presidency in 2012. He removes a letter from the top of a pile on his desk and holds it in front of me.

"You see this? We received this today from a prosecutor informing us of a 'checkup.' They are looking for evidence of extremism. So I have to fill this out, confirming that I am authorized to lead this group, how we spend money, and how we use foreign grants."

Indeed, Putin angered the United States and other western governments by threatening to scrutinize human rights organizations, forcing them to register as "foreign agents." The move was seen as a not-so-subtle effort by Putin to intimidate the groups and begin the process of shutting them down. In March 2013, the government raided some of Memorial's offices as well as the offices of other rights organizations. Pavel Chikov, who leads Agora, an umbrella group for human rights organizations, told my NPR colleague, Corey Flintoff, that groups were deeply worried about bowing to Putin's demand and registering as "agents" because, as he put it, "this means that we are spies of foreign government."

Robert tells me he received the threatening letter because he gets charitable contributions from the United States.

"The situation in our country is constantly worsening," Robert says. "I have this game. Whenever I hear about some new initiative like this"—he shakes the letter—"I hold it in one hand. Then I take a copy of the Russian constitution in the other. And I read that. And I'm surprised to learn about the country I'm *supposed* to live in."

The thirty-first of any month is an important one for democracy activists in Russia. Often people hold unsanctioned antigovernment protests. Often they get arrested. It is a symbolic display, because article 31 of the Russian constitution guarantees citizens' rights to public assembly.

"What we have," Robert tells us, "is not democracy. It is imitative democracy. We have all the external signs. We have elections. We have a parliament. We have legislation. All the accessories of democracy. But anyone with common sense here knows we live in an authoritarian state. Putin has learned that if he offers the accessories of democracy, his regime can be very hard to accuse. The regime does one thing very well: It doesn't listen. So there can be free speech, channels of communication. But normally in a democracy, those voices affect decision making. In this country that doesn't happen."

"But why do the *people* allow this to go on?"

"It's in the genes, David. Do you deal with power? Or do you live in a parallel world? Two-thirds of our society was shaped in Soviet times. And young people? There are young people who agree with Stalin's ideology. So for them it's not fear driving them, but something else."

Two people have walked into the office, waiting to sit down with Robert. The last thing I want to do is take his time away from people who truly need it.

"Just another question or two, Robert?"

"Sure."

"Where do things go from here?"

"I see several options. The first—there's a slow process where people, very slowly, develop a better understanding of the country they want to live in, what kind of power they want. I am confident this can happen, if there's no war or catastrophe."

"And other options?"

"Option two is the one many experts predict: confrontation. Different groups competing for the best way to overcome their disappointment. Not necessarily with guns. But a revolution. The thing is, any revolution leads to tragedy. Ties are broken. One set of rules is gone. Another set of rules is established."

Robert is getting eager now to attend to his other guests. As we stand up, I ask him if he feels that better days may be coming.

"I used to answer that question by saying I would not be working for this organization if I were not an optimist. I would like to believe those words. In truth, what makes me optimistic is my wife, my daughter, and knowing they have a bright future."

"Do you have trouble keeping that faith?"

"We'll manage that."

With that we shake hands, and Robert is already offering his next guest tea and a seat. Sergei and I quietly gather our things and walk outside onto the street to look for a taxi.

Talking to Robert makes me even more eager to return to Sagra, and to reconnect with Andrei. He and his family have tested democracy in Russia, whatever it is. And I wonder if he feels that he has overcome the barrier Robert mentioned between people and power—the feeling that as a citizen you can't interact with power in this country. It just exists and does its thing. And you do yours.

IT'S THE MIDDLE of the afternoon, and the sun is setting in Perm as Sergei and I arrive back at the train station—dragging all our luggage, since we didn't want to leave it in the storage room. Oddly enough there are no "friends" in sight. Maybe they have finally decided that an American writer riding the rails is no real threat.

Sergei and I are ravenous. We find a food stand outside the train station. I wait with our suitcases. The weather has turned bitterly cold—I desperately dig out my gloves, as my hands are already feeling numb. Sergei buys four beers, a bag of *piroshki* (the same pastries I tried to buy on the train—this time they have their filling), and *chechel* (a stringy, salty cheese from the former Soviet republic of Georgia). We board our train, chow down, and relax, taking in the scene out the window.

Over four hours our train moves into the famous but less-than-impressive Ural Mountains. Even with the benefit of daylight, they don't look like much—foothills, really, making you expect the giant peaks to arrive, but they never do. Symbolically, though, the Urals are an important marker. They divide Europe and Asia and mark the official beginning of Siberia. The borders of Siberia differ depending on who you ask—the official Russian region extends from the Urals to west of Lake Baikal, not even close to the Pacific Ocean. But most geographers and historians consider Siberia to be all of Russia east of the Urals—all the way to the Pacific, all the way to North Korea to the southeast and Alaska to the northeast. Russia as a country is already by far the world's biggest geographically. Siberia alone is 5.1 million square miles—meaning somewhere close to 1.5 United States of America (yes, including Alaska) could fit inside Siberia.

Aside from most of the place being very empty and very cold, it is hard to generalize about it. In fact, it's not always even cold. Parts of Siberia get horribly warm and bug infested during the summer months, making many people dream of the snow and twenty-four hours of darkness in the winter. The topography is different in different places. So are the cultures. There are scores of different ethnic pockets and native languages. The Siberia that borders North Korea is nothing like the Siberia that Sarah Palin marvels at, which is nothing like the Siberia that Sergei and I will see when we head farther east from here.

12 · ANDREI

WE ARRIVE in the Urals city of Ekaterinburg at 10:00 p.m. Andrei Gorodilov, who lives with his wife and son in the city (a half hour from his father in Sagra), is waiting for us in the parking lot of the train station.

"David, Sergei, zdravstvuyte!"

"Andrei, privet. Rosa tozhe skazala privet [Andrei, hi. And Rose also says hi]."

"David, look," Andrei says in his bit of English. He climbs into the driver's seat of his SUV, reaches into the console to the right and pulls out a fading Aeroflot boarding pass—with Rose's e-mail address scribbled on it: "I still have!"

I am really touched. "Andrei, she wishes she could be here."

"I will be glad to see her."

But that wasn't all.

"Vodka." He reaches into the glove compartment, and there is the third bottle of vodka I left to Andrei and his family: "I don't drink!"

I am really happy our first visit to Sagra was as meaningful to him as it was to me.

The three of us go to a sushi restaurant near the train station, attached to a hotel where we get two rooms for the night. Sergei, Andrei, and I are squeezed into a booth ringed by fake bamboo. Andrei is medium height, with a round face, brown hair, and bright blue eyes. He is sipping tea—he has already had dinner—as Sergei and I dive into bowls of soup.

We exchange news about our wives. Andrei tells me that his wife is starting her own business, selling replacement parts for excavation equipment. "I bought a property at a good price during the economic crisis," Andrei says. "But you know how long it took me to get the permits to make it a business?" He snaps his hands into motion, as if flinging documents, one after another. But now it looks as if the business will be in good shape to open. After the difficult legal battle over Sagra, things are going better for Andrei. His wife may get her business open—and his businesses are doing well. He imports excavation equipment from abroad, mostly South Korea, and he owns a store selling custom-made fur hats.

I am even more struck by the connection between us. Rose, like Andrei's wife, has dreams of opening a business, and after months of legal wrangling, she's close to opening a restaurant in Washington, D.C. What's more, like me, Andrei travels abroad a lot—we both realize that one of our favorite cities in the world is Busan, a South Korean port where he moves excavation equipment and I covered an international summit attended by former president George W. Bush.

"There really are special moments in life," Andrei says, looking at me and Sergei. "When you came last time, we spent time together, all of us, and I believe we grew wiser."

It's getting late, and we have an early start to get to Sagra in the morning. We pay the bill, and Andrei walks us to the lobby of the hotel. "Do zavtra [until tomorrow]," I say, before catching myself and noticing it's already 12:30 a.m. "*Do sevodnya* [until today]."

Andrei walks out into the cold to his car, and Sergei and I take the elevator up to our rooms for a few hours of sleep.

At 10:00 a.m. sharp Andrei is in the lobby, and we jump into his SUV for the half-hour drive to the village. It takes a while to get out of Ekaterinburg, a city of more than a million people that reminds me of Chicago—a population and cultural hub, with a more friendly vibe, not as intense or high-strung as New York, or in this case, Moscow.

I ask Andrei if we can stop at a grocery store to pick up some things to bring to his father. We grab sausage, pickles, and a bottle of cognac. I pay, Andrei grabs the bags from the cashier, and, smiling, hands me the bottle of cognac to carry. I get his message: Let's see some redemption. I carry it—carefully and successfully—to the car.

As we get closer to Sagra, the roads get narrower and less well traveled. We are now on the road where, in 2011, that violent gang was walking toward the village, with unknown intentions.

The story of what happened next has been widely reported in Russia, and has been a matter of some debate. Some observers wondered whether the villagers, including Andrei's family, went after the group of men because they were ethnically Azeri. People from Azerbaijan do face discrimination in Russia. Andrei, his family, and other people in the village have always said they were offended by charges of racism and maintained that this gang had been selling drugs in the community for a long period of time. And whether it was part of a turf battle or an effort to intimidate, the gang made its way up this road one evening. Neighbors saw them advancing, alerted people in Sagra, and a resident called the police. The police never came. And when the gang members approached the outskirts of the village, the residents were waiting, with pitchforks and hunting rifles. One gang member died in the melee that ensued.

As with so many cases in Russia's justice system, the police made an accusation—here blaming the villagers—and it appeared it would be an open and shut case. Viktor Gorodilov, Andrei's father, and his fellow villagers would serve time. Andrei took time off from work, found a lawyer, and began a public campaign to learn the truth and expose the police who, the villagers believed, were trying to cover up their own negligence in letting this gang develop so much power. The fight succeeded, and Viktor and other villagers are now off the hook.

Andrei's SUV is bumping up and down over mounds of snow as we make our way into Sagra, where the prevailing characteristic is deep snow. It covers the patchwork of unpaved streets, where dirt has been churned up by insufficient plowing. It blankets the rooftops of rickety wooden homes. Deep snow has all but swallowed the tarps that cover piles of firewood, perhaps the only resource here that's easy to come by, as this is a lumber town. Geese are wandering by, honking away. Smoke is rising out of chimneys. We pull up to a familiar house where we all met last time, the home of another Andrei, a friend and neighbor of the Gorodilovs.

Inside, the owner, Andrei, and Viktor Gorodilov welcome us back with bear hugs. Viktor, Andrei's father, looks like a lumberjack—a reddish-gray beard, balding, wearing a red flannel shirt and camouflage pants. The house is one level, all activity pretty much limited to a single room. There is a mattress—neatly made with a sheet and red blanket—on the floor in one corner, a pool table, an exercise machine in another corner, a guitar hanging on the wall, and a couch and table in front of a flat-screen television. The kitchen is noticeably lacking a sink. That's because water comes from a well into one place—the small adjacent room, where there is a toilet, shower, and sink to wash yourself as well as the dishes. Andrei's (the occupant) wife is a striking woman who is a spitting image of Angelina Jolie. I imagine her—like so many Russian women of modest means— putting on makeup and sprucing up in a cramped room like this. I see her makeup laid out in the same room as dirty dishes. All this is a window into the haphazardness of Russian life. Many villages are like this—in surprising stages of development. The streets are not paved. Homes have one room with well water. But then there is also a flat-screen television, and everyone owns mobile phones. The house is heated by burning wood, and cooking is done using an orange canister of gas that people have to replace every few months.

"Russia extracts a great amount of gas," Viktor notes wryly. His country is among the world's top energy producers. "And yet somehow they can't bring gas service to our village."

In so many Russian towns and villages I have visited, I had to forget all assumptions about democracy. For years people have lived under this set of unspoken rules—life will be hard, the government will provide few services, people in power might be corrupt but there's nothing you can do about it. Today a *few* people seem to be realizing, in small ways, that they *can* have a voice.

"Thank you, son," Viktor says, as Andrei passes the tray of pickles and meat over to him. "David, like this," Viktor says, putting a chunk of *salo* and a pickle slice on some brown bread. *Salo* is a Russian delicacy, and not a healthy one—it's basically cured pig lard.

It's mushy, salty, and to many people, delicious. I did learn to appreciate it, so I happily join Viktor.

"Andrei, Viktor, I wonder if we can reflect a bit more on what happened here in Sagra," I say, as we all chew—and chew and chew—our chunks of *salo*.

"The police," says Andrei, in midbite. "They tried to suggest this conflict was just a part of everyday life in Russia."

And that is sadly believable. Even just living in Russia for a few years, I adjusted to the lawlessness. It was not uncommon to see two men punching each other on a street corner, settling some dispute, then moving on.

"The truth?" Andrei says. "The police didn't want to admit there was organized crime here. They didn't want to admit there was major gang activity. That would have opened them up to charges of negligence and criticism. In Russia that's all anyone worries about—blame."

He takes a few chews of *salo* and pickle and gets more animated.

"In our country, sure, a person is equal to another person. But there are people who are more equal. They have connections to another resource—the police, or government officials. And they feel superior. The law is not one and the same for everyone. And that is not democracy."

He chooses his next words carefully. Sergei smiles as he translates them.

"In this case publicity was our protection."

"Okay Andrei, publicity is your protection. A belief that the truth can expose a corrupt power. Aren't those democratic values?"

"Yes," Andrei says, "and we have to protect them. When I studied at university, I was taught that the police, the authorities, should fulfill their duties for the state. Their only motivation should be, 'What can I do for the people?' But the state machine that we have works in favor of itself. I remember the lectures. They are supposed to work for the people."

"So a government for the people—"

Andrei cuts me off. He senses where I'm going. "But our Russian mentality has to be protected, too."

Russian mentality?

"You can't impose an ideology on a country. Other people often talk about Russians as lazy alcoholics. I'm not lazy. And I don't drink. And I don't smoke."

This accusation of laziness has him animated.

"In Soviet times the flight of stairs was cut off for a Russian person. He can't move up. If and when this formula changes—then everything will work, and we'll feel those values."

We are into a second plate of meat and pickles, refreshed from the fridge.

"So Andrei—what now? Are Russians just waiting?"

"This will all develop gradually. But no, we can't just sit and wait."

"You told me last time I was here that the answer is not a bloody revolution."

"Right, that would be death to our country."

"But the answer is also not to sit and wait."

"Civil society needs to be developed. We all have to take our own small steps."

Truth be told, that comes directly from the message playbook of

Putin and his cronies. They often say that Russia's citizenry is not yet "developed" enough to have true democracy.

"Did the experience here give you—personally—more faith in these values we're talking about?"

Andrei pauses.

"When all this happened, I made a lot of friends. And in our life the most important value is the human resource."

Now I'm thinking about the babushkas, who in times of tragedy turned to one another and found a true sense of community to get by. I'm thinking about Boris, and how his time in that cramped communal apartment with Gia was the best time in his life.

"Honestly, Andrei, what you want really sounds like what we have in my country. Isn't that ultimately the right choice for Russia?"

I have now opened up a whole new can of worms.

"You want to know something? I don't like your system of electing presidents."

Okay, the Electoral College *is* weird. Point for Andrei.

"And your congressmen all have the same names, don't they?"

He's suggesting the same families often dominate American politics. And he has a point here, too.

I have often reported on Putin's potential reign—if he wins reelection as president and stays in the Kremlin through 2024, he will have been in power either as president or prime minister for twenty-four consecutive years. While that is unheard of in the United States, I do take Andrei's point. I put my notebook on the table, and scribble names in order. "Bush Clinton Clinton Bush Bush Obama Obama Clinton Clinton."

I am pointing out that, if Hillary Clinton wins the presidency in

2016, there's the potential for a few familiar names to have occupied the White House over thirty-six years of American history.

"Neepravilno! [not right]" Andrei yells, laughing. Everyone else joins in.

But then I press Andrei on what really he dislikes about Western-style democracy.

"I don't understand why in European countries, they have gone so quickly from being so religious, so hateful of gay marriage, to enshrining it in their laws."

Andrei quickly backs up and says he personally has nothing against homosexuality: "It's just that you destroy a society when all of a sudden you invent something new. Something gets imposed by the mass media. And a country's people can lose their sense of purpose."

I'm beginning to understand Andrei better—and I admit it's disappointing me. I know Russians are averse to change. The anger and fear that Russians felt toward Mikhail Gorbachev and Boris Yeltsin for driving the country into economic paralysis was well reported. But somehow, challenging Andrei, a man who seems so close to appreciating democratic values, and hearing him recoil, hearing him express fear, underscores the complexity.

"Gorbachev and Yeltsin," Andrei says, just as I'm thinking about them. "They destroyed our country."

Now Viktor Gorodilov offers that well-known Russian signal that the serious conversation must end: alcohol. He pours shots of cognac. We end up drinking the afternoon away, laughing together in this hardscrabble Russian village. But I know Andrei has given me a lot to think about.

"David," Viktor says, pouring the second round of shots. "Russians really are optimists. But there's a proverb. It goes like this: 'Think about bad things. The good things will come on their own.'"

Think about bad things. The good things will come on their own.

What does this mean? I am in a room full of people who don't like Putin. They see their country as corrupt, and without a fair system of justice. And yet their patience is astounding. *The good things will come on their own.*

Father and son have a few more questions about America before the cognac sets in. "Twenty years ago," Viktor says, "if I had told you that in twenty years, America would have a black president, would you have believed me?"

"I would have," I tell him. Viktor's point seems to be that positive change comes with time. The thought I'm left with is how many Americans had to fight for that change. They didn't just wait.

We drink, and laugh, and drink some more for hours. There is nowhere in Russia I feel warmer than in this snowy village. Finally, in midafternoon, Sergei and I thank our host and say good-bye to Viktor. We step outside as Andrei spends a few minutes talking to his dad. The streets are so quiet—the kind of eerie silence that follows a big snowstorm, before people have come out to inspect the damage and shovel. I am standing in this village, thinking about how many villages just like this dot the hills around Ekaterinburg, and dot the Urals region, and dot this vast country. Hidden, struggling communities, each with its own set of challenges largely ignored by the government. Suddenly Andrei's fight for justice seems smaller, less consequential. Sergei, looking down a street covered with snow and dirt, seems as contemplative—and buzzed—as I am. "If this government would just *work*. They should build the roads in this village. The government should operate well."

A whistle shatters the silence, and a train flies by the village at high speed.

"Like the trains—they work," Sergei says.

A young boy from the neighborhood walks up to us on the street, looking curious. We learn his name is Maxim. Sergei reaches into his pocket and takes out a keychain—a mini-Kalashnikov rifle—he bought in the museum gift shop. He hands it to Maxim.

"Eto Kalashnikov," Sergei explains. Maxim shakes the gift around in his hands, then stares up at me. "Eto David," Sergei says. "Iz Ameriki." (This is David. He's from America.)

Maxim's eyes grow big. He smiles. And he reaches out and shakes my hand.

13 · POLINA

THE DRIVE BACK from Sagra to Ekaterinburg is quiet. I am in the backseat, behind Andrei, watching the rural landscape become more urban again. At each corner men and women, bundled up against the cold, wait for mud-covered buses to pull over—their tires splashing dirty snow in the direction of the bus stop—to pick them up. The crowd rushes onto a bus, the last passenger barely on board as the uncaring driver swiftly shuts the door and whisks his big vehicle back into traffic. There can be a rhythm to life on Russian streets that feels so devoid of emotion—people move as quickly as they can in the cold from one spot to the next, not smiling, not noticing other people, lost in their own thoughts.

Now the full-throated debate about the future of Russia back in Sagra is feeling almost intrusive, as if I was forcing these questions on people who don't want or need to think about them, and just go on each day getting by. But Andrei Gorodilov engaged. He asked challenging questions of me. And he defended Russia against this notion that it is only a matter of time before a Western-style system is imposed here. I have just never seen such a patient people.

The good things will come on their own.

. . .

IN THE 2013 debate over possible military action in Syria, President Obama made the case that the United States sometimes needs to engage, to help people elsewhere in the world—"That's what makes America different. That's what makes us exceptional." Putin then wrote an op-ed in the *New York Times*, saying he closely read Obama's comments and that he "would rather disagree." In Putin's view "It is extremely dangerous to encourage people to see themselves as exceptional." He added, "There are big countries and small countries, rich and poor, those with long democratic traditions and those still finding their way to democracy." Putin finished by writing, "We must not forget that God created us equal."

Putin is not someone I'm eager to take lectures from. But that exchange raised the very questions I was asking myself on the ride back from Sagra. Notably Putin suggested that Russia is finding its way to democracy. And no doubt he has benefited from using a "we're not ready for democracy" argument to justify some harsh policies that threaten human rights. Throwing people in prison for being gay is despicable and immoral. I'm all for lecturing—and shaming—Russia when it comes to an issue like that. But I realize I had gone into that house in Sagra thinking that I knew the best model for Russia, falling into the trap many of us fell into twenty years ago.

"Do you guys have time to stop at my house and meet my wife?" Andrei asks from the driver's seat.

"Of course," I say.

We drive into what appears, on its face, to be a ramshackle neighborhood behind a shopping center. But then we pull into one house that stands apart from the rest—far more modern looking. Andrei walks us into his home, and here is everything that was lacking in Sagra—a sparkling kitchen with marble countertops, polished wooden floors, a bathroom not just with city water service but a state-of-the-art shower with a computerized display.

For Andrei business has clearly been good. His wife and young son come in from the snow, bundled up in winter coats. Andrei starts speaking about Sagra, and I can see in his wife's eyes a look of, Are we still talking about *that?*

"You know, the people who suffered the most were my wife and kids," he says, boiling water for tea and unwrapping a cake to go with it.

"It really was outrageous," his wife says. "We were trying to lead a quiet life."

Andrei and his wife were apart for the larger part of a year, as Andrei stayed with his father in Sagra for weeks at a time, working on the case. And their older son was expelled from the local police academy—which Andrei is certain was punishment for his confronting local officials.

It is striking how Andrei was pulled into this other world for a year. Here he was, with a gorgeous house, stable work, and a wife fulfilling her dream to open a business. Then, all of a sudden, he is yanked into the darker, more vigilante side of Russia, having to defend his father in Russia's joke of a justice system. It's all a reminder of how precarious life is for everyone in this country.

Andrei got a taste of democracy at work. *Publicity was our protection.* But he didn't feel much incentive to do more with this case. He and his wife are just eager to get back to their routine, and not make more waves.

It's not just that Russians are built to endure. They are also wise. Many see their odd version of democracy today as flawed and dangerous. But this purgatory is perhaps as safe as they can hope for.

"Wasn't it Confucius who said a person shouldn't be born into a time of change?" Andrei asks. I'm not familiar with the particular quote, but I'm all ears. "It's the worst thing to be born into a time of change. We were children of perestroika. Born in one country, grew up in another, and now live in a third. And who knows what's next?"

Andrei emphasized back in Sagra that Russians are not lazy. But they are tired. At least his generation is. And so are many in Russia's younger generation, as Sergei and I were about to learn on our next stop to the south.

"Sergei," I say, as both of us have pieces of cake in our hands. "We have a meteorite to chase."

Feels odd just to say those words. After all, are we in some science-fiction movie? Role-playing at a *Star Trek* convention? No. In fact, while we were making our way across the country by train, a *meteorite* streaked across the Russian sky at low altitude, shattered windows, and scared the hell out of people in a large city, then plunked down in the middle of a lake. This just isn't normal!

The thing landed near the city of Chelyabinsk—only a few hours to the south. How could Sergei and I pass up the chance to go?

"The train to Chelyabinsk takes hours—I think you should take a bus," Andrei says. We heed his advice.

After saying good-bye to his family, Andrei drives us to the bus station in downtown Ekaterinburg. Evidently Russian traditions are not specific to one's mode of transportation, because Andrei grabs my suitcase, rolls it over chunks of snow and ice, and escorts us into the bus terminal. (Now I'm feeling guilty for the times when

I have pulled up to an airport terminal or train station and just let Rose out of the car, without going inside.) The bus terminal is pure chaos. There are indecipherable timetables hanging on the walls all over the vast room that echoes the sounds of travelers yelling at one another. As for the timetables, it's not just the Russian making it hard on me. Sergei can't figure out what any of them mean either. We eventually decode one and are reasonably confident there's a bus to Kazakhstan at 9:00 p.m. that makes a midnight stop in Chelyabinsk. (Some twisted version of "Midnight Train to Georgia" is now playing in my head.) We buy tickets, and we each hug Andrei.

"It was great to see you—and thanks for all your honesty."

"David, come back anytime."

Andrei waves as he walks out to the parking lot, and Sergei and I find a spot to wait for our bus.

THIS BUS makes third class on a Russian train seem downright luxurious. I swear, our driver looks just like the Moscow trolleybus driver who refused to let me pay. And he's just as cruel. Sergei and I stand at the door to the bus and ask if we can put our luggage in the compartment underneath. He shakes his head no.

"Where do we put it?"

He motions inside the bus. So Sergei and I lug our roll-aboards in and place them in the vacant seats next to ours, which moments later become occupied. And so our bus to Chelyabinsk involves Sergei and me being pressed up against our suitcases, squeezed into a seat. The bus jostles back and forth, hits every imaginable bump, and smells on the inside distinctly like an outhouse. I can't sleep a wink because my nightmare is missing our stop and being awakened by Kazakh immigration authorities asking me for a visa. (I once arrived at a small airport in Kazakhstan's neighbor, Kyrgyzstan, thinking I did not need a visa but learning on arrival that I did. I was held for six hours in the transit zone, a small concrete area with no air-conditioning—it was ninety-seven degrees—no food, and facilities that amounted to a hole in the ground. A fellow passenger sharing my predicament offered me warm Kahlua. I politely declined. At hour five having eaten no food and found no water, I took him up on his offer. Hence my pangs of fear about accidentally arriving in Kazakhstan tonight visa-free).

Our bus bounces its way into Chelyabinsk, and on first impression the stereotype that this is the armpit of Russia is spot on. In near-darkness, looking from the bus in all directions, we see endless oceans of industry, hulking towers and monster machinery rising over lots full of old trucks and vehicles caught in the orange glow of spotlights.

This city of three million people is among the most polluted places in Russia, maybe the world. The city has long been home to major industry—iron and steel plants, and a huge tractor factory— and a large number of Soviet tanks used in World War II were produced here. And while foreigners could not visit firsthand to know for sure, there was evidently a major Soviet nuclear research center in the region outside the city where a deadly nuclear accident occurred in 1957. In other words, this is not the nicest place to live. Then again, being a native of Pittsburgh and familiar with all the jokes and stereotypes of living in a dirty place, I come to Chelyabinsk with an open mind.

My former NPR colleague and Russia veteran Anne Garrels followed the story of this industrial city in a series for our network.

Anne reported, when she visited in 2008, that the city had closely followed the broader narrative of Russia.

In the 1990s, the economy of Russia fell apart. There was no demand for Chelyabinsk's goods; they could not compete on the world market, and the decrepit factories all but shut down. The city was bankrupt. Civil society, the ability of people to take responsibility for themselves, was in its infancy. . . . I returned this fall to find out what had happened to this city and region, more than a decade after I was first there. The changes are staggering. Thanks to the global economic boom in the intervening years, demand for Chelyabinsk's metals and raw materials saved the city. With new service industries, shops, restaurants, and everything that comes along with them, there is an emerging middle class. There is a profound psychological change. Residents credit former president, and now Prime Minister Vladimir Putin, with bringing stability and a renewed pride in being Russian.

But Anne found the boom ending, as the world was on the cusp of another economic downturn. "All of the signals of a crisis are here, but journalists writing about it have to be careful. Several local reporters are being investigated for what the prosecutor general calls 'inflaming a mood of panic.'"

Not even realizing that we have reached the bus station— because our bus just stops in the middle of a parking lot—our driver yells "Chelyabinsk" and Sergei and I and a few other passengers are quickly ushered off by our friendly driver so he can continue his journey to Kazakhstan.

We are able to wave down a car, a red Lada, a Soviet make that ceased to be produced in 2012, driven by an easygoing older gentleman named Oleg. I immediately inspect Oleg's dashboard and am disappointed not to see any videotaping device. And this seems an appropriate time to point out how so many vivid images of that streaking meteorite here were caught on tape, and beamed on the Internet around the world. It has something to do with Russians' fear of trusting anyone. If Russian drivers are ever in an accident—even the smallest fender-bender—they will keep their vehicles right where they are, even if they are blocking traffic on a congested highway. This is to avoid the other driver fabricating what happened. What's more, when police arrive, Russians doubt the cops will be fair—what if they accept a bribe from the other driver, or what if the other driver has connections with the police or local government? The solution? Many Russians install small video cameras on their dashboards to film everything. Sergei has one. I asked him about it once.

"So, how much memory do these things have?"

"Well, mine has about six hours. So it continuously copies over, but keeps the last six hours. So if anything happens, you can go back six hours and find the video."

Voilà! When you have thousands and thousands of drivers on the roads around Chelyabinsk, and a meteorite happens to streak across the sky, chances are there would be some damn good images caught. But even more shocking than those images was the fact that there was very little screaming or yelps of surprise from the Russian motorists. The comedian Jon Stewart, in a segment on *The Daily Show*, may have put it best when he aired one of the videos, noting the reaction from the driver—or lack of: "The dude in the car is completely unimpressed by a ten-ton death rock hurtling at mach 50 toward the city!"

And this made more sense as Stewart played a montage of more scenes captured on these video camera in Russia. There were motorists emerging from their vehicles after an accident, grabbing a baseball bat, and smashing up the windshield of the other car involved. There was a woman caught on tape stealing a bumper; a farm truck accidentally dumping a herd of cattle on the road; a Russian tank suddenly bursting out of a field and into the middle of a busy road.

It was therefore no surprise to Russians when a meteorite happened to land in the country—not even to me and Rose, then having lived there for just three years. Crazy shit just happens there. "Of course it landed in Russia," Rose said to me on the phone from home, as Sergei and I were still in Yaroslavl: "Rose, we've got to go to Chelyabinsk."

"Of course you do."

We are driving toward a hotel. Sergei asks Oleg if the meteorite is still all the talk in Chelyabinsk, a week after the landing.

"Oh yes," he says, chuckling. "There are still ads on television. One is for a new door. The ad has a wife saying to her husband— Honey, what are you waiting for to buy a new door? For the *next* asteroid?"

Oleg laughs at his punch line.

"I was home. My first thought was it was a missile. My second thought, maybe a plane crashed. My dog hid under the sofa. I couldn't even woo her out with sausage." (At least Russian dogs *are* freaked out!)

"There was no panic, no fear. A thousand people went to the

hospital, but they are okay. There is a problem now, though—people are being arrested for selling fake space chunks on the Internet."

Of course they are. What's more, Russian scientists are coming around asking people to donate the remnants they've discovered for research—and evidently there's been resistance because people don't trust that the scientists are not frauds.

We pull up to a hotel. Sergei asks Oleg if we can hire him tomorrow to take us around and inspect the meteor zone. He's thrilled for the business—and just a little stoked to be involved in our mission.

He picks us up at 9:15 a.m. sharp and suggests we visit Chebarkul, a small city situated on the lake where the meteorite evidently made landfall. The space rock flew over western suburbs of Chelyabinsk, shedding debris all over the place, then flew low over the city, shaking apartment buildings and breaking windows, before heading east and flying into the lake. Scientists have not yet found the largest remaining piece, but they did find a gaping hole in the ice, so the assumption was the meteorite plunged down deep into the water to its final resting place.

Chebarkul has a small downtown, with clothing stores, mobile phone outlets, and older people bundled up in fur hats and coats selling fish. We approach one woman, who introduces herself as Polina Skorobogatova.

"I saw it!" she says, knowing full well that this American radio crew had not come to ask her for directions to the *banya*. "It was heading over that building. It was a ball. I thought it was just the sunrise, but then"—she *claps* her hands together once to re-create the loud boom she heard—"and there was just black-and-white smoke. I was afraid. But just for a moment."

We ask if the community has recovered.

"I think this was actually a message from God," she says. "A message that our community is nice and deserves some attention. We have enjoyed the attention."

And Polina has moved on, suddenly far more interested in my clothing choices. I am not wearing gloves or a heavy coat. She suspects vanity.

"There are just old guys around here—no one to fall in love with you," she says. "Get a hat on, kid."

Sergei and I move on down to the lake, which seems surprisingly peaceful for the very spot on Earth that just swallowed a meteorite. We find one guy walking down a snowy path along the lake. Yes, he saw the meteorite. No, he wasn't stunned. No, he hasn't found any debris. No, he doesn't know where we might find some—but he suggests a village eighty miles away, back on the other side of Chelyabinsk.

Done.

Sergei and I climb into the car and ask Oleg to set course for Yemanzhelinka. The place is barely a village, more a depressing settlement that makes Sagra seem well developed. There are perhaps three or four feet of snow on the ground. The homes are wooden and uncared-for, painted in light blues and greens, with dark gray metal roofs sagging under the weight of the snow. This dying little place is sadly common in Russia, villages with staggering poverty, unpaved roads, rampant illness, alcoholism, and dwindling population that are largely forgotten by the government. We drive slowly through the village. I ask Oleg to stop to chat with a teenager who's passing by.

Sergei asks if he's seen any space debris.

"Oo-meenya, yees [I have some]!" he says, digging into his

pocket, then opening his hand to reveal a small black pebble, perhaps the size of a marble. I am not going to lie. The fact that this is—or at least may be—a chunk of extraterrestrial debris seems pretty cool to me.

"What are you going to do with it?"

"Show it to my friends. Keep it as a memory."

"Would you sell it?"

"Well, there are rumors that some guys are paying one thousand rubles [thirty dollars] per gram."

We learn his name is Viktor. As we talk, a few more young men saunter up the street, exchange firm handshakes, and inquire about the fuss I'm causing.

One of the guys, Ivan Kichilin, throws me an accusatory glance.

"You know, I have a friend who asked if the U.S. knew this meteorite was going to hit Russia three days ahead of time—and didn't say anything."

I make clear I know nothing about that. And Ivan flashes a half-joking smile. He's twenty-one with closely shaved black hair, an easy smile but dark, tired eyes.

"Seriously, some guys are doing some shady business trying to sell fake pebbles." Ivan is speaking to me but directing his message to Viktor, almost fatherlike, suggesting *he* not get into any shady business. I'm impressed with Ivan and begin to sense that he is a guy who could teach me a thing or two about Russia.

"Sergei, can you see if we could meet Ivan for tea or something tomorrow? I'd love to talk to him more."

Sergei translates. Ivan thinks it over, looking me up and down, then agrees. "There is one little café in town—maybe you saw it coming in. I'll meet you there."

We exchange phone numbers and plan to call Ivan in the morning.

I was beginning to feel I had exhausted my interest in a meteorite—strange as that may sound coming from a *Star Wars*–obsessed child of the eighties. And while I don't necessarily believe God sent this thing to southern Russia, I get a weird feeling that trailing this space chunk brought me into contact with Ivan for a reason.

14 · IVAN

CALLING IT a café is generous.

The parking lot is empty, and the gas pumps haven't worked for years. There is a one-story wooden building, with a ramshackle outhouse attached. Sergei and I walk inside to find four wooden tables, no customers, and a woman watching an old TV behind the register. She and another woman back in the kitchen look up at me and Sergei as if we've arrived from outer space. Think old Western movie, where a stranger arrives in a dusty town and walks into a vacant bar, feeling very out of place, fearing a duel at any moment. Except here there's no sunshine or tumbleweeds, just bitter cold and giant heaps of snow. I try to act natural, inspecting a pink, creamy salad that's available for purchase in a glass case. Sergei tells me it's a Russian dish called "herring under a fur coat"—it usually has herring, mayonnaise, beets, egg yolk, and garlic. The salad is wrapped tightly under plastic wrap. A handwritten note says, "Don't touch with your hands." Wouldn't dream of it, actually.

As we are at the counter, the door swings open and two young men walk in, with the casual, careless strut of guys poised for a fight but wanting to show no fear. One is Ivan, the other a young man I don't recognize from the day before.

All four of us silently shake hands.

"Ivan, thanks for coming," I say. Sergei translates. Ivan nods. I ask if everyone wants tea. Nods all around, and I order four teas from the woman at the counter.

I felt a personal connection with Andrei Gorodilov in Sagra. He is my age, a businessman, world traveler. There's no natural connection here.

"This is my friend Evgeni. I asked him to come with me."

"Of course," I say.

Ivan is wearing jeans and a sweater with thick black-and-white horizontal stripes. He seems nervous. Evgeni is wearing an all-black coat, zipped up to his chin. He has a menacing look and snakelike eyes, light-colored with small dark pupils. In fact both of these guys seem menacing at first glance—and very much like young men across Russia. On the streets in Moscow and elsewhere, there's a certain look to many young men: strong, tough, intimidating. I have interviewed some, but only now realize I've shied away from many, feeling no welcome mat.

Often it has been younger men who ask that I don't use their last names on air, for fear of retribution against them or their families. Before the recent election that would return Putin to the presidency, I spent time in Tver, a gritty railroad town north of Moscow. A twenty-eight-year-old named Pavel was working as a veterinarian but driving a taxi on the side to make enough money to survive. He was excited to vote against Putin—but frightened that being quoted saying so could get him punished at work. "It's time for us to have new leaders," he said. "These people are in power too long, and they're starting to get brazen." I also met a forty-two-year-old factory worker named Mikhail. He said he sleeps better the less people know about him, so he also gave just his first name. He makes seven hundred dollars a month building railroad cars and lives with his wife and two daughters in an apartment assigned to the family during Soviet times. Life is fragile, he said, but he gets by and doesn't want to mess with a good thing—well, a workable thing. That's why he was ready to support Putin. As he put it, "It's better to have someone who is tested, or else someone will come along and start making a mess." I recall thinking in Tver how younger Russian men display this certain toughness. In some cases maybe it's a veneer. Whatever it is, Ivan and Evgeni developed it at a young age.

The woman brings four cups of hot water with tea bags to the table. The cups have cranberries and green leaves painted on them.

"Sergei, let's just start with the basics. I want to hear about Ivan's life."

Sergei dives in, and Ivan—speaking softly and methodically—begins to speak.

"I grew up here. I know everyone here. Never thought about leaving, and don't like the fuss of living in a big city. You know, we are interested to know about the USA. We know it from films. Are there villages, places like this?"

I now see that curiosity was one reason Ivan decided to come.

"My wife is actually from a village about this size," I tell him. "In a state called Ohio. And she often talks about how much she liked growing up in a small, friendly place."

"You know, when we were young, there was another life here. The tractor factory was busy, people were rushing around. Something has changed. Now people try to live in the big cities. But my friend Evgeni and I, we stayed. I'm not leaving this place. It's my motherland. I was in the army. I served in the North Caucasus. Many of them would say how much they love living in the big city. My grandmother always used to tell me people here live a friendly life, live in houses in a village, know people. But we are losing that Russian spirit. You have to understand, there used to be stability. Now I don't have this feeling."

"Well, how did this stability get lost?"

"Remember, Ivan?" Evgeni says. "We were talking about this the other day."

"Yeah, people in the Soviet Union lived at one economic level. Now we have division in our society. And this division makes people tough, like beasts. Wealth has brought selfishness. Wealth means a person is not helping his friend. This is what's being lost. I experienced a lot of hardship. I lost my parents. And now it's hard to live here. I lost my parents before I was eighteen. But it makes it easier to endure hard times when you lose a person."

His mother died of cancer when he was sixteen. His dad died of cancer when he was eighteen—perhaps related to his work at a dirty machine factory in Chelyabinsk.

"I am proud of my father and his work. And the plant did everything. We didn't have to pay a kopek for his burial."

Evgeni smiles and pats his buddy on the shoulder.

"All I have is my grandma and two friends." Ivan looks at Evgeni. "Everyone else I pushed aside because I knew what to expect."

Ivan was eighteen, an orphan but done with school, which made him eligible for his mandatory year in military service.

"I always wanted to serve in the army. But after losing my mom and dad, I didn't want to go."

"Did you ask to get out of it?"

"Yes. And their answer was no. I was in a fury. What could I do? I went to serve. And I never regretted it."

"Why don't you regret it?"

"As an American, I don't think you understand what it's like there. There is not a single person who supports you. They want to break you. There are people who morally break you, and emotionally break you."

At this point I can't help but think about the black-and-white images I've seen of Russian young men fighting in Chechnya in the two wars in the 1990s. Russia's soldiers were known to be fighting machines, killing brutally and dying often. Then you would see these photos of them taking a break from the battlefield, cigarettes hanging from their mouths, teenagers, so hardened at such a young age.

"It takes time to show what you are worth," Ivan explains. "But it makes you stronger."

He describes his training in southern Russia. His commanders, he says, deliberately put ethnically Caucasian men together with Slavic Russians, hoping ethnic tensions would boil over and they would beat one another up. That was supposed to get them ready for battle.

"I considered it the right thing to serve in the army. Difficulty brings people together. I think what the Russian army achieves: It makes *Russians*."

It makes Russians.

With Ivan I feel I am listening to a single voice amid the "millions and millions strong" in Russia's outer provinces—Shishkin described this as the second of two "nations." Tucker described it as "popular Russia." And it's about more than geography. Even amid the trendy cafes and fat paychecks in Moscow, there are many people toiling and seeking strength. I'll never forget a former military doctor in Moscow named Sergei Pichonkin. I waved him down for a ride. He gets a pension of four hundred dollar a month and looks for potential passengers on the streets to supplement that income. When I asked how tough life is, he turned around and stared at me in the backseat. "Here I am, giving a ride to an American journalist. What do you think? Is this a good thing?" With that he turned to face the windshield again, I shut the door, and he drove off. From him, from the guys in Tver, from Ivan, I detect a determination to feel strong, and appear strong. But from Ivan I hear something more: a respect for the predicaments that molded his strength—and the *people*. Russians "want a tough hand," Sofia Pinsker once told me. She's a twenty-two-year-old college student in the Siberian city of Novokuznetsk who said even younger Russians display an old tendency—to look for role models, leaders, who exude strength. "Even if he was bad or cruel—for example, Ivan the Terrible—it didn't matter and it doesn't matter. He is our father, our king, and that's all. We are supposed to do what he tells us."

Ivan says his harsh military training made him "Russian"—which I take to mean strong and impenetrable. His words bring to mind Orlando Figes's book, *The Whisperers*. In it he described interviews the historian Catherine Merridale did with Russian World War II veterans. "These men's vocabulary was businesslike and optimistic, for anything else might have induced despair . . . It would have been easy . . . to play for sympathy or simply to command attention by telling bloodcurdling tales. But that, for these people, would have amounted to a betrayal of the values that have been their collective, pride, their way of life."

"What do you think of your government, Ivan?"

Ivan, having lost both his parents and endured a punishing year of military service, doesn't play for sympathy. And he's businesslike.

"There are not enough honest people running this country."

"In America people might say then it's time for a protest."

Evgeni laughs out loud. "Ochen interesno [Very interesting]!"

"People get used to living in difficult situations here," Ivan says. "If the cup of anger gets filled? Then you have 1917."

Evgeni is still holding on to my protest question.

"In our family" Ivan's friend says, "it works like this. Husband comes home, wife gets angry, husband gets up and goes to work; then it repeats. That is the only kind of 'protest' we have. You just think about the hard life we have. You think there's time to think about revolutions? You think anybody's worried about a revolution?"

Ivan is starting to tear up, and I'm not sure why. It doesn't seem that the conversation about politics took him here. Maybe he was holding it in when he spoke about his parents. But this tough young man is suddenly vulnerable in a way I never expected.

"Our government oppresses us," he says. "But we love it. Our country—we love it."

There is desperation in his voice. Maybe desperation to hold onto something: His friends, his grandmother, his village, his image of a Russia that protects him.

It's easy to forget he's only twenty-one.

"From childhood we decided that *we* would stay together in life," Evgeni says.

I ask Ivan what he dreams about.

"I have a great wish to travel. But it's not possible."

There's no money left. Ivan rents his own place. He and Evgeni do odd jobs around the village to get by.

"I would love to own my own business," Ivan says. "It would take a certain sum of money—maybe five hundred thousand rubles [seventeen thousand dollar] to get started, rent a van. I have a driver's license." He pauses. "With all the difficulties in life? Will never happen."

We have been sitting for more than two hours. Our tea is cold. I ask if anyone wants more, but everyone declines. The woman behind the counter has been watching an old Soviet movie on the television all this time.

"So what do Americans think of Russians?" Ivan asks.

First impression, I explain, is a country full of people who don't smile much. But when you spend time, as I tell him, you see the warmth and friendship on the inside. Both young men smile. But Ivan presses on. (Who's the journalist here anyway?)

"What was your worst moment living here?"

"My wife and I were used to living in a country where you can rely on the police if anything happens. I didn't have that confidence here if, god forbid, anything happened to me or my wife."

Now it's Evgeni's turn. "Okay, so was there a worst *moment?*"

"Fortunately nothing happened to either of us."

"So," Ivan says proudly, "your worst fear about Russia never came true."

"I guess not."

Ivan smiles. "In our country we don't assume anything about our police. If something happens on the streets, better not to call anyone. Because it's better to keep your record clean."

I tell these young men how grateful I am to have met them. All thanks to a meteorite.

"There has been a joke on the local radio," Ivan says: "We are never happier than when a meteorite lands in the morning."

I don't even know how to respond to that.

"I was so curious to meet a foreigner," Evgeni says. "And you know we joked about how maybe you and this meteorite were not accident."

"Oh, like somehow I rode on this meteor——"

"Konechno [of course]!" Evgeni says, laughing.

He stands up, and so does Ivan. I ask if I can snap a photo of them. Ivan drapes his right arm around his friend's neck and with his left hand, makes a peace sign for the camera.

That photo is never being erased.

Sergei and I exchange hugs with the two young men, and say good-bye. Then Ivan Kichilin and Evgeni Barandin walk out of the café as they came in—with a tough-guy strut, marching back into their world.

Sergei and I lean back in our chairs, both moved by the last few hours. For Sergei, I know that hearing about Ivan's military service was not easy. His son, Anton, has such big dreams of being a physician and traveling the world. He doesn't know yet if he can go directly to a residency, or has to do his year in the military first. Clearly that year can change a young man.

The Russian army makes Russians.

Maybe it's true, in a way. I have no idea how Ivan's life might have been different if he had not lost his parents. But he's a smart, personable, creative young man. Suffering the tragedy of being orphaned—then being beaten down and rebuilt in the army—

hardened him. He self-imposes limits on his dreams, accepts his place, and wants to believe his country—his motherland—for all its flaws will protect him. It's hard to bemoan such genuine faith.

There are millions of young men in Russia, each with a different story. But I would hazard a guess that many share something with Ivan—difficult upbringing, maybe the loss of a father at a young age, economic hardship, and a year in the military. Through all that, young men emerge stoic. I imagine many, like Ivan, see no other way.

Sergei and I pay for the tea and go outside, where Oleg has been waiting in his car, probably by now on his thirtieth cigarette. Despite our invitation to join us, he said he preferred to wait outside.

Sergei and I decide to take a night off from serious conversation. Oleg drops us off on the main promenade in downtown Chelyabinsk. It is a welcoming pedestrian mall, especially welcoming for a city known for being so dark and dirty. As is the case often on cold nights in Russia, there are no pedestrians to be seen. Usually it's just that everyone is keeping warm inside. And that is what Sergei and I find as we wander into an Irish pub called the Fox and Goose.

I head directly to the bar, but notice that Sergei is still at the hostess stand. I had forgotten, since moving away from this country, how Russians generally dislike sitting at bars. Sure enough, the bar here is empty. It's too casual, I guess. And the restaurant experience should be a serious affair, involving a table with seats.

I digress: Rose, the former bartender, did a guest stint at a Moscow restaurant. The goal was to encourage members of the American Women's Organization to try the place. Rose was a big draw. The bar area was overrun with customers. People filled the barstools, and others stood behind. This left the Russian staff at the bar totally confused. They kept serving drinks to people standing, and asking Rose, "Where is that person sitting?" Rose would say they weren't sitting. The staff member would say, "Then we cannot serve them—there is no way to put their order in the computer." Just like Rose's butter.

I cave to Sergei's wishes and we take a table beside three Russian men who are so drunk on beer and cognac they're barely conscious. Sergei and I don't quite get to that point, but after a few beers, we take our own crack at Russian politics. Sergei has listened closely to my line of questioning. He knows that in Moscow there is an impression that Russians are antigovernment, ready to take to the streets. That's not the case in the country at large.

"You know, David, I have a friend who likes Putin. He always says to me, if you want to meet nice people, go to a rally in Moscow. But nothing's gonna change."

We're on our third beers.

"But what kind of government do we have? Capitalism? No. Socialism? No."

I do wonder what it's like to live in a country in such a state of uncertainty.

"Stalin, I would never support him. But he was the right man for the job in his time. No one stole anything."

Sergei, like me, is looking deeply at a country—its people, its problems, its future. The difference is, this is his own country. We talk about the people we've met—Nikita's parents mourning the loss of their hockey-star son, Alexei's mom staring at us as we walked down the stairs away from her apartment, and tough Ivan, tearing up out of the blue.

It is almost lights out for me and Sergei. We wave down a cab in the bitter cold and return to our hotel. In the morning we need to buy train tickets for our onward journey, which becomes a freshly complicated affair. I check out a map and notice that the southern route of the Trans-Siberian Railway goes west to east through Chelyabinsk—good news—except that when it heads east from here, it passes through a small section of Kazakhstan. We have two choices: visit the Kazakh consulate here, apply for a transit visa and wait who knows how long. Or take a circuitous route back up to Ekaterinburg, then eastward again. We choose option two.

The train station in Chelyabinsk the next morning is far less welcoming than the city's pedestrian mall. It is a concrete block of place with no signs to tell you anything—where you buy tickets, where you catch trains, what time it is.

"This is strange," Sergei says, as we walk around outside.

It's actually not. This kind of disorder no longer surprises me here. I've just come to live with it. Accept it. God, I sound Russian.

15 · TATIANA

HAVING NO VISA for Kazakhstan means an extra twelve hours of train travel.

Through the night we straddle the Ural Mountains, from Chelyabinsk back up to Ekaterinburg. Then we bend southeast, emerge from the Urals, stop for a long layover in Tyumen, then move deeper into Siberia. The train stops less frequently. The landscape is more rugged and picturesque. As hours pass the scenes become more captivating—maybe just because you need something to do. There is endless snow stretching to the horizon. Then forest. At sunrise and sunset, streaks of light cut through the trees and the snow glows in orange. We pass villages with little wooden homes. Some look abandoned—not rare in a country where many villages are losing population and dying. Some have smoke rising from the chimneys, and I imagine Viktor Gorodilov inside, in his plaid shirt and hunting pants, warming his hands by the wood fire. Or Ivan, orphaned as a teenager, alone in the small house he rents.

Deep in these thoughts, I suddenly feel a burst of pressure from the chilly window that my head is resting on and a loud hacking sound as another train flies by in the other direction. Within seconds the train is gone and peace is restored.

"I am driving across the plain of Siberia," Anton Chekhov wrote during a trip—by carriage—in May 1890:

> *I have been transformed from head to foot into a great martyr.*
> *This morning, a keen cold wind began blowing, and it began*
> *drizzling with the most detestable rain. I must observe that*
> *there is no spring yet in Siberia. The earth is brown, the trees*
> *are bare, and there are white patches of snow wherever one*
> *looks; I wear my fur coat and felt overboots day and night.*
> *. . . Well, the wind has been blowing since early morning . . .*
> *heavy, leaden clouds, dull brown earth, mud, rain, wind . . .*
> *brrrrr.*

Siberia, this vast and forbidding geographic expanse, has been the fascination of Russian writers, the torture chamber for Russian exiles, the gold mine for Russian energy companies, and the savior for Russia at large. Paradoxically, cold and forbidding lands have *helped* this country survive. As Fiona Hill and Clifford Gaddy write in their book *The Siberian Curse*, Germany lost its first major battle in World War II because thousands of its men were starving and freezing. Napoleon in 1812 fled Moscow, then faced an impenetrable enemy: the Russian winter:

> *Winter and snow are particularly Russian phenomena,*
> *captured in poems and novels and in the broadly-recognized*
> *images on lacquer boxes—of fur-clad figures bundled against*
> *the elements, troikas or sleighs drawn by three horses, expan-*

sive stretches of birch or pine forest laden with snow, and squat
wooden peasant huts around a stove to beat back the elements.
'Russia' conjures up associations with Siberia, permafrost, and
vodka to warm the flesh and boost the spirits on long winter
nights. Winter (Zima) is even a place in Siberia, a small town
and stopping point along the Trans-Siberian Railway from
Moscow to Vladivostok.

But myth and poetry are one thing. Reality is another. And Hill and Gaddy argue that the Soviet Union's obsession with moving people to Siberia, building up cities and industrializing in harsh and isolated places, is at the core of Russia's economic problems today: "If Russia is to be governable and economically viable, it needs to 'shrink' itself. Not by divesting territory but by organizing its economy differently. The objective is to reduce distance and create new connections. People will need to migrate westward on a large scale, and large cities in the coldest and most remote regions will have to downsize."

Moscow seems so very far away as we push eastward. The feeling of disconnect grows, making it seem unsurprising that having people scattered in such remote places is a drag on a nation's economy. Politically the disconnect works in different ways. Many people in Siberia feel little if any relationship to Moscow and the Kremlin, and throughout history, people have felt relatively more free to think for themselves. And yet, distance is also an impediment for any serious opposition movement to grow and thrive.

Sergei and I are still in third class. On this train we both have top berths. I am still horizontal, quietly resting my head against the window. Sergei is up. He has climbed down and made tea. He is sitting on the lower berth. The man there is still sleeping but has shifted his legs to give Sergei a corner to sit on and enjoy his tea. Sergei has his hand on the spoon in his glass so it doesn't rattle. He is worried it might wake me up.

I OFTEN WONDER how many gallons of tea are consumed daily on a Russian train. Every car has a big cauldron of water, in Russian, a *titan*. It's like a modern-day samovar, a traditional device in Russia—usually ornately made of brass—that heats water with wood chips and churns out damn good tea. The samovar on the train runs on electricity—as does the train itself. Which raises the question: What is all the coal for? At many stops the *provodniks* shovel coal into a storage cabinet located on each train car. As I've learned, coal heats the train. And it makes sense. Look outside. The landscape is rugged, empty, and cold—at times twenty or thirty degrees below zero Fahrenheit. If a train breaks down and the electricity goes out in a place this remote, passengers could freeze to death. Except that the heaters would keep working—on coal. But I've noticed a downside: The heating in train cars is not easily controlled. To keep things remotely close to a certain temperature, *provodniks* will add more or less coal to the heating system. I have a guess this is why the trains get oppressively hot overnight—hot as in you rip off your sheets and begin using them to wipe sweat off your face. I imagine the *provodnik* getting ready for bed herself, not wanting to disturb herself overnight by having to add more coal. So she loads as much as possible before going to bed. Yes, she probably thinks, that will take care of things.

Sergei and I have been traveling for about two weeks now.

Passengers have gotten on and off, and Sergei and I are now joined by a pleasant, older couple, Tatiana and Oleg. They are two of the thinnest people I've ever met—but bursting with personality. He has wavy gray hair, she has short hair—dyed bright red.

"You are David? From America?" Tatiana says, trying her limited English.

"Yes."

"It is funny. I ride the train in 1972. And there was an American David with me. A student. Harvard. He was coming from Japan. With his visa he had to stay on train the whole time crossing Soviet Union. We talked about America, about Soviet Union."

"This is crazy, but I went to Harvard."

Tatiana laughs. "This is crazy! You know he gave me gift for Oleg. Two packs of cigarettes. Marlboro."

What a reminder about how this train, and this famous train route, have endured for so long. It has been the spine of this country, even as the body around it transformed and evolved. The train has seen a lot.

"Where are you going?" Tatiana asks.

"Ishim."

I wish I could say that Sergei and I had a good reason for planning a stop there. In truth I had told Sergei we had seen enough big cities—I wanted to choose one of the smaller Trans-Siberian stops, a town where the train pulls in, dumps a few passengers, and continues on its way within minutes. The challenge if you're disembarking is to get your stuff and yourself off in time, before the train is on its way again.

"We are going to Ishim too!"

"Really? We thought this would be a good place to stop."

"I am going to give you a phone number for a friend of ours who works at a museum—her name is Tatiana," this Tatiana says. Sergei takes down the number, and we tell her we're grateful.

"Tatiana, I hope in another forty years you meet another David from Harvard."

"Yes!"

The weather has taken a turn as we pull into Ishim. The wind is whipping around in all directions and heavy snow is falling. Tatiana, Oleg, Sergei, and I climb down the metal stairs into this mess, feeling as if we are skydivers who just stepped out of a plane into a powerful jet stream. "Good-bye!" I yell, waving to the lovely couple as they march off into the meteorological abyss.

Sergei and I find a rusty red car with a taxi light taped on top and a man sitting inside. We open the door and dive in. The driver revs his engine, spins his tires a bit, and we're off, at high speed. The driver does not seem to be respecting the weather conditions. In fact, everywhere I look, people seem unfazed by this blizzard. At home, in Washington or New York—even in winter-proof cities like Boston and Chicago—I swear conditions like this would have schools closed, drivers warned to stay off the roads, power down, and people in an all-out panic about whether they bought enough bread, milk, and toilet paper. There are probably three feet on the ground already in Ishim and more snow is piling up.

Totally routine.

Sergei turns back to me from the front passenger seat.

"David, what's the name of the hotel you found?"

I look down at my notepad. "Hotel Tranquility."

16 · NADEZHDA

WE DRIVE perhaps fifteen minutes out from the center of Ishim—which didn't look like much of a center, as it was—and suddenly pull off the two-lane road onto a bumpy path. Our driver is swerving around what appear to be small factory buildings and abandoned trailers, then pulls to a stop in front of what resembles a farmhouse. It's a small building with an A-frame roof.

"David, we're here."

"Okay, Sergei."

We pay the driver and pull our luggage along; the roll-aboards are cutting a path through deep snow.

A pleasant young woman inside the Hotel Tranquility tells us she has a room for two people, for eight hundred rubles (twenty-seven dollars). She shows us the shared bathroom and shower in the hallway, then brings us to the room—it is about the size of a second-class train cabin, with two single beds within spitting distance of each other and a nightstand in the middle, with a vase of flowers. All I can think is, what an upgrade from our sleeping quarters last night! I settle in, while Sergei handles the always-elaborate check-in process. I hear his boots clunking along the empty hallway returning to our room.

"David, we have a problem."

"What's up?"

"I asked Oksana to register you as a foreigner with the local immigration authorities. She said she has no idea how to do that."

"Well, we decided this is important—we need to do it at every hotel, right?"

I am sure it has as much to do with the weather and being tired, but Sergei and I are both pretty annoyed about this. Perhaps Sergei even more so. He walks back up the hall, and I hear him speaking—sternly but respectfully—telling Oksana that every Russian hotel is supposed to be able to do this, and that I could be in big trouble with the authorities if it's not done. Sergei then returns.

"David, all she can do is talk to the owner. And she gave me the owner's e-mail address. I will try to e-mail her. Her name is Nadezhda."

"Great. They have Wi-Fi?"

"Oh. No. I asked about Wi-Fi. Oksana didn't know what I was talking about."

With this I calm down. So does Sergei. I think we both realize we were being jerks—waltzing into a hotel in a small town in rural Russia, expecting them to have Wi-Fi and to be able to register a foreigner immediately. Oksana is doing her absolute best—and she can't think we're very pleasant. And I realize how happy I am to be in a place that has never seen a foreigner—or heard of Wi-Fi.

Sergei and I turn in and get some much-needed sleep. We are awakened by—wouldn't you know it?—sunshine, streaming through the window. Sergei takes a towel and washcloth and heads up the hall to use the shower. He comes back with news.

"David, you will not believe it. The owner of the hotel is here. Nadezhda. She stayed up all night reading about how a hotel should register foreigners. She has spoken to the local immigration authorities. They gave her instructions."

"Oh, Sergei."

"And she brought a portable photocopy machine this morning to copy your passport. She said she was very sorry for the trouble. And she thanked *me*, because she is grateful now to know how to register guests from other countries."

I am touched—and angry at myself for being frustrated last night.

"David, Nadezhda is also offering to drive us into town—should we say yes?"

"Of course."

"She has one request: She would like to take a picture of us. She would like to begin a display of photos of honored guests. We are the first."

I shower and pack. Then Sergei, Nadezhda, and I pose for a photo in one of her guest rooms. I thank Nadezhda profusely.

"Nadezhda—ogromnoe spasibo."

It's quite a photo. Nadezhda looks best—she's an attractive blond, perhaps in her forties. She's wearing a bright red sweater, with a gold Orthodox cross hanging around her neck. Sergei and I are in our Trans-Siberian uniforms—we packed light, so our outfits become familiar. I am in jeans, a blue sweater and gray scarf. Sergei is in jeans and a tan sport coat over a plaid shirt.

The three of us walk outside and load into Nadezhda's Nissan SUV. The driver's seat is on the right—a telltale sign we are making our way East. Russians in Siberia try to import cars from Japan if they can, because they are generally cheaper than Russian- or

European-made cars. The only downside is that you drive on the right side of the car—and also the right side of the road.

The hotel looks nicer in the sunlight—a bright yellow-and-brown building with white windowsills—but the neighborhood does not. We pull out of the parking lot into the industrial wasteland— abandoned vehicles buried in snow and empty industrial buildings with gaping holes where windows used to be.

Sergei asks Nadezhda about her life. "She is saying there have been some sad events," he leans around to tell me from the front passenger seat. "But she doesn't like to talk about it much."

We do learn that Nadezhda lived with her husband for fifteen years, but they divorced. She is raising two daughters on her own— they are seven and thirteen.

"There is a quote from Lenin—*Uchitsa, uchitsa, uchitsa* [Study, study, study]," she says. "Not for me. God meant for me to work, work, work."

Nadezhda and her husband owned two hotels together. When they divorced, she kept one—the Tranquility—and now runs it herself. On the side she also decorates cars for weddings. In Russia weddings are elaborate—at times gaudy—affairs. Couples go over the top to deco- rate cakes, and vehicles. To Americans, Russian wedding dresses are hideously over the top. Rose actually kept a blog, and one of her favor- ite things to capture was the craziest wedding dresses in this country.

"I make the fabrics and the artificial flowers to go on the wed- ding limousines," Nadezhda says. "This is a small town. At wed- dings I'll often ask couples how their parents are doing. They'll say, 'oh, my mother and father drink too much.' It's a terrible thing."

Ishim looks better in sunlight, with a fresh coating of snow. Trees line the streets. It's too small a place to have any large buildings—in downtown there are mostly two- and three-story structures with flower shops and restaurants. The place reminds me a bit of Lancaster, Pennsylvania, where I went to high school. Ishim has the same population—around 65,000 people—and the same feel. Big enough to have some energy, small enough to feel tight-knit.

Nadezhda pulls up to a restored building that is the city's museum. Since we have checked out of the hotel and have a night train, we doubt we'll see Nadezhda again. Sergei and I thank her and say good-bye, then head into the museum to meet Tatiana, the friend of the Tatiana we met on the train.

Tatiana Savchenkova is a local history and literature scholar, a larger-than-life woman with crooked yellow teeth and straight brown hair down to her chin, who speaks as loudly as Marina from the *sanatoriy*—and wants just as much to be our tour guide.

"Let's start!" she says, beginning a dizzying tour that takes me and Sergei into every room of the museum. She must be six feet tall, waving her finger near my face as she tells me about the famous poet from Ishim, how Ishim once hosted a world's fair for Asian and European merchants, and how this remote city in the snow, for reasons still not clear to me, came to be known as Siberia's Italian city.

After our trip through the museum, Tatiana calls a taxi. The three of us climb in, and she directs the driver to a pleasant spot near an attractive Russian Orthodox church. Onion-domed Orthodox churches are a dime a dozen in Russia—every city you visit has one, or eight, and if you visit, typically an elderly woman inside will greet you and explain why this church and the religious icons inside are particularly important in Russian history. It is easy to grow weary of visiting yet another church in yet another Russian city. But then you recall how the Soviets wiped out religion—and you quickly get a warm feeling, seeing so many Orthodox believers appreciating what they have and are able to do today. Here in Ishim the bright blue onion domes, bathed in sun, look perfect in front of the snowy white backdrop.

"Come here." Tatiana walks us over to the statue of a woman in the church courtyard. "Her name is Praskovia Lupolova."

The figure has a scarf wrapped around her head. She's bundled in a coat, wearing a long skirt. One foot is in front of the other, as if she's walking. And she's carrying a walking stick.

"Her family was sent here to Siberia," Tatiana says. "She could see how much her father was suffering. So she decided she would walk to St. Petersburg. Alone, as a young girl. She could have died. In fact, she fell somewhere and nearly drowned."

Hearing this woman's story is making me feel very weak for feeling so cold at the moment. I am taking notes as Tatiana speaks, but the cold has frozen the ink in my pen, and my notes grow more and more faint.

"Praskovia walked for more than a year. When she finally reached St. Petersburg, she was received by the czar. He was impressed by her deed, and allowed her family to return to their homeland in Europe—what is now Ukraine. She vowed that if the czar saved her father, she would enter a convent, which she did. She died in that monastery in 1825. Her story amazed Russia."

And me.

There's an engraving beneath the statue: "To Praskovia Lupolova, who showed the world the deed of a daughter's love. Ishim—St. Petersburg, 1803–1804."

Tatiana stands next to that statue with a visible sense of pride.

"Unfortunately the Soviet authorities did away with religion—and with Praskovia's story."

"The story was banned?"

"Yes."

"It wasn't good to talk about people who did heroic things that were inspired by religion," Sergei adds.

Tatiana has family roots going back generations in Siberia. And she *is* proud of that. She goes it alone these days—her husband died of cancer in 2000. She says she has a toughness that's not unrelated to her Siberian roots. We have now—mercifully—headed back to the warmth of the museum to continue our chat.

"I would like to give you an interesting fact," Tatiana says. "When the Decembrists arrived in Siberia, they realized they could use their talents and responsibilities in ways they never imagined."

The story of the Decembrists is one of the most epic and colorful tales in Russian history. In December 1825 some Russian army officers—many of them princes and dignitaries in their own right—led a revolt against Czar Nicholas.

It failed.

The Decembrists, as the revolutionaries came to be known, were sentenced for their deeds—a few executed, others imprisoned. Many were exiled to Siberia. For some that was refreshing—for one thing, because they were still alive, but also because it offered a fresh start. After suffering through several years in labor camps, some of these men settled here, and their wives, who could have remained in the West, enjoying lives of royalty, joined them in exile. It wasn't an easy road. When one of the wives, Princess Trubetskaya, "first caught sight of her husband's emaciated, bearded face and filthy, tattered convict's smock held up by a length of string," she fainted.

In his book *The Decembrists*, Mikhail Zetlin writes that another woman, Princess Volkonskaya, "was allowed to visit her husband in his cell. She found a tiny cubicle, six feet by four, filthy and with a ceiling so low that she couldn't even stand up. The prisoners were so covered with vermin that the ladies had to shake out their clothes after every visit." But things improved. Princess Volkonskaya rented a house in the city of Irkutsk, and her husband, once a prince, was released a changed man. He "preferred the company of his peasant friends," but the princess "gave parties, balls and masquerades that were attended by all the local society."

The Decembrists who settled in Siberia were by and large embraced by the locals, and their legacy has lived on here. Many people credit the Decembrists with bringing the region arts, literature, sophistication, and a can-do attitude.

"They began educating the Siberian people," Tatiana tells me. "They opened schools and grew new types of plants. They constructed railways and developed natural resources. They no longer had to fight the czar. And they realized they loved Siberia, and loved the people of Siberia."

"Was part of it a sense of freedom out here?" I ask.

"I think so, yes."

"Is that spirit of freedom still here?"

"That feeling, that sense of freedom, lives on in people here, I know it. We feel like no one can make us do what we don't want to do."

Those words linger in my mind as Sergei and I wrap up our time at the museum. I reach into my pocket to give Tatiana a business card, and find something unexpected: my room key from the Hotel Tranquility.

After saying good-bye to Tatiana, Sergei calls Nadezhda, who says she was hoping she might see us one more time before we leave town.

"Oh, you'll be seeing us again," Sergei says, smiling. "David still has the key to his room."

Nadezhda says she'll swing by the museum to pick up us in fifteen minutes. Standing in the lobby, I ask Sergei a bit more about Nadezhda. Sergei is a fiercely loyal person. I occasionally wonder if he has conversations in Russian with people we meet and doesn't translate everything, knowing the person is saying something private, hoping it won't be passed on to me.

I tread delicately.

Sergei tells me that Nadezhda and her ex-husband have remained friends—they just had to be apart.

"I bet it had something to do with alcohol," I say.

"I'd say yes. She just got tired of it. And she did what my mother could never do."

He pauses. I remember how Sergei's mom stayed with his father through the alcoholism and at least several beatings. Sergei is speaking quietly.

"You know, my sister and I are two years apart. If my mother had made the decision, I wouldn't be here today."

"You're two years younger than your sister."

"Right, and that was the time she thought about leaving my father."

"Before you were born."

"And if she had done it at that point, I would not be in this world. Part of it was a woman, with two kids, in the Soviet Union. If she left, where was she to go? Where would she live?"

These are different times. And I take nothing away from Sergei's mom and the strength she must have shown in a difficult marriage. Yet Nadezhda's decision to leave, to go off on her own, to raise two daughters and run a hotel, impresses me.

We see Nadezhda pull up outside in her SUV.

"Nadezhda, sorry about the key," I tell her. "But you know I just kept it to make sure we would see you again."

She smiles and drives us to a pub in town. As we get out of the car and walk toward the entrance, I snap a photo of one of Ishim's main streets. It's this straight, snowy road, getting smaller and smaller off toward the horizon, with a brilliant pink-and-orange glow in the sky above as the sun sets.

We head into the pub and grab a table.

"Nadezhda, tell me what it's like to run a business in Russia."

She smirks. "Oh, it's complicated."

"In what way?"

"You can never figure out what the authorities are requiring. Like a fire escape. I want to do what the law says. So I go to this government office and say, 'What do I need to do?' They're not helpful at all. They say it's all on the Internet, look there. But it's not."

This was always one of Rose's chief gripes about life in Russia—especially for women—as she contemplated opening her own restaurant. Once she got home to the United States and began the process, she realized it was harder than she ever imagined. But having seen what aspiring entrepreneurs in Russia go through made her grateful.

"Now that I'm doing this," Rose told me at one point, "I will say, there are days at the permitting office or other government buildings in D.C. when lines are long, people are confused, and I just want to scream, 'I'm back in goddamn Russia again!' What's funny is, you could say I'm up against the downside of democracy—here, everyone has an equal voice. Three neighbors were against my place and were almost able to stop me from opening. But I have it so much easier. I have nonprofits that fight to help women opening businesses. There's networking.

Entrepreneurship is encouraged. I was able to get a loan from the Small Business Administration. I really don't think Russians have much of this. Or any of this. If I were a woman in Russia, trying to start a business, I would feel like there was no recourse if someone wanted to take advantage of me. If someone is bigger and more powerful and they want to extort money, they can do it. Nobody will stop them."

In 2012, two students at the University of Pennsylvania's Wharton School of Business, Florentina Furtuna and Anna Ruvinskaya, looked at the small business climate in Russia and published a study called "Small Business in Russia: Drowning in a Sea of Giants." They found business owners routinely "face corrupt officials who have the power to deny licenses, permits, office space and access to supplies unless substantial 'gifts' or bribes are offered."

Paradoxically, efforts to stamp out crime and corruption seem to be making problems worse. One small business owner told the authors that "in the early 1990s, the gangs of bandits that controlled most of the markets during the period of organized crime seemed to be more humane than the current government officials; they had a certain threshold that they abided by; now these corrupt clerks can take even the last piece from our mouths."

Nadezhda, in Ishim, is fighting to survive in a system where bureaucratic corruption feeds off the chaos. If officials are never clear about what's actually required, they can say someone is wrong—at any time. And likely collect either a fine or a bribe.

"I ended up paying 75,000 rubles [$2,500] to upgrade my fire escape," Nadezhda says. She did everything she could to follow the regulations, but different regulations called for different requirements. In the end, hoping to avoid fines, she built the best and safest fire escape money could buy. Just like she stayed on the phone overnight with an immigration officer, learning every detail she possibly could about the rules for registering a foreign traveler.

"Do you wonder if the money ends up in the wrong hands?"

She's smiling. "There are so many 'fines.' Many are incredibly expensive. They can just show up and do an inspection. You don't even know what they're looking for. I wish they would just help—help me understand what the actual rules are."

"My wife is going through the process of opening a business at home. And I'll say the process has been hard. But I feel like one thing she has is certainty. She pretty much knows what is required, and then she has to figure out how to get there."

"I wish we had that kind of stability."

Sergei is worried about the translation here. "Maybe we've heard a lot of people talk about political stability in Russia—maybe Nadezhda is talking about a different kind of stability," he says.

Or maybe not. Perhaps it's all intertwined. In this crazy, unpredictable, unfair country, maybe what Russians really do starve for is stability—not just political stability, but stability in their own lives. In marriages, friendships, and businesses.

When I've pressed Russians—like Andrei Gorodilov—on why they don't push for change in their country, and they answer "because they want stability," I tend to scoff.

But then I look at Nadezhda. She craves stability—and is fighting for it. And in a way she's calling the bluff of the local authorities. They have this elaborate web of rules and regulations set up to confuse and mystify, so they can come after her on a whim. Rather than cave to that, she spends a sleepless night researching every detail she can to learn how to register a foreign guest at her hotel. She works overtime to figure out how to design a fire escape that will pass muster in any inspection.

Her strategy is time consuming, expensive, and not fool-proof. But she's trying. So was Andrei, when he fought off the local prosecutors who were ready to throw his father in prison and call it a day.

Publicity was our protection.

I wonder if these are the smaller battles that could someday begin to create cracks in the entrenched foundation of power in this country.

I REMEMBER true low points while covering the power structures in Russia. In the summer of 2010 wildfires ravaged parts of central Russia, destroying entire villages. Critics quietly raised questions about whether Putin had made recent policy changes that slowed the federal response to natural disasters. Those allegations never became much of an issue, and what's more, Putin turned the events in his favor. He arrived at one burned village, Verkhnuya Vereya, a few hundred miles east of Moscow, and promised residents that their houses would be rebuilt before winter arrived. He had cameras installed in the village to chart progress on state-run television. "There's one, two, they're everywhere!" the excited deputy governor told me when I visited, pointing out the cameras on telephone poles, as construction crews buzzed around, erecting new houses as quickly, it seemed, as you can place pieces on a Monopoly board. It was hard to see this as anything but a ploy, a charade, to burnish the image of Putin and his ruling United Russia Party and protect them from any political fallout. This was underscored as I chatted with residents of the village, still recovering from the scare of the fires and not all that optimistic about the sturdiness of their new homes. One woman, who barely outran the fire and survived, said, "They should have spoken to us to find out how we wanted these houses built. They promised they'd talk to us individually. But that never happened. They're building without us." Her brother, whose own house up the street was destroyed, said the foundation of his new structure looked so weak he expected it to sink when the spring rains came—notably, after the cameras were shut off.

Then there was the story of Viktor Kondrashov, a young developer in the Siberian city of Irkutsk. He's a former fashion model with wavy blond hair, an infectious smile, and a knack for politics. He rose up in the Communist Party—the main opposition in today's Russia to Putin's United Russia Party—and stunned the establishment in 2010 by winning the mayoral race in Irkutsk. Putin's party won a landslide victory overall in local and regional elections that year, but support was beginning to fade, and Kondrashov's victory in a city so large was a blemish. I arrived in Irkutsk and spoke to residents who felt they had sent a loud message that democracy is alive in the country. "I do go to elections, but what's the point?" one woman said. "They always have everything decided." This time, she proudly declared, "We were mistaken!" In his office Kondrashov knew he had pulled off something special. "This never happened in the history of Irkutsk—so many cars at polling stations. I managed to stir up this part of the population, people who never went to elections, who were indifferent." But something bothered me toward the end of our interview. I asked Kondrashov if he worried that the ruling party might retaliate somehow—perhaps threatening to cut off services or funding to his city, perhaps by intimidating him. "There are risks," he said. "I'm simply going to observe the law, not going to steal, not going to take bribes." I had one more question: If United Russia presented him with an invitation to join them, a not-so-subtle way of saying things would be better for the city if he joined Team Putin, would he accept? Putin's party, after all, controls the levers of power, the money, the domestic security services—they can make offers that are hard to refuse and make life difficult for people who don't accept. The mayor took a moment, and the smile left his face. Yes, he finally said, he would consider joining United Russia, if it was in the best interest of the city.

Within weeks, United Russia posted a message on its Web site that Viktor Kondrashov, the mayor of Irkutsk, had declared his support for the party and would be formally joining as a member soon.

IT CAN BE so tempting to look for the big battles in Russia—big elections, big rallies, an Arab Spring. And it can be deflating when you don't see Russia rise up, when you see what looks like a citizenry that's lazy or resigned. But maybe this is overlooking the smaller battles. Spending time with Nadezhda is leaving me with this feeling of hope. She and Andrei may be trailblazers. But over time, if more people feel as emboldened as they do to challenge power, even in small ways, maybe a corrupt government will begin to weaken, maybe their outdated strategies for clinging to power will become less relevant.

Nadezhda's spirit of freedom and survival in this Siberian outpost has me more excited to head deeper into this region and meet more people. And to see Rose, who I know will love hearing about Nadezhda.

"You know, when we checked into your hotel last night, I never imagined we would feel so much warmth here."

Nadezhda smiles.

She shows me photos of her daughters on her iPhone. Her seven-year-old is in a dress, ballroom dancing with a seven-year-old partner.

"He loves her. We are ready to make him her husband!"

I can tell she misses marriage.

"My daughters are truly what makes me happy."

I show her a photo of Rose, and she immediately zeroes in on her wedding band, a silver ring with tiny diamonds that belonged to my grandmother. "Why do you wear silver wedding rings?"

I explain that in the United States, wedding rings can be of all sorts, not always gold, as is the case in Russia.

It's time for our train. Nadezhda drives us to the station and—of course—walks us in to make sure our train is on time and we know where we are going. For both me and Sergei, this is the toughest good-bye so far. Sergei and I often talk about how, on our reporting trips, we so often pick up new members of an extended "family"— strangers so much more welcoming and friendly to us than they need to be. This makes us feel incredibly lucky.

"Ogromnoe spasibo [Thank you so much]," Nadezhda says, standing in the middle of the small train station.

"Spasibo, Nadezhda. Do vstrechi," I say—until our next meeting.

She walks back outside, and Sergei and I quietly board our train.

We have two lower berths reserved on this night train to Novosibirsk. Two young guys are sitting on our berths, one just mixing hot water into a cup of instant soup. We tell them not to rush at all, stay seated, take your time.

Sergei and I sit down with them. Over in one of the berths across the aisle, an older man in black dress pants and a zipped gray jacket is snoring, on his side, beside an empty forty-ounce bottle of Russian beer. He rolls over, squints, looking perhaps at Sergei.

"*Hehhh.* What time is it?" he asks in Russian.

"Eight fifteen," Sergei says.

"Where are we?"

"Ishim."

He nods, moans, and returns to sleep.

The night seems so peaceful—which in Russia can only last so long.

As we speed along into the night, I hear an increasingly loud clanking next to my head. I'm worried about the structural integrity of the window. Especially given the severe cold outside, you do develop some sense of security that, if nothing else, this train will protect you from the elements—you know, like a pressurized airplane cabin protects you from altitude shock and instantly freezing to death thirty thousand feet in the air. It is only a slight exaggeration to say that the wall of this train feels just as vital to your well-being. So you can understand my anxiety when the window rattles more, then develops a cold wet coating of water, then begins to release a stream of water onto my pillow. In darkness I see Sergei is experiencing the same problem. He has built a dam of blankets to stem the flow of the water on his side of the window. I do the same.

It's not ideal. But it's stable.

17 · YET ANOTHER SERGEI

I WAKE UP on the train a half hour before arriving in Novosibirsk and can think of only one thing: how excited I am to see Rose. She has been working around the clock preparing to open her new restaurant but was able to escape for a week to join me. She lands in midafternoon.

The weather is ominous. There appears to be more snow piled up outside than there was in Ishim, far more than anywhere along the trip. And it looks bitterly cold. Rose will be just thrilled.

This trip has not been nearly as cold as in 2011, when I had a close encounter with frostbite. We were in the city of Ulan-Ude, near Lake Baikal in eastern Siberia. Sergei, Rose, and I hired a driver/guide named Yuri. The retired construction engineer was wearing no gloves with temperatures hovering around thirty below zero Fahrenheit and a stiff breeze blowing. I wanted to be as tough as Yuri.

The problem was not my hands, though, but my feet. Yuri's van had odd amenities, including flowing green curtains and green fabric covering the dashboard, but it lacked reliable heat. During the drive, cold from the floor seeped through the soles of my boots, which were winterproof only by the standards of the department store in New York where I bought them.

At one stop Yuri looked at my boots and gasped. He then grabbed a spare pair of knee-high boots—*valenki* in Russian—made of tightly packed felt and noticeably lacking style. The word for this type of Russian boot—the singular form is *valenok*—is the same word used in Russian to describe a "hick" or "country bumpkin." That did not dissuade me in the slightest. I wore Yuri's *valenki* the rest of the day, and I can only imagine how much pain I was spared. Chekhov, on his travels, wrote of relying on these felt boots in Siberia—and that was in *May*. And so, here I was, in one sense—the only sense—walking in Chekhov's shoes.

Even with that recovery, my feet were a dark shade of blue when we returned to the hotel, and I had to run hot water over them for a good half hour before normal color and the ability to feel returned. The way of life in Siberia is built around cold. Unimaginable cold. And many say that trading secrets for survival, helping one another, made people closer and formed the foundation of communities here.

All that said, I was hopeful Rose would arrive on a warmer day, for her sake and mine.

Novosibirsk is Russia's third-biggest city, with more than 1.5 million people. Approaching it from the west reminds me of coming up to Denver from the east, passing miles of flat empty land until suddenly this frontier-feeling city pops up, with its urban sprawl and tall buildings.

One sign of hitting a major urban center is cell phone coverage, which kicks back in, and a parade of unread e-mails arrives. One is from Olga Granovskaya, a professor of political science I interviewed in 2011 in Vladivostok. I had a wonderful visit with her and her husband at the end of my last Trans-Siberian trip and I had been corresponding with Olga, eager to meet her again. She had written about how the radio piece I produced last time from Vladivostok generated a lot of discussion on local news sites, with many people suggesting that the comments Olga made criticizing her country were a figment of my imagination. I had asked Olga to send along the comments so I could read them. But in this new e-mail there was something surprising.

> Dear David,
>
> You can read all the comments here. But they are in Russian. I can help you to translate them when we meet. We had not any problems because of the interview. Putin is not Stalin, fortunately. But a man from the KGB called my father-in-law (who is a German and an honorary consul of Germany in Vladivostok) and told him that his wife gave an interview to American radio. My relative informed them that it was not his wife but his daughter-in-law. So, I know KGB is not sleeping. Do not think that your visit would be inconvenient or frustrating. If so, I would not invite you.

I always assumed after interviewing people in Russia that they might get a phone call, a subtle warning, from the FSB. But this is the first concrete evidence. It really bothers me. I reported from Tripoli, Libya's capital, when Mu'ammar Gadhafi was clinging to power as NATO bombs were falling on his city. Government spies were everywhere, tracking journalists, eavesdropping on interviews. Each time I spoke to a citizen—especially if he or she said anything critical of the regime—I honestly worried that that person would be hounded afterward—interrogated or worse, punished. That happened here in Soviet times.

In today's Russia I worry less about a person's well-being. People are generally free to speak their minds in public. Still, the element of fear remains. A follow-up call like this may not intimidate Olga's father-in-law, a Western diplomat. (In fact I can't help but smile thinking that the FSB really chose the wrong guy here!). But calls like this do intimidate many people. Without a fair and reliable system of justice, what's your protection if you're a citizen?

While the culture of fear in Russia today doesn't compare to that of Soviet times, while there are far fewer victims, the threat is real. Oleg Kashin is a business reporter for a respected Russian newspaper, *Kommersant.* He often wrote critically of the government and in the fall of 2010, was beaten outside his home and nearly died. His attackers, among other things, severed one of Kashin's fingers and broke several others—a clear message to a man who types words for a living. Doctor's induced a coma following the attack, and fortunately Kashin survived. The government, outwardly at least, gave Kashin its full support and said his attackers would be found. But more than anything, it was another reminder to Russian journalists—and other citizens—that you can be in danger if you step out of line, and there may be no reliable place to turn for justice.

What a strange purgatory Russians live in. For so many years they could not travel freely and took a major risk if they wrote or said anything critical of the government or anyone well connected. There were severe limits on where people could work and who could own businesses or property. Today many of those restrictions are gone. Life is more free and open. And yet the fear remains. The risk remains. In a way, maybe clear limits of toleration are less fearsome than erratic limits of toleration. Uncertainty about being punished is more intimidating than certainty. You are always just left to wonder.

Sergei and I arrive in Novosibirsk, find a hotel and collapse for a nap. I awake in midafternoon and jump in a cab to meet Rose at the Novosibirsk airport. She walks out the International Arrivals door with a camping backpack on her back, looking stunningly energetic after traveling for the better part of two days. I'm feeling a tad guilty for begging her to come, since she only had a few days to spare. But I've missed her a ton.

She jumps into my arms and I grab her backpack. Then we walk toward the doors.

"You know how I told you it's been warmer on this trip than I expected?"

"Greene?"

"Yeah, not today."

We step into the cold, and it hits her like a ton of Russian bricks. The gush of wind blows her hair back, and she immediately reaches for her gloves. "Oh, it's all here. It's all still here. Good *God.* How did I know I'd arrive on the coldest day? If you don't think Russia has it in for me! I'm already starting to not feel my lips. It's already starting."

We get in a cab, and I don't even know where to begin: "I have so much to tell you."

"I can imagine."

"I really missed you in Sagra. Andrei *really* missed you in Sagra. He still has the boarding pass where you wrote your e-mail and phone number."

"That is so sweet. You know, Sagra is where I realized that I don't like Moscow—but I like Russia. Those are the people I was waiting for when we got to Russia. They invited us into their homes. They had no indoor plumbing but spared nothing to show us hospitality. They put vodka on the table, and food—pickles they pickled themselves. And they couldn't care less about Moscow—the millionaires and the Bentleys. I knew Moscow wasn't the real Russia."

AND YET, FOR better or worse, Rose and I spent our three years living our daily lives in the "Moscow" Russia, the world of trendy cafés and fat paychecks. My reporting took me to speck-on-the-map villages and brought me in touch with people living on the brink. But living in central Moscow, socializing in journalism and diplomatic circles, we generally met Russians who were part of the urban elite, people working as lawyers, bankers, or executives in energy companies, many of whom benefited from Putin's economy but were out on the streets protesting his authoritarian leadership style. And that's a paradox you discover in many younger, more well-off Russians. They are educated, have traveled the world, and find democratic principles and values appealing. Then again, they're still pulled by the cultural forces in their country that have defined their thinking and who they are. And what's more, at the end of the day, any complaints they have about the state of Russian society must be weighed against the fact that they themselves are doing quite well.

And so Rose and I cursed the piles of wealth in Moscow and scoffed at Russians who loved to strut out of designer boutiques showing off stunningly expensive new fur coats or order seven-hundred-dollar bottles of champagne just to say they did. And while I'm happy to say we didn't live in that world, we probably intersected with it more often than we did with, say, Ivan's existence in his village outside Chelyabinsk. I remember Rose once returning from shopping at one of the fancy grocery stores in Moscow to report that she had made her "first Russian friend!" She and Natalya met in the checkout line. Natalya, like Rose, is in her thirties. She speaks flawless English, went to college in the United States, works for a technology company and is often on the road, shuttling from Moscow to her home city of Novosibirsk, to spots around Europe, or to the United States. Rose often had lunch or dinner with Natalya, and she would come to parties with us at the homes of journalists and diplomats. When Rose told Natalya that she was flying into Novosibirsk to meet me for part of this train trip, she told Rose we had to meet her friend Alexei.

A few hours after Rose lands, she and I walk into a palatial café near Novosibirsk's train station. Suddenly, nothing says you're in Russia—this could be some trendy hotspot in London, New York, or Buenos Aires. The walls are artistically-distressed gray stone, the ceiling is corrugated metal, with rows of bright light bulbs hanging from wires. At a wooden table near the back, we see the man Natalya described—her friend Alexei Kamerzan—waiting for us. He gets up to greet us and shake our hands, a Bluetooth earpiece still firmly in his left ear, where it would remain planted throughout our conversation. Alexei is thirty-five, with thinning brown hair and some deliberate style choices: perfectly trimmed five o'clock shadow and a button-down opened just so to display some chest hair. His story is a reminder that Russia has produced its share of winners. Alexei's mother worked for a state carpet company during Soviet times. When the Soviet Union collapsed, many people who were either smart or lucky—or both—rushed to start private companies in their areas of expertise. His mother opened Carpet World, which Alexei helps run today, putting his business degree from the University of St. Thomas in Minnesota to good use. He was in the United States from 1999 to 2001. Now, back home in Novosibirsk, he spends days in meetings with big shots who are buying his family's carpeting—their big new contract is with the recently opened Marriott hotel in the city.

"I'd say my mother is officially the head of the company," Alexei says, pushing his lips into a half-joking smile. "But I do all the work."

He is sitting facing Rose and me. We settle in for a few cups of coffee as the café begins playing the Tears for Fears tune "Everybody Wants to Rule the World."

"I just traveled to Lebanon," Alexei tells us. "In my childhood, I watched the terrible news saying Beirut is hell. I was just deeply impressed and surprised when I saw it because we only hear about Lebanon when it's in trouble."

And he feels like Russia gets a bad rap abroad as well. I tell him the impression among Americans is that doing business in Russia means constantly bribing, assuming you have the connections to get in the game at all. He tells me only roughly half of the business transactions in Russia are dirty, involving some kind of bribes.

"To an American, that sounds like a lot," I say.

"I know, I knooow," he groans. He explains that *his* family's business is on the up-and-up, and he wishes more businesses were following suit. "Russia—it's not as clean as the United States. But I'd say not as dirty as Asia or Africa. Somewhere in between. But we don't pay much attention to this. I know it's not really good. But it's part of a long heritage—not just from Soviet times, but even earlier. Look, I know how American society built itself. I know how Russian society built itself. It's a different culture and different philosophy here. It's not like, 'Hey, let's just build democracy.'"

Alexei calls himself a fan of democracy, not so much a fan of Putin. "Some days I like him, some days I don't." A day he didn't came in 2012 when Putin signed a temporary ban on the adoption of Russian children by American families. Alexei didn't see how it made sense to prevent Russian babies from finding loving homes. "That's like saying, 'Let me cut off my finger to try and make you uncomfortable.'"

"And on days when you like him," I wonder, "why do you like him?"

"He's a strong leader. This is the first thing people like about him because they're so tired of weak, stupid people. Like Khrushchev, a real village guy. Brezhnev was vulgar, just an old crumbling person. And Gorbachev? He said too much and did almost nothing."

On balance, Alexei would rather Putin be gone. He voted against him in the last election "just to show that we're not satisfied with some of the stupid politics," he says. Alexei's pretty sure the election was rigged. He agrees with critics who said Putin and his allies made sure—by forgery, or pressuring voters in some districts—that he had enough votes in a first round to avoid a run-off.

"It was an issue of image. He didn't want it to look like he wasn't strong enough to win [in the first round]. So they forged the results at least 10 percent. Anyway, he would have been President. But we were deceived by fake results, so it was unpleasant."

Unpleasant. If, Alexei added, there had been two candidates running and votes were forged to actually change who was elected, he may have taken to the streets. But this didn't rise to that level. He wasn't stirred up.

"It's not such a big deal. Unpleasant, but not such a big deal."

There's a window into what Putin is managing: something resembling a democracy, a system that keeps him in power and makes people such as Alexei—educated, and potentially influential if made angry enough—satisfied, happy, and so far, quiet. This makes me think that if Putin oversteps—if he outright steals an election, say—people like Alexei would join forces of protest in Moscow, and the government could have a problem on its hands. It would be not just the middle class of Moscow rising up but also the middle class elsewhere in Russia, people with means and embarrassed and chagrined to live in a country where freedoms are restricted. That could bring the clash of ideas—potentially violent—that Robert, the Memorial activist in Perm, predicted as a possibility. But if Putin keeps his authoritarian ways in check—enough—he may have latitude. And it may be years before Russia sees any true political change, depending on the wishes of the younger generation.

For now, Alexei spends as much time as he can on the road. He and his grad school friends have met up in Colorado a few times, taking on the slopes at Aspen and Vail. He also has a videography business on the side—a recent video, shot on a snowy mountain, had young Russian women flying down a slope on skis and snowboards, wearing nothing but bikinis. Alexei himself made a cameo— shirtless. Last check, his video had gotten over seven million hits on YouTube. "I'm not a fan of skiing, tried it once and that was it," Rose tells him. "Even the hot instructor couldn't get me to like it."

"You just have to keep trying," Alexei says, putting both hands out, palms up, for emphasis, "until it gets fun. The whole thing is fun. You have the skiing. Then the spa, the sauna, the swimming pool in the open air. Recently, I started snowboarding too. I'm still dreaming of trying heli-skiing." (That would be when a helicopter drops you and your skis off in a remote spot on the mountain.)

At the moment, he's gearing up for his next adventure with some friends—a road trip from Russia, through Central Asia, into China, across Laos, Vietnam, and Cambodia, and eventually to Malaysia. "We are driving to the most southern tip of continental Eurasia," he declares. It is tempting to frown on his excessive lifestyle, especially in a country where wealth is concentrated at the top and so many people scrape by. But as Rose and I would remind ourselves, Alexei, Natalya, and other Russians like them are in many ways success stories, discovering the fruits of personal ambition in a place where that wasn't really possible not so long ago.

It seems the only thing Alexei's starving for is children. His sister, who lives in Dubai, has a son. "My mom adores him and spends a lot of time there." Alexei pauses. "And I'm thinking about this because it's time. You know, whenever I see my grandmother she's like, 'I have to talk to you!' And I did watch this Russian comedy recently, where the guy was saying 'I don't want to get to my son's prom in a wheelchair.' And this is what I'm saying . . . if I have children when I'm forty."

Right now, he lives alone in an apartment his mother bought in 1995, shortly after she started the carpet business.

"There are so many girls to choose from in this country," Rose says. "They're beautiful. Come on."

Alexei smiles, pausing for a few seconds before abruptly changing the subject. "Okay, you can type my name in YouTube and find all my videos. And you can follow me on Twitter."

He has to run. His phone rang twice already, but he didn't want to interrupt our conversation to answer it. "Okay guys, it was real fun," he says, shaking my hand, hugging Rose then heading outside.

Leaving the café a few minutes later, I tell Rose about the people she's missed on the trip: Nadezhda and her struggles running a business, Ivan in Chelyabinsk, the babushkas, and the ominous e-mail from Olga in Vladivostok.

"Do you think seeing her again is dangerous?" Rose asks me.

"For me or for her?"

"Either, I guess."

Rose has always been level-headed about these things—more street smart than I am. I can sometimes take more risks, thinking it's worth it for the sake of the story. But I never want to put anyone else at risk.

"Well, I remember the guys who followed us in Vladivostok," Rose says. "They were idiots. Harmless. If that's who is calling Olga's family, it's probably okay. Just be careful, Greene." Arriving at our hotel, we stop by Sergei's room, and Sergei literally jumps. "Rooose! It is so good to see you." They hug. We really were a family for our time in Russia, and now the family is back together.

We do a bit of exploring together in Novosibirsk, then head in the evening for the train station, where I break the news to my wife.

"So, one difference I haven't told you about yet. Sergei and I have been traveling third class. And, um, we have third-class seats on this train. I don't think you've been in third class yet."

"No, I haven't," Rose says, smiling.

It is honestly not my imagination—the train experience with Rose on board, coincidentally or not, seems far worse than anything Sergei and I have experienced so far.

Our third-class car on this train is No. 19, the last car of the train and a solid ten-minute walk down an icy platform. As we arrive at the steps of the car, a passenger is rushing out carrying a mangy-looking dog in need of a potty break. We step into the car and its passengers are predominantly young men from Central Asia. In many ways Central Asia is to Russia what Central America is to the United States—scores of young men pour across the border looking for reliable construction work or other jobs to make money for families back home.

I would say of the dozens of people on this car, all are men, except perhaps one or two.

"It's all going to be Okay" I tell Rose unconvincingly.

"You don't have a guy staring at your breasts." I think she's over-reacting until, indeed, I see one man on his upper berth laughing and motioning to his seatmate as he cups his hands over his chest.

Rose brings out a bag of jelly beans and offers it to the man who's sharing the four-berth space with us. He declines, but Sergei takes a few—his first jelly bean experience. "Do I chew?"

"Yes—you'll like them," Rose says. "Sergei, can you take a photo of me and David? Because, if we get divorced, this is going in the file." She's not done. She pulls out her iPhone, clicks Record on the video function and points the thing at the two of us, with her arm around me. "Hi, future children. If David remains married to me long enough for you to be conceived, then this is for you. Your father made me ride third class on an overnight train in the winter in Siberia. Who does that?"

We eventually settle in. Rose takes an upper berth to sleep, and I do feel guilty, noticing a lot of eyes pointed at her—harmlessly, I believe, but probably annoying.

I wake up last—Rose and Sergei are up, looking out the window as we approach Krasnoyarsk. The great Russian writer Anton Chekhov called this Siberia's most gorgeous city, and you understand

246 · MIDNIGHT IN SIBERIA

why. The city is tucked into a river valley, surrounded by gorges and snowy mountains rising in all directions. We have only a day here, and we were told the one thing not to miss is the Stolby Nature Reserve just outside the city.

And here I emphasize again—try not to ask why in this country. In this case, why would it be so difficult to arrange a visit to the area's number-one tourist destination?

Rose and I are in the backseat of a taxi as Sergei negotiates with the driver.

"David, you said Stolby Nature Reserve?"

"Right—or maybe national park?"

Sergei and the driver discuss.

"He doesn't know about it."

"It's supposed to be a very popular park."

"Da, da, Stolby Park!" the driver says.

"Yes." We may be getting somewhere.

Lots more animated discussion in Russian in the front seat.

Rose is smiling, not having experienced the joy of Russian chaos for a while.

"David, he says maybe it's closed. Maybe you'd like to see the hydroelectric dam instead. It's very interesting."

"Okay, tell him we appreciate his advice. We'll think about it."

He drops us at a hotel, where we leave our belongings and inquire at the front desk about Stolby Park. She says of course, any cab driver will know how to take you there. You can take the "air vehicle" (which I interpret as a gondola) or walk seven kilometers, no problem.

Great. We find a taxi.

Sergei asks the driver—another Sergei—if he can take us to the gondola.

There's a lot of discussion.

"You missed this, right, Rose?"

"Uh-huh."

"David," Sergei says. "Sergei says it's not quite a gondola, it's more of a lift?"

"Like a ski lift?"

"Yes."

With no ski equipment handy, and not enthusiastic about walking seven kilometers in the cold, Rose hatches an idea. "Could we ask Sergei if he could drive us as close to Stolby as possible, so we can have a look?"

Sergei asks Sergei.

"He says he thinks you might like to drive to see the hydroelectric dam instead."

Oh, man.

"Could we stop at Stolby first on the way to the dam?"

This seems like a plan, and Sergei pulls out of the hotel parking lot, drives maybe ten minutes, and pulls over. He rolls down a window and calls over to a police officer. They begin speaking, and Sergei gives us a play-by-play of the conversation.

"He's asking if the road to Stolby is open. . . . No, nope. 'Remont,' it's under construction."

Sergei the driver rolls up his window. "Okay, plan" he says, then unloads a mouthful in Russian to Sergei.

"David, he suggests we go to an overlook to see a view of the area, then we go to the hydroelectric dam, which he says is very interesting, then we come back."

Rose and I are officially ready to let go of Stolby.

"Sounds good!"

Russia being Russia, the chaotic confusion suddenly turns serene and enjoyable. Sergei pulls over at a scenic overlook where the parking lot is full of limousines—wedding parties. Rose is overjoyed—more pictures for her wedding dress blog.

Sergei, Rose, and I hike out to a spot overlooking a stunning valley. There is a platform surrounded by red metal fencing, and I snap some of my favorite photos from the trip—wedding couples posing, the mountains and valley behind them, with wind blowing through the brides' veils—the red from the railing, the white from the dresses, the black from the tuxedos are gorgeous in front of the natural backdrop.

"Yeshcho raz, yeshcho raz [Another time, another time]!" one groom keeps yelling to the photographer, urging him to snap more shots of his bride. This scene—newlyweds surrounded by their families and friends, laughing and celebrating—makes all the bad thoughts I was having about Russia melt away. Rose is feeling the same.

"I can't believe we're in Russia," she says. "Feels like somewhere else."

"I know," I say, as we walk back toward the car. "But it makes me angry. This all feels so free and hang-loose. And then I think about what people here are sometimes up against."

I think about the beating of Oleg Kashin, the trouble Nadezhda goes through, the call to Olga's family from the FSB. Why can't everyone just let people in this country *alone*? This is still on my mind when we return to the car, and begin driving toward the well-hyped hydroelectric dam.

Sergei, our driver, is in his forties, a pleasant, stocky guy with brown hair who seems eager to chat. He talks to himself while driving. "Spasibo, spasibo," he says when other drivers let him into a lane. "Oh, yolki palki!" he says whenever we go over a bump.

I tell Sergei how I was struck by the free spirit and joy I witnessed at that overlook.

"Sure, a person feels free if he has means," Sergei our driver says. "When a person gets up in the morning, what does he think about? His job and making money for his family. Today people don't feel secure that they can do that. Compare this life to socialism. Our old life was comparable to what countries like Sweden and Finland have today. But here? Bureaucrats are the only people who live good lives, and they don't care about common people."

He graduated from a university in Krasnoyarsk and became head of a transportation company. But his job evaporated during the recent economic crisis. "So I decided why not work as a taxi driver? I have to support my family—my wife and seventeen-year-old daughter."

I point out that many people in the United States lost jobs and struggled through the economic crisis, and Sergei doesn't deny that. But his wish for socialism as the solution fascinates me. He doesn't want a less intrusive government—in fact, he wants government to be more involved, just more responsive to the needs of the people.

"You know, we had our chance in perestroika. The setup of our society changed. That was our moment to develop some kind of democracy. Instead our economy was converted in a way that just put bribes in the hands of officials—right into their pockets."

Bribes are a way of life, he says. If you're recovering from surgery in the hospital and want your bedsheets changed? Bribe. Want an appointment with your kids' teacher? Bribe. Need your car inspected sooner? Bribe. Want the paperwork to open a new business actually processed by the local authorities? Bribe.

"They began a new society, just not with the right people," Sergei says. "We need to start from scratch. Putin lost his moment to establish a national idea. The idea was going to be to fight corruption."

"So now you're looking for a new national idea?"

"Who's looking for it?" Sergei says, throwing his hands up—briefly—before returning them to the wheel. "We won't be able to get out of this. We have a cancer."

We have a cancer.

I'm now really into this conversation. Sergei seems tired, but is dutifully translating for me, which I appreciate, especially after I told him I wanted to avoid any deep interviews for a day or two. Rose—victimized by jet lag—is asleep on my shoulder.

"So you want your daughter to leave this country because you think there's a cancer?"

"Yeah, she says no way she is going to live here. We are trying to get her to study in Prague. She can't see herself in Russia. She can see what is happening."

"Sergei, why is this resignation so deep—why can't there be another revolution, some kind of change?"

He takes a long pause.

"Don't you forget—it's not like Putin taught economics or something. He was a spy. He was taught to handle spies in other countries. You don't play chess with him. Groups who tried to organize in this country—many of them are now behind bars."

And so the path of our winding conversations takes us here—fear.

We drive down a long hill, make a turn, and there it is—the hydroelectric dam. I'll admit it's damn impressive. A hulking structure not unlike Hoover Dam in Nevada. Rose wakes up, and we all trudge outside for a few photos. Then we are back in the car, heading back to the city.

"Sergei, it was hard for me to see all those wedding parties having such fun, feeling so free, and then be talking to you about the difficult situation in the country."

"Yes, it's complicated. We have a saying, actually. Have a drink in the morning, and the whole day ahead of you can be free. Have something to drink in the morning, and the whole day can feel like a holiday."

"Drinking helps you forget reality?"

"I am just saying everything is brighter colors for a person when he is drunk."

Sergei takes us for a drive around his city, then drops us off at a restaurant so we can grab dinner before our evening train.

We pay Sergei for his services. Then I ask if I can write down his last name for the book. He stiffens up, and declines.

"You never know what tomorrow will bring," he says.

I say thanks anyway, and we start to get out of the car. But then Sergei says something else.

"Chort poberi [Oh damn]!"

He pauses.

"Sergei Komarov," he says. "Let the world know me."

Let the world know me.

Those words carry power. The power of a man who, before my eyes, overcame fear.

Sergei Komarov felt an instinctive reaction—fear—that many Russians feel every day at different moments. And he decided to take the risk.

He decided to play chess this time.

18 · TAISIYA

SERGEI, ROSE, AND I board train No. 44 in Krasnoyarsk just
after 1:00 a.m.

It is packed full, but thankfully with a more balanced
male-female ratio than our last train. We have a twenty-one-hour
ride to Irkutsk, the gateway to Russia's romantic Lake Baikal.

Many passengers are asleep, so the three of us are as quiet and
unobtrusive as possible, trying not to bang our roll-aboards and
backpacks into anyone's feet. All our efforts are spoiled when a
mousy little blond *provodnik* decides to come yell at us.

"You come from a plane? Too much luggage! You must have a
document to bring so much luggage!"

Sergei screams back at her in Russian. Then she walks away,
grumbling to herself.

"What does she want, a bribe, Sergei?"

"Probably."

"Should we pay something?"

"No."

This is not the end of her.

As we are preparing our berths, a woman across the aisle from us is desperately looking for her lost pillow. This is no small thing. On a Russian train anything lost can be the responsibility of the *provodnik*. Once she takes your ticket and hands you a pillow and sheets, it is your responsibility to hand them back to her before you leave the train. Or *she* could be held responsible.

The *provodnik* is summoned and immediately zeroes in on us as possible culprits. She begins to tear into our unwieldy pile of luggage to see if a pillow happens to be buried somewhere. Not finding one, she yells at the woman and says she'll just have to make do without one.

And as if she has not made our night unpleasant enough, around 3:00 a.m., I happen to be awake to see her pass through the aisle in the darkness and trip on someone's bedsheet. She curses and immediately turns all the lights on in the train car, leaving the place illuminated for the rest of our sleeping hours. Well, at least she won't trip again.

As the sun comes up I look across at Rose in the opposite upper berth. She's awake and reading. Below me is Sergei, and below Rose is another passenger—a Central Asian man, sitting on his bed, looking out the window. The landscape has changed—less forest, more open landscape, shrubby, like the ranchlands of Texas. There are some distant mountains.

"Honey," Rose says.

"Yeah."

"I think we should talk to him." She motions to the guy below. "If he is on his way to Russia for work, it could be really interesting. Don't you think you need to talk about immigration in your book?"

"Why don't you interview him? You can ask Sergei if he minds translating."

Rose climbs down, chats with Sergei, and the two of them begin chatting. I'm listening intently from above, with my notepad.

"Where are you from?" Rose asks.

"Uzbekistan."

He's in black athletic pants and a black wool sweater with gray stripes. I would guess he's in his forties, a peaceful, worn-down man with skin tough like leather and a thin mustache. In a rack above his berth are a pack of cigarettes, matches, and a tube of toothpaste.

"Where are you going?"

"Khabarovsk." It's a city in Russia's Far East, the last big stop before Vladivostok.

"How long are you going to stay there?"

We may have reached the limits of his Russian.

"He doesn't understand," Sergei says.

"Does he speak just Uzbek?"

"Yes," Sergei says.

"I'd like to see Uzbekistan sometime," Rose says, to no avail. "Leave it to me to interview a person who doesn't speak Russian or English."

The four of us sit peacefully.

"Anyone want tea?" Sergei finally says.

Rose and I say yes, and Sergei makes a trip to the samovar.

"Do we have anything to go with tea?" Sergei says. I reach into a bag and pull out a chocolate cake we grabbed at some train station behind us. We motion to our seatmate that he is free to dig in. I begin to cut the cake with a spoon, and our friend pulls out a knife—a serious knife, a knife that's a foot long and clearly designed not for food preparation but construction work, if not killing animals.

I thank him and chop the cake into perfect pieces.

We motion again for him to take a slice, and he holds up his empty teacup. The implication is clear: Who in their right Russian mind would consume cake—or do much of anything—with no *tea*?

I take it back. We all do share a language.

"Sergei, how is your family—Tania? Anton?"

"Really well. Thank you for asking, Rose."

Sergei tells her about Anton's hope for a military draft deferment so he can complete his residency program.

"Oh, Sergei. I'll keep my fingers crossed for him. He worked so hard. When we were in Moscow, I feel like we never saw him sleep."

Anton's future is clearly weighing on Sergei's mind. He tells me and Rose about his own military service—which was a close call. In Soviet times the requirement was two years, not just one. Sergei interviewed with a unit that was seeing call-ups to Afghanistan. It was 1981, and the Soviets were beginning an invasion that would end in failure and thousands of casualties.

"Some of the men from that unit were sent. Some said they would see fifty guys—then just five would be left." Somehow Sergei was deployed instead to the Caucasus region as a Soviet border guard.

"I guess you said the right thing in that interview."

He nods, taking a bite of cake.

Hours pass. Rose and I do some reading and napping. Sergei is on his laptop, picking up faint Internet signals here and there.

Finally our train pulls into Irkutsk. I am so excited to get in a taxi and get to Lake Baikal. It's truly one of the world's natural treasures. Nestled in the mountains, the lake is the deepest body of fresh water in the world. It resembles Lake Tahoe—in fact, the two are considered sister lakes—but to my mind Baikal is even more breathtaking. In the summertime the lake reflects the green mountains and blue skies "like a mirror," Chekhov wrote. In the winter it's majestic in a different way—near the shorelines the surface of the lake is frozen, a clear, reflective blue-green surface that looks like an abstract painting. Farther out on the lake, snow—fresh, brilliantly white, untouched snow—extends like a quilt to the tree-covered mountains that shoot up at the horizon. As I wrote earlier, seeing Baikal was enough to lift the spirits—albeit briefly—of a gulag prisoner trapped in a boxcar, peeing through a wooden crack. And the legacy of the Decembrists runs deep here. Local legend has it that on their journey to exile some of the Decembrists stopped on the shores of Baikal, waited for the lake to freeze, then rode across on horseback. Even today the freezing of Baikal is a significant event. Once solid, the lake becomes a playground. People take hovercraft across the ice—or even cars and trucks. The bravest ride across on bicycles.

We pile into a taxi in Irkutsk and head for the lake. History is on Rose's mind.

"Don't forget I always told you I'm like a Decembrist wife," she says.

She did always tell me—half-jokingly—that escorting me to Russia for several years and making the best of it was not unlike the women in the nineteenth century who, rather than leave their husbands, followed them to their Siberian exile.

I just nod, accepting Rose's point.

The shore of Baikal—the village of Listvyanka—is an hour's drive from Irkutsk. And we arrive on a cold, sun-splashed weekend afternoon that could not be more welcoming. There is a festival on the ice. Families are grilling fish, playing music, and frolicking. Kids are running around ice sculptures and coming down ice slides.

All over, people are selling *omul*, a delicious local fish caught in the lake. You can buy the fish raw or smoked.

And then there are the *nerpa*. These pudgy freshwater seals—they look like fat black torpedoes with whiskers and eyes on one end—are Baikal's mascot.

One attraction in Listvyanka is a "nerpinarium"—a Sea World for nerpas. Parents and their kids are piling in for the show—along with me, Sergei, and Rose. In a large swimming pool—ringed by tourists—nerpas are doing tricks. One paints. Another plays the saxophone. They even do math (the trainer yells out "Three plus one!" and a nerpa claps its flippers together four times.)

Afterward, like a family after a full day at Disney World, we sit for beer and kebabs, grilled outside, and talk about the warm feelings. "This really is Russia at its best," Rose says. "All those cold days in Moscow, all the frustration, nobody smiling: it's so easy to forget all that here. Look at these families, these cute kids all bundled up running around. It's so sweet."

"I know how short this trip was for you—and a shitload of flying. But it meant a lot to have you here, to experience this place together one more time."

"I'm glad I came—really. I always told you I didn't spend enough time out of Moscow when I was here. It's like a different world."

"I know."

"You know what strikes me here?" she says. "I just look at these families here on the lake—and it's damn warm here for February. It's just pure joy. I don't think anyone appreciates a nice day like Russian do, honestly. I feel like they don't expect the day to be nice. And when it's nice, they don't expect it to last. That what we're looking at out here in the sun—joy."

It's not all joy here on Baikal.

There have been fierce environmental debates about this lake. UNESCO has Baikal on its World Heritage list, for its natural beauty and unique habitat. But across the lake from where we are standing, in the village of Baikalsk an old paper mill is still operating, pouring gallons of dirty chemicals into the pristine waters every day. Environmental groups pushed for years to close down the plant— and it did close for a time—but Putin insisted on keeping it open. At one point Putin visited Baikal for quite a stunt. He plunged into the depths of the lake in a minisubmarine and said over the radio from underwater that everything looked clear to him—"I could see with my own eyes . . . there is practically no pollution" (as if pollution lurking in the water is visible to the naked eye).

There was another side to the debate. The paper mill is the major employer in the region. Nearly 10 percent of people in the city of Baikalsk work there. When Sergei and I visited to do a story, we met an elderly woman on the street. I asked what the factory means to her, and she just kept saying, "Food . . . food . . . food." The city's mayor, Valery Pintayev, said that when the plant was shut down for a stint, he saw a dead community. "There were no lights on in houses. People ruined themselves drinking. They stood at my window demanding jobs. Now the social tension is gone."

But the World Heritage program continues to threaten Russia, saying if they don't close the plant and stop polluting Baikal, it will take the lake off its list of World Heritage sites.

On this day, in this spot, Baikal seems beautiful, reminding me of the warmth and poetry I felt on many days living here. We find our hired driver and make the drive back to Irkutsk, then call it an early night. At 5:00 a.m. the next morning, I take Rose to the

Irkutsk airport, kiss her good-bye and send her on her way to the United States, to get back to work on her restaurant. It's just Sergei and me again, and I taxi back to the hotel to meet him. We have an afternoon interview with a woman named Taisiya. She's a local activist in Baikalsk who, we're told, has been fighting for the paper mill to close, as well as needling the local authorities in other ways.

Sergei has reserved a hovercraft—yes, a hovercraft—to take us from Listvyanka across to Baikalsk. I'm not sure what to expect. In our taxi Sergei is on the phone with Andrei—our hovercraft captain—who is explaining where along the lake shore we should have our taxi driver take us. We pull up to a little restaurant with what appears to be a dock—of sorts—frozen into the ice.

My only previous hovercraft experience was on the English Channel—from the slower boat I was on, I watched a sturdy vessel, carrying hundreds of passengers, flying slightly above the unfrozen water from Boulogne, France, to Dover, England. This is a different kind of hovercraft. I hear what sounds like a motorcycle engine roaring closer, and Andrei pulls up on the ice behind the restaurant. He's in a small blue-and-white vessel just slightly larger than your average station wagon. This thing is definitely jury-rigged. There is a massive fan on the back, with what looks like an automobile muffler hanging off it. The steering wheel inside is straight off a Lada. There are eight seats inside, with fading orange seat covers. All in all this looks like a minivan someone drove to Woodstock, super-glued on top of a pontoon.

Andrei motions for us to get in, so we load our suitcases and ourselves on board and settle into the orange seats. And away we go. Andrei is all business, in aviator glasses and a camouflage snowsuit.

The ride is surreal. Closer to the shore the ice really is like glass—

with cracks—and I can literally see plant life through the surface, making me wonder about the ability of the surface to hold an object as heavy as ours. Then we speed farther out onto the lake—with mountains rising on both sides—and the ice is covered with more snow. Andrei is at full throttle, and we're bumping over snowdrifts, with the back of the craft occasionally thrusting back and forth like a violently wagging tail.

I can only imagine the Decembrists—some of whom were princes—going from their royal surroundings in St. Petersburg to crossing this remote snowscape on horseback. If anything drove home that they were beginning a new way of life—this, along with the stinging cold, probably did the job.

After ninety minutes Andrei slows things down and pulls up to—well, not much. He leaves us at an empty spot on the shore, promising that we are close to Baikalsk. We pay him five hundred dollars, deciding his fee was enough without any additional tip. Maybe this was a mistake. As he leaves us Andrei spins the rear of his hovercraft around, and the big spinning wheel blows our luggage about ten feet into the air and into a snowbank.

We collect our things, and Sergei uses his cell phone to find a driver willing to pick us up. It takes a while for them to locate us. Then we're on our way to meet our activist.

Taisiya Baryshenko is sixty-nine. She has short blond hair, bright red lipstick, tinted glasses, and is wearing a blue sweatshirt and sweatpants as she brings us into her apartment. It's a comfortable place, full of plants and stacks of books. She raised two daughters and a son after she and her husband divorced.

"He started to drink. So I asked him to just leave us alone."

Taisiya is quite a talker—the kind who picks up speed as she goes on, making it increasingly harder to get a question in. But I'm impressed by her energy.

"Putin is the enemy of Baikal," she says, insisting that the paper mill must close. "I've lived here for five years now. And there are just few people who care."

And apathy angers Taisiya as much as anything the government has or hasn't done.

She pulls us over to her computer and begins playing a video. It's her and a local television reporter entering an apartment that's in horrendous condition—trash and old plates of food are littered everywhere. "A two-year-old child died in here—he had been sleeping on a board," she says. No one in the community has held the family responsible, nor has anyone shown much interest in the case.

"And so I made a video about it."

Her Internet is slow. She says the authorities have hacked into her accounts, following her activities, and things have moved slowly since.

"I'm trying to bring people around in some way. But many people aren't interested. They are just waiting, waiting for something readymade to happen."

WHEN I HEAR Russians vent about apathy, I always wonder what exactly they wish people would fight for. And often the conversation turns nostalgic, revealing a determination not to fight for something new but to preserve what made Russia special in the past. In Moscow I met a thirty-three-year-old activist who leads the Baikal program at Greenpeace. He scoffed at Putin's submarine stunt: "It's just plain stupid. You cannot see chemical substances in the water, like you can't see radiation. It's the same thing as standing near a nuclear bomb and saying, 'Well, I don't see anything.'" I expected the activist, Roman, to be most emphatic about the environmental damage the plant was causing and how he sees this kind of pollution as immoral in our day—not that he doesn't believe that—but Roman was most passionate about something else: how Russia may be letting go of something that makes people proud. He remembered his teachers in the 1980s preaching about symbols of Soviet pride, "And Baikal was one of them," he said. He was disappointed that Russia was not taking better care of a national treasure. Vassily Zabello, who worked at the polluting paper mill for twenty-six years, told me he desperately wanted it to close. Like Roman, he told me he was devastated by the idea that Russia might fail to safeguard a national treasure. If the government can't find a way to bring jobs and support to a city—and if polluting Baikal is the only answer—then a "great, enormous country [is] acknowledging its helplessness." (At the time of this writing the plant had just been closed again. That, of course, had happened in the past before the place was brought back online. A union boss from the plant told the French Press Agency that the closing would create an "abyss of poverty and unemployment.")

SCIENCE was also always a source of Soviet pride. And I was moved by a story about protecting that legacy in St. Petersburg. Amid all the horrors of World War II, one of the worst was the German blockade of the city—then known as Leningrad—which cut off food and supplies and starved hundreds of thousands of people. At a place called the Vavilov Institute, a dozen scientists were holed up with a large supply of grain that was important for research into food supplies. Rather than eat any of the grain, they starved to death protecting it. Seven decades later, when I visited, there was a new and *seemingly* less potent threat: The importance of these plants was emphasized to me by scientists in Britain and the United States. And yet, under a law that allows the government to sell off neglected property, local officials were considering selling the property to wealthy real estate developers. The head of the institute's gardens, Fyodor Mikhovich, got wistful when I interviewed him, focusing not just on the potential loss for science but on what it said about the country. "What will we, the Russian nation, have to be proud of if we ourselves destroy this?" Then he got nostalgic, saying that Communist leaders in the Soviet era would never have let this collection come under threat.

As for Taisiya's frustrations, she's speaking at lightning speed, bemoaning how Russians today favor apathy over activism because, she says, there's far less pride: "They don't want to struggle. And many people say to me—aren't you *afraid*? You'll be *killed*. But I won't change my convictions or principles."

"I've been thinking a lot about the Decembrists being on Baikal. Does their spirit live on in you?"

"I've always been proud of them. *They* were not afraid. They were sent to exile because they cared about freedom for their country."

"Well, what's the solution for today's Russia?"

For once Taisiya pauses. She walks over to her bookcase and pulls out a book. It's called *Generalissimo*, by Vladimir Karpov. It's a biography of a man whose face is unmistakable on the cover. "Do you know who this is?" she asks.

"Stalin?"

"Yes, Stalin."

I'm unsure where she's heading.

"In this moment, now, now I'm not saying we *need* Stalin—"

"Okay."

"I'm not saying that. But we need a person *like* Stalin. So people don't steal. So people aren't corrupt."

"Taisiya, it is worth having the bad sides of Stalin to get whatever good there may be?"

"I'm not talking about having repressions. That was not right. It was very bad."

"So, maybe there's a better option for Russia besides—another Stalin?"

"I'm not saying we need Stalin. But we need discipline. We need order."

I came to visit Taisiya expecting to get a vision toward Russia's future. Here is a woman who has been inspired to take on the government, to challenge power. I am stunned to hear that she—of all people—has Stalin nostalgia. What a reminder of how complicated this Russian puzzle really is.

IN HIS 2007 BOOK, *The Whisperers*, Orlando Figes wrote how nostalgia for Stalin was steadily growing, especially among older people, who remember a time when "their lives were organized and given meaning" and "everything was clear, in black and white, because Stalin did the thinking for them and told them what to do. . . . Nostalgia for 'the good old days' of Stalin reflects the uncertainty of their lives." For Putin, Stalin nostalgia is a useful tool, and according to analysts he's manipulated it to his advantage. Lev

Gudkov, director of the Levada Center—perhaps the only respected independent polling firm in Russia—wrote in a 2013 report cited by Reuters that Putin, after coming to power in 2000, "launched a comprehensive program to ideologically reeducate society. Putin's spin doctors did not deny that Stalin's regime had conducted mass arrests and executions but tried to minimize these events while emphasizing as far as possible the merits of Stalin as a military commander and statesman who modernized the country and turned it into one of the world's superpowers." (In 2013, Putin's government threatened to close the Levada Center, saying the polling firm was violating the law by not registering as a "foreign agent.")

Today there seems to be less fear than in Stalin's time, but still fear. The safety net is gone—people certainly struggle more for jobs. Corruption is rampant. There's no system of justice. A democratic experiment in the 1990s was seen as a disaster. And democracy seems like a risk—a big change. So many people have told me they've had enough chaos in their lives already—so they crave stability. And so what's left? Stalin?

Well, Stalin without the repressions, Taisiya emphasizes. She truly believes that's possible.

19 · IGOR

WOMEN WERE CARRYING their babies up to a barbed-wire fence, staring longingly into a place where there was no killing.

It was the summer of 2010. Sergei and I flew from Moscow to the border between two former Soviet republics—Kyrgyzstan and Uzbekistan—to report on an ethnic killing spree. There were clashes between ethnic Kyrgyz citizens and the ethnic Uzbek minority in southern Kyrgyzstan, and Uzbeks by the thousands fled to villages along the border, hoping to cross into Uzbekistan. But the Uzbek government, seeking to avoid a refugee crisis, sealed off the border.

The images were appalling. Mothers, children, the elderly packed into border villages. Makeshift hospitals were set up in churches to treat those wounded in the violence—they could not be transferred to hospitals because the hospitals were run by the Kyrgyz government, and they feared being harmed rather than treated. In one stunning scene Sergei and I witnessed, several residents of an Uzbek village took the corners of a blanket and carried a badly injured man—he had multiple gunshot wounds—up to the border fence. An ambulance arrived on the Uzbek side, and a medical team got out and approached a hole in the fence. They stared down the Uzbek border guards who were supposed to keep that border closed. Those guards stood motionless as the villagers passed the injured man through the hole in the fence to the Uzbek medical team. They rushed him to the ambulance and sped away.

Hundreds of people were killed in the violence, and thousands were displaced and to think—it may be Josef Stalin's fault.

In the 1920s Stalin drew the borders of the Soviet Central Asian republics, and the lines made little sense. They looked haphazard and divided people. For one, a sizable population of ethnic Uzbeks was left over the border in southern Kyrgyzstan. The most generous theory is that Stalin was careless. But academics have often wondered if Stalin hoped to foment chaos—to reduce the chance that a republic could ever come together as one unified people and challenge Soviet authority. What's more, chaos meant the republics might often need help to bring stability—they would have to turn to Moscow.

That legacy may still exist. Even though these are now independent countries, even though they have relationships with Western countries like the United States (the United States, over Russian objections, has an air base in Kyrgyzstan that it uses to move troops into Afghanistan), they still look to Russia—in an almost paternal way—to come to the rescue. Indeed, Kyrgyzstan's president asked Moscow to send peacekeeping forces to quell the violence in 2010.

The terrible ethnic conflict came to mind when Sergei and I made the stop in Baikalsk, when Taisiya, the local activist, grabbed the Stalin biography from her bookcase and said *he* is the kind of leader Russia needs today. She's not alone. Especially among older Russians—and as Taisiya demonstrated, even among those who criticize the government and push for change—Stalin nostalgia is growing.

Andrei, in Sagra, looks at socialist countries today with envy. Ivan, the young man with the meteor pebbles, says if he'd lost both his parents in Soviet times, the government would have done so much more to help him. For seventy years this was a country where the government could come to your rescue. But rescue from what? Maybe that was Stalin's magic. He created the feeling of chaos, fear, and confusion so people—from Central Asia to the streets of Moscow—needed him, needed government. They had no other choice.

And today people *do* speak of a sense of loss. When Sergei and I rode the train in 2011, we stopped briefly on the train platform in the Siberian city of Amazar and met a sixty-two-year-old woman named Inna Khariv. She was receiving a small government pension—three hundred dollars a month—after working on a mink farm in the Soviet Union. She looks back fondly to Soviet times, when she felt cared for by a government that provided education, jobs, and health care, and also felt a sense of national purpose.

"You can argue with me, but this is what we had—we lived with it—we had one faith, one goal," she said, adding that in today's Russia "nothing holds us together."

Now she is no fan of Putin. But she hasn't seen anyone come forward since Soviet times showing promise to take the country in a positive direction: "I lost my faith in this government, and I lost my faith in our youth. We do not have a replacement, [there's] no worthy replacement for us."

After the Soviet Union fell, Boris Yeltsin took a stab at more Western-style democracy, and Russians saw nothing but economic disaster. Putin came to power and amassed huge support. Russians saw a strong leader who could restore order, end the chaos. And for a time he succeeded. Putin made many Russians wealthy and gave the economy a huge boost, using the country's vast energy resources. But now the forward march of Russia—wherever it was going—seems to have stalled. Putin has slowly been losing support, and something is stirring—the protests in December 2011 showed there are people, a minority, ready to take to the streets and fight for broad change. In reaction Putin clamped down on dissent, targeted human rights organizations, and brought more fear back into society. So what now?

People are frustrated, angry, and not satisfied with life. But that isn't driving all that many people to the streets with protest banners. For many the reaction is to turn inward, and protect the people around them—family. Andrei protected his father, and in doing so learned that "publicity was our protection." Nadezhda has fought to run a successful business, to make money to raise her daughters, and in doing so has learned to call the bluff of local authorities who try to earn bribes by creating more confusion than people can handle. These fights matter. The more people like Andrei and Nadezhda realize their individual rights, their power in the face of authority, the more Russia may change.

I think about the history of the United States. To imagine people elsewhere in the world checking in on us in 1796 and wondering why we hadn't fully developed our system of government yet seems ludicrous. It's been twenty-one years since the Soviet collapse—any criticism we lodge at Russians could be a tad premature. There are dangers, of course. Much of what we've heard from people could play into Putin's hands. He loves to talk about how Russians are not *ready* for true democracy. Maybe that's true, in a way. But if so, it's not because they are ignorant or naïve or unsophisticated. It is that they need time—and deserve it—to figure out their own path. The danger is that a leader, like Putin, uses that to justify anti-democratic policies, which he has already done in some cases.

On our first train trip Sergei and I sat down in Ekaterinburg with Yekaterina Stepanova, a professor of law and philosophy who had closely followed Andrei Gorodilov's fight in Sagra. She said that what we witnessed there was a small step in a long process. The key was not just for people like Andrei to realize their individual rights, but for the younger generation—people born after the Soviet collapse—to learn the power of the individual. The more that happens, she said, the more an authoritarian system becomes obsolete. "What we have now," she said, "is not the history of a new Russia. It's still the history of the Soviet Union."

I have not gotten any clear sense of what the younger generation wants or will fight for. None of the young people we met—Zhenia in Nizhny Novgorod, Dima in Yaroslavl, Ivan in Chelyabinsk—are clamoring for Western-style democracy. They love their country, love Russian traditions and don't seem rushed to sort out the future. And Alexei in Novosibirsk, thirty-five years old, running a family carpet business and making videos on ski slopes, says he would clamor more urgently for a different political system in his country only if things got a lot worse. Sergei and I carry on our journey east from Lake Baikal, which is the last major milepost in Russia, before reaching the Far East and, ultimately, the port city of Vladivostok. We are in the dining car of the train, a place with brightly colored curtains hanging on the windows and Western techno music blaring from a radio at the bar. We find a seat at a table with fellow traveler, Igor Zakharov. He's forty-four and runs a company in Irkutsk that builds electric boards for power stations. Igor tells us the government can be a major impediment for him. He desperately needs a specific part made in the United States by General Electric. Even though that part has been approved for use by countries around the world, the Russian government is still working through the bureaucracy to approve it. This has set Igor back. What he says he *does* need his government to spend time on is helping Russian-owned businesses like his succeed by keeping out competition from Chinese firms.

"But that they won't do," he tells us.

Igor has brown hair, slightly graying, and a rotund figure. He is eating *solyanka*—Russian soup made with beef—a crab salad with mayonnaise, and some vodka. He treats us to some of the vodka, and we raise our shot glasses: "To a new friendship," he says. Clink.

Igor is wearing a long-sleeved shirt that catches my attention. Written in black letters, in vertical top-to-bottom rows, in English, it says: "The past is now part of my future. The present is well out of hand."

We all smile.

The shirt was a gift from his twenty-two-year-old daughter, who liked the message, though she had to translate it for her dad when she gave it to him.

"What does the message mean?" I ask.

He takes a long pause. "It means, there is my grandfather, my father, and me. And my daughter."

He stops there, a man of few words. The shirt seems to remind him that different generations of his family have lived through different times. Whatever past generations have seen and learned will shape his daughter's life. As for him, there is little work that can be done.

"Why is the present out of hand?"

"The present—it's me."

"And you have no control?"

"It is possible to control oneself. But nowadays it is difficult to control the overall situation because it has been constantly changing."

Intimidated by the change all around, clinging to any small sense of control that can be found. This is not the first we've heard of this.

Our next stop is Birobidzhan, a Far East city not far from the Pacific coast. Sergei and I planned an eight-hour stop there before getting on our final train.

Birobidzhan is the capital of Russia's "Jewish Autonomous Region"—yes, it's still called that. It was one of Stalin's other geographic creations in the 1920s, a place to both relocate Russia's Jewish population and, he hoped, draw Jewish communities from outside the country. Hoping to attract the masses, the government had a gorgeous train station constructed—the work of forced laborers. The masses never came, but the Jewish population became modest for a time. Yet the place was an embodiment of Stalin's cruel whims. As the BBC described, "The first Jewish settlers arrived in 1928—20 years before Israel was created. They had come to the virgin lands of the Far East to build a new city, and set up a national homeland for Soviet Jewry with Yiddish as the official language. But less than 10 years after the creation of the Jewish Autonomous Region, Stalin began to crack down on Jewish culture. The government head was executed, Yiddish books were burnt, and Jewish schools and the synagogue closed down."

Once Israel was created, many Soviet Jews fled there, and the Jewish population of Birobidzhan became all but nonexistent, making the name of the region almost laughable.

But today, still, when you arrive at the train station in Birobidzhan, the first thing you notice is a gigantic menorah outside. And, a few blocks away, a statue commemorating the play *Fiddler on the Roof.* There are several synagogues in town, and the leaders swear that the region's Jewish population is slowly growing today.

We stop by one synagogue, and sit down with the young rabbi, Eli Riss. He's Russian-born, but spent some years in the United States, in an orthodox congregation in Brooklyn. He returned to Birobidzhan and feels he is serving a population of not just Jews.

"There was an older guy in town who started coming by recently," Riss says, as we sip tea together in the meeting-and-activities room of the synagogue. "He said, 'Well. I live in Birobidzhan. So I should think like I'm Jewish."

So I should think like I'm Jewish.

Inna, on that train platform, felt nothing holding Russians together. Igor, with his T-shirt, felt part of a generation that has no control. And this man, clinging to whatever identity is locally available. What a sense of emptiness, of wandering.

20 · OLGA

LATE IN THE AFTERNOON, we drag our suitcases past the snow-draped jumbo menorah outside the station in Birobidzhan and board the train for the last time.

It's train No. 002, the *Rossiya*, the train that leaves Yaroslavsky Station in Moscow as an old Soviet march echoes through the hall. Sergei and I were not able to take that train out of Moscow, but we make sure to ride it on our final leg. The train is decorated, on the outside, like Russia's flag—a light shade of blue, red, and white. The *provodnik* seems a little more formal—and a little more friendly. We splurge a bit on this leg, because there is no third class—just closed cabins.

This overnight leg of the journey flies by—perhaps because the digs are so comfortable, I sleep peacefully for hours. After heading east from Birobidzhan, our train makes a hard right turn southward, down a narrow patch of Russia that lies between China and the Pacific Ocean. Early in the morning, as the sun rises, we pull into Vladivostok. The station sits right alongside the city's bustling harbor, which flows into a bay and out to the Pacific. It's a cold morning, but bearable, with an ocean breeze pulling in some moist, warmer air. Sergei and I walk down the platform and pay our second visit to a special monument.

It reads "9288"—the number of kilometers you travel on the Trans-Siberian Railway from Moscow to this point. I feel pretty lucky to have completed this journey—twice.

Sergei and I walk up a hill from the station, dragging our suitcases over ice clumps, to a hotel and rent a room. He quickly showers and calls a taxi to go to the airport. He has to catch a flight to Moscow to get back to work—with NPR's new correspondent there.

"Sergei, what else can I say but thank you? I know this won't be our last adventure together, though."

"No, no way, David. Please, please tell Rose I send my best again. And wish her good luck with the business. This is very, very exciting."

Sergei went above and beyond to make me and Rose comfortable, secure, and fulfilled in our years in Russia. He took enormous pride in doing that. He would truly do anything for me. What's more, he was genuinely interested, personally, in the reporting we did—all the stories, including those on this train trip.

I consider him one of my closest friends in the world. But I often do think about how, in some ways, he is an enigma to me, surely as I am to him. There's a distance—some of it, surely, because of the language barrier. Near-perfect as Sergei's English is, I know he misses some of the nuance in my random thoughts and bad jokes. But when he and Boris would gossip or talk about how and why we were reporting a story the way we did, I could sense a puzzled curiosity on their part, not unlike feelings I sometimes had toward them. Close as I am to Sergei, I don't think I'll ever fully understand him in the way I do friends from home. To me, it's a reminder that culture matters—everywhere, but especially in Russia, a place I'll also never fully understand.

And I do worry about Sergei. He has a stable job with NPR, but Tania works at a sock factory, and we know how uncertain manufacturing jobs are everywhere in the world, especially in Russia. And Anton's bright future in the medical field could be halted at any moment if the government swoops in and forces him to go into the military.

"Sergei, tell Tania and Anton hello—and please, please keep me updated on Anton and the military service. I am keeping my fingers crossed."

"Thank you, David."

We hug in the lobby.

"Fly safely," I tell him.

With that, Sergei pushes the silver handle down on his roll-aboard suitcase, lifts it up to carry it down the stairs outside, and climbs into the backseat of a waiting taxi.

I spend the afternoon walking around the city, which has the feel of San Francisco. Hills packed densely with houses and buildings overlook a harbor with several attractive bridges. The city streets are full of cheap Chinese goods. The main hotel is the Hyundai, a headquarters for South Korean businessmen who come through in droves. There is a direct ferry from here to Seoul, but it takes hours more than it should, because the ferry has to bypass North Korean waters.

There is, however, the Pyongyang Café. I've been before, and decide to return on this night for dinner. The restaurant, I have come to learn, is owned by the North Korean government and operated as a form of propaganda (and profit making). It is an irony that I am heading here to dine—and support the regime in Pyongyang—on the very day the North Koreans unleashed rhetoric threatening to nuke my home country.

The place is attached to a hotel, decorated with pastoral scenes of the mountains in North Korea. There is a bar area, with a large television used for karaoke, but right now, to play bizarre scenes from a recent concert in Pyongyang—the audience is clapping as men in military uniforms march around a stage with Disney-like characters (no sign of Dennis Rodman so far.)

My server is named Elena. She has fashion-model looks and is dressed in a traditional North Korean flowing gown. In limited Russian I ask where she's from. "Pyongyang," she says. In limited English she asks if I'm British. After a dinner of kimchi and Korean barbecue, Elena and two other servers do some karaoke. They sing several songs in Korean, and several in Russian, all while dancing and gesturing in unison.

A Russian couple—actually, the only other diners left in the place—make the bar area their dance floor as the women keep up their singing. The guy, I come to learn, is Mikhail, a plump gentleman, perhaps in his fifties, wearing a white sweater and brown scarf. His wife, Sveta, is becoming increasingly annoyed with Mikhail, who is drunk and becoming increasingly interested in the North Korean women singing. He is dancing around them with one hand in the air, and they are doing their best politely not to notice.

"*Beeeauuutiful*, right *beeeauuutiful!!!*" Mikhail yells to me in English, knowing I'm American and also hoping I might join in his appreciation for our entertainers. I quietly nod and applaud.

The manager of the restaurant—who, I imagine, is in charge of limiting her staff's movements during their temporary employment outside North Korea, not to mention limiting their contact with drunk Russian men like Mikhail—is moving herself closer and closer to the scene.

Mikhail orders a bottle of champagne and a bottle of whiskey from the bar. He opens the bottle of whiskey and pours shots for me and for himself. Then he opens the bottle of champagne and pours glasses for the manager as well as the three servers.

"Korea, America, *Russia!*" he cries out, noting the diplomatic success we seem to have achieved by sharing a dance floor. "So interesting. Cheese!" (I believe he meant "Cheers," but he's trying English, so I've got to give him a pass.)

We all clink—the North Korean servers raise their glasses to their lips but seem to have gotten a "don't drink it" look from the manager.

This does wrap up one of the more unusual nights of the trip. Then again, I think back. During this journey I chased a meteorite and touched a piece of it, baked in a *banya* with a drunk veterinarian, watched fat seals do math, and financially supported a regime that's a sworn enemy of my country.

My friend Chandler once asked me if I love Russia, or if it fascinates me? "I think I'm fascinated," I told him. "I may love it. I do like the chaos. Anything can happen. But I can't imagine what all that means for people who live here—especially people who don't have money."

I do believe all that. This is a wild, entertaining place full of culture, creativity, and craziness. I understand why Russians go to the United States and find it boring and too controlled. Here, it's the Wild West, for better or worse. Worse, surely, if you have to live here with little means. For those with wealth the place must feel like an electrifying vacation where any amount of adventure or luxury is possible. For people without money, the chaos must be a cruel existence, because life can feel so uncertain. Little is possible, and little seems fair. I have kept that in mind at every stop on this journey, tempering the fun and wild moments with a dose of reality.

IN VLADIVOSTOK in 2011, Sergei, Rose, and I met Olga and Dmitry Granovsky, married and both thirty-nine years old. They each had previous marriages that ended in divorce. He's a musician, a fashionable, confident guy who wears rock-star–looking sunglasses. Olga is a professor of political philosophy at the local university, a warm, generous middle-aged young woman with an easy smile. Last time we spoke, Olga told me she was disappointed in Russia's government. She and Dmitry thought often about taking their four children to live in another country. "Our society is sick," she said. "It's ill. It's not healthy. We have no society." Still, she said, her family loves life in Vladivostok—the coast is beautiful, they enjoy vacationing to some of the islands to the north, they certainly felt no impulse whatsoever to join the antigovernment protests raging in Moscow around the time we spoke.

Rose and I felt a close connection with this couple—akin to what I felt with Andrei in Sagra. We could see ourselves in them—in our thirties, happy with our jobs, enjoying our friends, the local music scene, and vacations together. The difference, of course, is that Rose and I don't live in a society we see as "ill."

Dmitry picks me up my hotel in the afternoon. He's wearing the sunglasses I remember. "It's great to see you again," I say, climbing into the passenger seat—on the left side in his Japanese-made car.

"Olga is at home," he says, speaking impeccable English like his wife. "She hurt her foot. But we can bring you over, and we can all have dinner?"

"Sounds great."

I know that in Russia, going to a friend's house doesn't mean just dinner—it often means hours of eating, drinking, and socializing. And I'm fine with that.

We stop by a takeout place, and Andrei runs in and grabs some sushi and a Hawaiian pizza. "I'm also going to cook some meat— but want to make sure we have enough."

Then we drive outside the city to a massive apartment complex that is one strange stepchild of Russian bureaucracy. Dmitri explains that the government built this new complex of skyscrapers as housing for military veterans. But far fewer veterans than expected actually took advantage. Of those who did, and received units for dramatically cheap prices, many decided to make an extra buck by renting to nonmilitary families. This is how Olga and Dmitry got their place—not exactly what the government intended. But decisions were made somewhere in the government, forms were signed, a program was set in motion, money was passed, Olga and Dmitry got a nice flat for their family and a military vet somewhere got some extra dough. Who's asking questions?

As we walk from the car to the building, Dmitry tells me not to say anything too critical of the government in the corridors, as there are some former military guys who may get too interested in my visit. But once we walk into the apartment, and remove our shoes, it is an entirely free environment. Olga limps over on crutches to hug me. I feel as welcome here as I do in friends' homes in the United States.

We sit around the table. A radio next to the refrigerator is blaring American pop music. Olga and I are digging into some sushi and pizza, washing it down with champagne, as Dmitry stands at the stove cooking pork.

"Smells amazing," I say.

"It's some Asian spices. Spanish pork"

"You eat pork?" Olga asks me.

"Yeah!"

"Ahh, but you're Jewish." Dmitry has a good memory.

"I guess not a really good Jew."

I fill them in on my trip across their country—Moscow, Yaroslavl, Nizhny Novgorod, Izhevsk, Perm, Ekaterinburg, Chelyabinsk, Ishim, Novosibirsk, Krasnoyarsk, Baikal, Birobidzhan and finally here to Vladivostok.

"Did you hear about the meteor?" Olga asks.

"I *chased* the meteor."

"You know, a friend of mine at Stanford University wrote me and said, 'I hope you haven't been hit by the meteor.' I laughed, thinking, you know how far we are from Chelyabinsk?"

"Like five thousand miles," I say, from experience.

Dmitri says Americans often ask where he's from. "And I would say, you won't be able to guess. And they'd say try me. And I'd say I live less than 500 miles from Japan, less than 150 miles from North Korea, and less than 50 miles from China. Now tell me where I'm from." No one ever guessed Russia.

Dmitri was actually going to school in Alaska when the Soviet Union fell: "I was seventeen."

He heard about the news in his country, and was so optimistic about going back that he declined the chance to apply for an American green card. He says a lot about his country today has turned out worse than in Soviet times.

"Back then, everyone had the ability to get an education. It was no problem for a family to have two kids, or five kids. Didn't matter. There were free schools, free medical service, everything. So to some extent, it was easier. Now you may be able to get everything, you just have to overpay—twice as much as in the U.S. for the same medical services, same insurance."

"Do you wish you had gone for that green card in 1991?"

"I guess not. I know a few people from my age group who moved there as green card holders, or got citizenship. Lived there five or ten years. And I don't hear a lot of cool stories. Often, they're not smart enough or wealthy enough to integrate into your society."

It reminds me of one of the first conversations on this trip—with the passenger who had just gotten back from Thailand. As a Russian he felt different, and out of place. And Dmitry is painting such a sad picture. He's saying there are Russians who can't afford a comfortable lifestyle at home—but also don't feel like they have the money or smarts to adjust to a Western society.

Dmitry, knowing English, having spent time in the United States, would have as good a chance as any Russian fitting in and finding happiness in a country like the United States. But even he doesn't have some strong pull to make such a move.

"We love Vladivostok," Olga explains. And her life isn't easy. The shrinking population in Russia has meant fewer students at universities. Her school has been desperately trying to recruit foreign students, from China and elsewhere. But they've also had to squeeze budgets. She gets paid 26,000 rubles ($880) a month in salary as an assistant professor. She can get an additional 10,000 rubles ($330) for every thirty-two hours of special lecturing—but says she doesn't get that payment until the administration confirms that her students have completed all required homework for the course—added bureaucracy, added delays.

She spent a semester in 2012 teaching at the University of California, Berkeley, and loved every minute of the experience.

"Were you feeling, I wish I could be a professor in the U.S.? Were you conflicted about that at all?"

"I don't know. I know I want opportunities to go there whenever I want to. Really, I just want to write my book and become a full professor and have enough salary to travel when I wish. I'm not sure I want to be a professor at an American university. But it was an interesting experience."

Olga's book, and her research, focus on Western political philosophy.

"How do you explain the current Russian government in the context of political philosophy? What *is* the political philosophy Russia has in place?"

Olga smiles, and gives this some thought.

"They are trying to separate people."

"Why is that a good strategy for the government?

"Because when people are separated, they don't care deeply for anything—except for themselves."

Whether it's some premeditated strategy by Russian leaders, or a product of history, Russians do seem to struggle to unify behind a vision, to share a sense of hope for something.

I think about Stalin dividing Central Asia, fomenting chaos and division, forcing ethnic groups to plead to Moscow for help. I think of Boris and Gia, the warmest friendship, strained when Gia's family moved to a different part of the Soviet Union, further complicated when Georgia became its own country. I think about Alexei, crippled, alone, and helpless with his mother in that apartment in Nizhny Novgorod, ignored by the state. Igor, with his T-shirt advertising the lost generation he feels a part of. Inna, on the train platform in Amazar, and Taisiya in Baikalsk, remembering Soviet times as a period when people believed in *something*. Ivan, in that hardscrabble village, praising the state for making him a soldier, loving a government that also drives him to tears. The people we've encountered have so much depth, their lives are full of poetry, pain, and laughter, and yet in so many cases something is just missing. When it comes to the future, there's just no faith.

"You get used to knowing nothing about your future here," Olga said. "Everybody knows something about their future."

"Except Russians?"

"Exactly."

"Why?"

"History. We get used to changes and transformations and not being aware of the future. We are the lost generation, the broken generation, the generation of changes and transformations. We get used to it." (Unbelievably, the soundtrack to our conversation, coming from the kitchen radio, is "Another Day in Paradise," by Phil Collins.)

"Why do you call it a lost generation?"

"Because we grew up in a different country, with different values. We didn't know we had to buy anything or make money to be successful. We weren't linked to any markets. We believed—or our teachers told us—we would always live in a communist society.

But then our society became capitalist—a wild capitalist society. Different country, different system. It's strange. So our generation is lost, I think. It is not easy."

I ask Olga again if I caused any problems by coming last time, drawing a phone call to Dmitry's father-in-law from the FSB.

"Pffft!" Dmitry says, as in, "Like we *care!*"

"We are not afraid of anything," Olga says. "They can do nothing bad to me."

Olga, Dmitry, and I spend several more hours polishing off the pizza, sipping champagne, taking smoking breaks on the balcony. They tell me I'm welcome back anytime, and I promise to bring Rose back for a double date.

Olga and I hug at the door, and Dmitry calls me a taxi. It's a car, not a train, but Dmitry still walks me downstairs, outside, making sure I'm comfortable in the backseat before closing the door and waving in the cold as I drive off.

My flight out of Vladivostok is early the next morning. Before going back to my hotel I stop for one last drink in town. I'm sitting at the bar, when a young, blond Russian woman walks up on stage. They turn down the DJ music for her to perform. A small crowd gathers around her—she's clearly known locally. And she does have a beautiful voice as she sings her first tune—Mariah Carey's "Hero"—with a thick Russian accent.

21 · VITALY

IT WAS MEANINGFUL for me to spend time with Dmitry and Olga again. They remind me of the assumptions I made about Russia. I assumed, as a young American watching the fall of the Soviet Union from afar, that Russians would immediately feel liberated and determined to grab onto my country's system as fast as they could.

The story is so different, and far more complicated. In an unfamiliar country, it can be easy to say, okay, that's a point of view that seems foreign to me, but the person I'm listening to is so entirely different from me, I can't empathize. But then there're Olga and Dmitry—people I connect to, and empathize with, in so many ways. That makes their outlook more powerful to me personally. Olga and Dmitry appreciate Western countries like the United States. But they don't long to live there. They don't see some superior form of politics they wish Russia had. They have some nostalgia for Soviet times, seeing it as an era when the government provided some bedrock services and guarantees for its citizens. As for the future, they can't see it clearly yet. Not a single person we met on this trip could. But no one said, I'm satisfied with the system in Russia—let's leave it as is. As an American, sure, I'd love to make some tweaks. But all in all, if a Russian writer came and asked me, I would say I'm pretty proud of what I have. No one in Russia said that. Still, so many people want and expect change.

But when? And what will it look like? Olga and Dmitry and so many other people showed an unimaginable willingness to wait—patience as long and hard as a crazy five-week train journey across all of Russia. Maybe that patience comes from learned endurance, a fatalism that anticipates difficult times, and a tendency to grab onto whatever feels safe, not wanting to shake things up and induce chaos too quickly. And so perhaps this will be a long but fruitful process. Perhaps the small battles we saw will go on. The young generation of Russians will learn about individual rights and freedoms, and ultimately that will lead them to deciding on a system that will make them proud.

THE TROUBLING REALITY about Russia is that for any sense of optimism to arrive, for people to feel hope, inspiration and a drive to bring positive change would mean escaping years—generations—of history. History and culture matter. Everything I heard on this trip—the feeling that strength comes from endurance, the fear of chaos and thirst for any sense of stability, the lack of faith in the ability to shape the future—are emotions and feelings that may well be embedded in the Russian soul.

The Decembrists are remembered as some of the rare few in Russia's history to rise up and try to break apart the system that ruled the day. They failed, and faced punishment and exile. Yet, amazingly, not all of them felt unjustly treated, or felt that the chance to change the course of history had slipped through their hands.

Mikhail Zetlin quotes one of the Decembrists, Yakubovich, who was writing in a journal in 1843, two decades after the failed revolution.

The 20th year of exile, of persecution, poverty and hard work is about to begin. Oh God! Give me the strength to do my duty as a citizen and a man and to add my contribution to the annals of sorrow of the Fatherland. Do not let this contribution be sullied by pride and egoism, but let it find its expression in love and truth. I am a very sick man. I am 59 years old . . . the end is approaching, the end that heralds the dawn.

But what *is* the dawn in a place where someone believes it is his "duty" to contribute to the "annals of sorrow" in his country?

Mikhail Shishkin, the great modern-day Russian novelist, struggles to see the dawn.

"To call people to the barricades in Russia is beautiful, but senseless," he said in a 2012 interview with the Web site Russia Beyond the Headlines. "We lived through all this already in the early '90s. All revolutions take place in the same way—the best people rise up to fight for honor and dignity, and they die. On their corpses, thieves and bandits come to power, and everything comes full circle. The same thing happened during the Orange Revolution in Kiev. The same thing is happening right before our eyes in the Arab world. Apparently, in Russia a new generation has grown up who want to experience the barricades. All right. They will experience them. And they will be disappointed."

But Andrei Grachev, a longtime adviser to former Soviet leader Mikhail Gorbachev, isn't so sure. When I asked him about Russia's future, he pointed to August 1991. Hard-liners in the Communist Party had carried out a coup, forcing Gorbachev from power. Thousands of people took to the streets outside parliament, waving anti-Communist flags in support of reformer Boris Yeltsin. Tanks were on the streets, but the military refused to fire at the protesters—some soldiers placed flowers in the barrels of their guns.

Yeltsin came to power. But his efforts at reform are seen in Russia not only as a failure, but as a big reason why people have such little faith in democracy. And yet, when I spoke to Grachev recently, he refused to believe that what those protesters fought for is dead. As he put it, "There is fire under the ashes."

Whatever the future holds, I am grateful to have had the chance to experience this country, to be touched by so many lives and stories, to have learned so much. I can't believe, looking back twenty years, that I saw Russia as a cold, oppressed, backward country, emerging from decades of terror and on the cusp of enjoying the wisdom of America's way of life and system of government. If nothing else, I for one, now understand that Russians may well want— and get—something else. They're taking time to figure that out. I can't predict what will happen, but I'll certainly be thinking about and rooting for the people I've met.

Suffice it to say, the story of Russia is far from finished. So perhaps it's fitting that while Vladivostok is the obvious last stop on this journey—the end of the train line, the window on the Pacific—my thoughts tend to wander back to the middle, where the trip was far from complete.

After our detour to Chelyabinsk to follow the meteorite, and our realization that we could not travel east, since that would require a visa for Kazakhstar, we took the train north to Ekaterinburg, east to the city of Tyumen, where we stopped for the day, then on to Ishim.

During that stop in Tyumen, Sergei and I took a ninety-minute drive through a raging snowstorm to find a rehabilitation center for drug addicts. Russia loses tens of thousands citizens each year to heroin addiction, and there are believed to be more than two million people actively using. It's a devastating epidemic and a big reason Russia was eager to work with the United States in Afghanistan— that's where much of the poppy that flows into Russia is produced, and Russia's government has been desperate to curtail it.

Sergei and I walk through knee-deep snow into a ramshackle building and a living room with old rugs and couches. On the wall, there's a painting of the sun, shining over a pasture covered with flowers. A sign on the wall, translated into English, reads, "If pain today, look ahead to tomorrow."

Nine of the people in the rehab program have agreed to meet with us—six men, three women. They're in comfortable sweats and T-shirts, sitting before us on couches. They talk about how they got here.

"I started smoking dope when I was fourteen," says a young man named Vitaly. "When I was fifteen, I started using heroin. And I was diagnosed HIV-positive."

"I was selling drugs at seventeen," says a nineteen-year-old named Paulina. "I could see I was dying."

"I started smoking when I was fourteen," says Kate. "It was the only thing that made me happy."

Drug addictions aren't unique to Russia, of course. But the director of the program, a thirty-three-year-old named Natalya—a recovering heroin addict herself who is HIV-positive—says that when people reach for help in Russia, it's nearly impossible to find:

"When it comes to disabilities, when it comes to drug addictions, in our society, it's simpler to put a fence around these people than to help them. I travel to other countries. I ask people about the drug problem, and people will say how sad and awful it is. Here? People think it's better to just take addicts to an island to execute them. And the government is really not guilty. It's the Russian mentality. A Russian starts thinking about how to help a disabled person, or an addict, only if the person appears in *his* family."

Another young man, on the couch directly in front of me, is also named Vitaly. He's noticeably thin, though not in an unhealthy way—he almost looks like a ballerina. As I speak to the others he keeps staring at me, listening intently, until it's his turn.

"Since my childhood, I danced. I traveled and performed in the U.S.—in Florida. Miami and Orlando."

Sergei translates, then asks him, "You speak English?"

"A little."

Vitaly gives it a try. "I start drugs in fifteen years old. I lose everything." He pauses. "May I speak Russian?"

Of course, we tell him.

He explains that after his trips abroad as a child dancer he performed around Russia—but began trying drugs in the dressing rooms. He couldn't stop and ended up on the streets instead of in performance halls.

"What was the drug, Vitaly?"

"Heroin. My mother wanted the police to lock me up. She didn't know what to do with me."

He finally found this rehab center but escaped from the program. Twice.

Now he's back for a third time, at this cold outpost, miles from anything, with every excuse in the world to feel hopeless. But he doesn't. He says he's going to see the program through this time. He's determined the world hasn't seen the last of his Russian dance moves.

"After rehab, you're going to dance again?"

He goes back to English.

"I really hope. Really hope and trust in this."

"What kind of dancing?"

"Ballroom."

"You know, my wife, Rose, really wants us to learn ballroom dancing. Maybe you can teach me sometime?"

He wiggles his hips and arms on the couch. "Cha-cha-cha," he says. The room erupts in laughter. "It's easy," he says.

"Maybe for *you*, not for me!"

The two of us exchange smiles and agree to stay in touch about scheduling that first lesson.

End of the line. This statue occupies a nondescript spot on the train platform in Vladkvostok. But the number is significant: 9288, the number of kilometers traveled from Moscow, where there's a statue marking the zero-kilometer mark. In between, gallons of tea and dozens of boxes of instant noodles consumed, new friendships formed, and a vast country better understood. (*David Gilkey/NPR*)

ACKNOWLEDGMENTS

SHORTLY AFTER RETURNING to the United States from Russia, I got an e-mail out of the blue from Howard Yoon. He introduced himself as a book agent and wrote that he was interested in talking to me about a series we had aired on NPR's *Morning Edition*. It was called "Russia by Rail" and it chronicled a three-week journey on the Trans-Siberian Railway. Howard and I met for a long night of eating, drinking, and conversation. He was convinced I could do the journey again for a book about life in modern Russia. He saw the train as a perfect setting—readers could come on board with me, get comfy in the compartment, make stops, meet people, and then return to the familiar confines of the train as the journey continued. He envisioned the book as part travel adventure, part sociological look at an important country at an inflection point.

Here's the thing: I thought Howard was nuts.

I just did the trip for the radio, I said. But a book will be a totally different experience, he told me. I was just starting a new job at *Morning Edition* and had no time, I told him. This is not an opportunity to miss, he told me. He finally convinced me to write just a few paragraphs, which he reviewed. He liked them. So he told me to write a few more. And a few more. I knew what he was up to—but I became a willing victim of his manipulation. Within weeks, we had a book proposal. And back to Russia I went. I am enormously grateful to Howard for his instincts, for his belief in this idea and in me as an author, for his many edits and endless advice, and for his friendship. He and his partner, Gail Ross, are so much more than agents.

David Berarducci is so much more than a landlord. In my fantasy, I imagined writing my first book in some little old shack on a fishing wharf in New England that happened to have Wi-Fi. That's what I googled—and the one place that showed up was David's serene little rental on Cape Cod. In my nightmare, I imagined losing my unfinished manuscript somewhere in the process. That also happened. Margaret O'Connor (who lives at my old address and thought that package looked like something important when it showed up in the mail) and Andrea Messina (who babysat the manuscript for weeks) saved the day.

I am lucky to work for a company, NPR, that could not have been more supportive. The book never would have happened without that first radio series, which never would have come together without producer/editor Laura Krantz and editor Chuck Holmes.

Chuck: You, Eric Rubin, and Fiona Hill have so much more important things to be doing than reading a friend's manuscript, at different stages of writing. But the three of you were so willing and generous.

I swear, there is no one in the business of news photography better than David Gilkey. I'm grateful for our time together in Russia and for your willingness to let your photos live in this book.

Some of my dearest friends—Chandler Arnold, Joe Levin, Jed Howbert and Sean Strasburg—took time away from busy lives to fly to Russia and experience the place with me. I'm grateful for all your reflections and insights, a few more vodka-induced than the rest.

Norton took a risk on this first-time author and made me believe in myself as a writer. I owe Mitchell Kohles for the many e-mails answering my most basic questions (so I write my changes directly on this thing called a "proof"?). My editor, Maria Guarnaschelli, was passionate about this project from day one. I love how she shared in the journey with me, asking the right questions, enjoying the surprises, and learning about Russia at every turn. Maria taught me about writing—how to find a voice, without forcing it or getting in the way of letting stories tell themselves.

I have really supportive families—the Greenes (Doug, Sally, Jackie, and Jose) and Prevites (Rose, Albert, Maggie, Joey, Jeanne, Becca, Peter, another Peter, and yet another Peter)—who put up with my endless obsession with all things Russia. My father, Doug, has been my primary editor since the first papers I wrote in grade school, and I hope he found this book to be an improvement. My late mother, Terry, believed everyone had a story to tell, and her inspiration is felt in this book and in my career.

I leave this project humbled and awed by the strength and will displayed by so many people in Russia, who opened their doors and lives to me in ways I never would have done myself for a stranger. While in Russia, Rose and I were so far from family, but we never felt that way because of Boris and Sergei. They would have done anything for us.

This book truly belongs to Sergei as much as it does to me. Sergei, I learned so much wisdom from you. I value our friendship more than you know and cannot wait for our next adventure together. I really feel like the two of us, as a team, *can* "do everything"!

And there really is too much to thank my wife for. She put her entire career on hold and dove with me into the unknown. I had the immediate benefit of a journalism community in Russia—Rose landed in the country with no automatic support network and no promise of work. She made the best of it, while supporting me in every way. Rose, your curiosity about people, your respect for friends and strangers alike, your street smarts, and your hunger for adventure all made me a better journalist in Russia and better able to write this book. Now back home, you are owning and running a successful restaurant, with not a minute of free time—and yet you somehow found the time to read, edit, and talk me through the tougher moments. I am eternally grateful—and promise we will never vacation anywhere with a temperature below 70 degrees Fahrenheit.

INDEX